GLEANING FOR COMMUNISM

GLEANING FOR COMMUNISM

THE SOVIET SOCIALIST HOUSEHOLD IN THEORY AND PRACTICE

XENIA A. CHERKAEV

CORNELL UNIVERSITY PRESS
Ithaca and London

First published 2023 by Cornell University Press

Library of Congress Cataloging-in-Publication Data

Names: Cherkaev, Xenia A., author.
Title: Gleaning for communism : the Soviet socialist household in theory and practice / Xenia A. Cherkaev.
Description: Ithaca [New York] : Cornell University Press, 2023. | Includes bibliographical references and index.
Identifiers: LCCN 2022057757 (print) | LCCN 2022057758 (ebook) | ISBN 9781501770234 (hardcover) | ISBN 9781501770302 (paperback) | ISBN 9781501770241 (pdf) | ISBN 9781501770258 (epub)
Subjects: LCSH: Property and socialism. | Communism and individualism—Soviet Union. | Informal sector (Economics)—Soviet Union. | Soviet Union—Economic conditions. | Soviet Union—Social conditions.
Classification: LCC HX550.P7 C4487 2023 (print) | LCC HX550.P7 (ebook) | DDC 335.430947—dc23/eng/20230201
LC record available at https://lccn.loc.gov/2022057757
LC ebook record available at https://lccn.loc.gov/2022057758

Make friends for yourselves by means of unrighteous wealth, so that when it fails they may receive you into the eternal dwellings.

—Luke 16:9

CONTENTS

Acknowledgments   ix

*Note on Translation and Transliteration, Scope,
Images, and Names   xv*

Introduction: Households and
Historiographies   1

1. The "Soviet" Things of Postsocialism   29

2. Gleaning for the Common Good   65

3. Songs of Stalin and Khrushchev   88

4. *Chuvstvo Khoziaina*: The Feeling
   of Being an Owner   116

Conclusion: Russian Socialism   139

Notes   145

References   161

Index   185

ACKNOWLEDGMENTS

I read somewhere that first book authors tend to thank everyone they have ever met in the acknowledgments, and this is puerile: a sign of intellectual intemperance. But maybe this is because first books take so long to write. This book took nearly one-third of my life. Over these years, it has taken me across countries, institutions, collectives, and conversations—too many to name. My deepest gratitude goes to the people who argued with me and twisted my conceptual optics, listened to my stories, and told me theirs. This book has become what it is through these meetings, and I have become what I am.

I must thank two people in particular without whom this book would not have been possible: Elena Tipikina and Amiel Bize.

Had Tipikina not existed, this book would not exist either. It precipitated from our endless conversation like a mineral formation. I am grateful to Tipikina for being my conduit to conversations throughout the Russian-speaking world, and for the immense personal labor she invested in this text; for reading all of its multiple drafts multiple times, attending not only to its logical arguments but to style also and voice, for teaching me how to write in the process. (I thank Google translate for making this possible.) I thank her for gleaning dead penguins and Soviet schoolbooks, and for all the other creative mayhem we cultivated together while this book was being written.

Amiel Bize gave this book its theoretical framing. In 2017, we organized a conference panel together on the subject of "The Ethical Parasite," where Amiel's talk conceptualized gleaning as a way to understand economies of remainders. This idea suddenly gave rhyme and reason to my disorganized thoughts about the Soviet economy, and I am immensely grateful to Amiel for letting me glean it. Proprietary rights remain hers, gleaning is mine only by custom. Meanwhile our adventure into fents, vails, chips, and scrapings continues. And it will certainly bring about new plentiful harvests—stay tuned.

I must also thank the institutions without which this book could not have been written. It began in the Anthropology Department of Columbia University, with the generous support of a Dissertation Fieldwork Grant from the Wenner-Gren Foundation. As a fledging book manuscript, it found support at the Harvard Academy for International and Area Studies. It came into its own at the Anthropology Department of the Massachusetts Institute of Technology, where I taught in 2019, and at the History Department of the Higher School of Economics, St. Petersburg, where I am presently working. Support from the Basic Research Program of the National Research University Higher School of Economics is gratefully acknowledged. My deepest gratitude to these institutions for providing me with a material base.

Many people have helped me think about things as I moved through these institutions. Thanks to my advisers and friends at Columbia: Elizabeth Povinelli, for attending to doubt that swirls around axis points; Rosalind Morris, for attending to fragments; Paul Kockelman, for revisiting status and contract; and to Claudio Lomnitz, for gleaning the debris that historical formations leave behind them when they recede, like old swamps. I am grateful to Naor Ben-Yehoyada for our discussions of *usufruct*, and to Mick Taussig for being a Sphinx. And I am grateful to all the people I knew in New York whose thought continues to structure mine. Especially, but not exclusively, thanks to Natalia Mendoza, Erin Yerby, Ana Miljanic, Manuel Schwab, Daniel Richards, Aarti Sethi, Fırat Kurt, Maria del Rosario Ferro (AKA Sayo), Elizabeth Gelber, Bruce Grant, Jasmine Pisapia, Gustav Kalm, and Dan Kendall.

At the Harvard Academy for International and Area Studies, I thank Tim Colton and Jorge Dominguez for their intellectual presence, and Bruce Jackan and Kathleen Hoover for their administrative labor. I owe a great debt of gratitude to Serguei A. Oushakine, Andrea Muehlebach, Douglas Rogers, Jessica Pisano, Naor Ben-Yehoyada, and Ajantha Subramanian for their insightful comments on the first full draft of this manuscript at my "Author's Conference," and to Jeremy Morris, who sent wonderfully useful comments even though he could not make it in person. I thank the Harvard Academy for bringing me to Boston, where many good people helped me think about Soviet history and Sovietologists. Thanks to Oleg Kharkhordin, Brandon Schechter, Yevgeniy Zhuravel, Susan Taylor, Dilan Yildirim, Katya Popova, Marwan Sarieddine, Rishad Choudhury, Tatiana Chudakova, Adam Leeds, Jason Cieply, Anna Ivanova, Philipp Chapkovski, and Maria Sidorkina.

Personal connections being as they are nonlinear, I have my St. Petersburg based friend Nikolai Ssorin-Chaikov to thank for having circled me back to Boston, this time to MIT. Around 2018, Nikolai invited me to tag along with him and his out-of-town friends Stefan Helmreich and Heather Paxson to the Dmitry Mendeleev Apartment Museum in St. Petersburg. A friendship began with this visit, fermented by Mendeleev's interest in cheese, from which two concrete projects then sprouted: a coauthored essay about cheese-making cooperatives and the etymology of quark, and a brief stint of employment at the MIT Anthropology Department. The quark and cheese essay has become my basis for thinking about how this book fits into a longer intellectual history of Russian nonmarket modernity, and my time at MIT has led to more friendships and conversations. I am especially grateful for having gotten to know Kate Brown, Elizabeth Wood, Danielle Carr, Bettina Stoetzer, Grace Kim, and Anthony Zannino.

The Higher School of Economics is my academic home in St. Petersburg as I finish this book in the company of wonderful colleagues. Thanks to Nikolai Ssorin-Chaikov, Tatiana Borisova, Igor Kuziner, Maria Staroon, Elena Kochetkova, Galina Orlova, Kirill Chunikhin, Adrian Selin, Alexander Reznik, Feliks Levin, and Nikita Karbasov. And also to Igal Halfin who is often here virtually, via video call. Thanks to the National Library of Russia and to the electronic library Nauka Prava, an indispensable tool for studying Russian legal history.

Several workshops and conferences—and their organizers—deserve special thanks for making this book what it is. Thanks to Nikolai Ssorin-Chaikov for bringing people together in St. Petersburg, in the *Anthropological Kruzhok* seminar and in the many conferences where materials from this book were discussed: "Towards an Institutional Ethnography of Late Socialism," "Late-Soviet Institutions," "Reassembling the Social: Revisioning Revisionism of Soviet History and Post-Soviet Anthropology," "The Soviet Legacy, Its Practices and Discourses," "(Post) socialism as the Post-Social." As the final draft of this book was coming together, I was fortunate to present a talk at the UC Berkeley History Department, and I am grateful to Victoria Frede for the invitation. I thank Harvard Anthropology's Political Anthropology Working Group for being a constant source of ideas, discussions, and friendship—and I particularly thank Dilan Yildirim for organizing. Thanks to Yanni Kotsonis for inviting me to present at NYU's Jordan Center, and to Anne O'Donnell and Juliette Cadiot for inviting me to their "Economic Histories of Russia and the Soviet Union" workshop. Thanks to Dina Omar for an invitation to speak at the Anthropology Department at Yale, and to Andrew Johnson for inviting me to the "Regimes of Visibility" workshop at Princeton. Our discussions gave this book a new optic. Thanks to Oleg Kharkhordin and Maria Sidorkina for inviting me to their panels at the Association for Slavic, East European, and Eurasian Studies meetings, Elizabeth Gelber and Amiel Bize for co-organizing panels at the American Anthropological Association meetings with me; thanks to Gustav Peebles and Julia Elyachar for being discussants. Above all, thanks to everyone who engaged my work at these get-togethers. I hope that you will see traces of our conversations in this text.

Beyond institutions are places that bring people together. I am grateful to this project for bringing me to St. Petersburg and into its many collectives. Particularly for my friendship with Katya Vidre, Volodia Katznelson, Elena Basner, Marina Shusterman, Larissa Zagrebina, Ira Maksakova, Pavel Lion, Kseniia Brailovskaia, Yury Ermolov, Andrei Shabanov, Nikola Samonov, Eline Helmer, Volodia Rybalko, Andrei Shishkin, Daniil Dukhavin, Alexander Gladky, Vera Noskova, Tatiana Ponomarenko, Igor Panin and everyone else at the Borey Art Gallery. In another place and time, before I took root in St. Petersburg, I used to live in Salt Lake City. I am grateful for the friendship of people I met there years ago, who have known me since before I became an anthropologist and whose words and thoughts are also everywhere in this book: Holly Bromley, Joshua Hardyman, Robin Steiner, Mike Dringenberg, and Jo Tietze. I am grateful that my family sprouted me into this world and that they still put up with me. Thanks to my parents, Andrej and Elena Cherkaev. Thanks to Annie Cherkaev, my sister.

Back to the beginning and on to happy conclusions. I am delighted that this manuscript found a home at Cornell University Press. My heartfelt thanks to the internal and external reviewers for their kind words and thoughtful comments. My gratitude to Jim Lance and Clare Jones for taking this project on and for making it into a book, to Jennifer Savran Kelly and Mia Renaud, and to all the other editors, designers, and marketing specialists who worked on this project. Thanks to Elina Alter for putting together the index.

My most joyful gratitude to Mike Dringenberg for image that appears on the cover.

Without all the people here named, this book would have been unrecognizably different—if it had come to fruition at all. Their traces cling to it like potters' handprints do to a vessel of clay, like a storyteller's traces retain every time the story's retold. Here, I have organized people into neat geographic and institutional piles, but these divisions are completely irrelevant. Some people have since moved elsewhere, others have known me across several places and times. Best you now take your pen or pencil and black out all the divisions until this acknowledgments page is just a long list of people: a house party of my imagination, with wine and whiskey and accordion music. Everyone here knows someone else at the party, and please bring along friends I forgot to mention. I hope that by morning everyone will know everyone else.

Thanks, friends.

NOTE ON TRANSLATION AND TRANSLITERATION, SCOPE, IMAGES, AND NAMES

Wherever possible, texts are cited in published English translations. All previously unpublished translations from Russian are my own. Transliteration follows the Library of Congress style, excepting some commonly used transliterations of proper names. Throughout the book, I use the term "socialist household economy" interchangeably with its direct Russian transliteration *sotsialisticheskoe khoziaistvo*.

This book is a historical ethnography of a political morality of collectivist use-right. Mediating between the stories people told me about Soviet times in the 2010s and Soviet legal theories of socialist property, it traces this political morality through three key transformations of Soviet civil law during the 1930s, 1960s, and 1980s. This legal focus leaves some important economic reforms outside the scope of the book, including the 1965 Kosygin-Liberman reforms, which paved the way for perestroika reform theory but did not themselves alter property law.

Photographs in this book are my own unless otherwise marked.

Following anthropological convention, ethnographic subjects have been anonymized.

GLEANING FOR COMMUNISM

Introduction
Households and Historiographies

I wander around, by myself I just wander around
and I don't know what do with myself
and there's no one home, nobody's home
I'm as leftover as a pile of scrap metal.

—Viktor Tsoi, "The Idler" (1982)

Studies of the Soviet project often begin with an image of failure, so I will begin with my own; this book is the outcome of a project that seemed theoretically promising but turned out to be utterly untenable. In 2010, I came to St. Petersburg, Russia, to study whether local assumptions that certain well-used things are emotionally warming could be understood as popular commentary on the specifically post-Soviet experience of disposable goods. I reasoned that people who were used to conditions of material scarcity may be struck by the repetitive silence of disposable things, which are made to be used once and thrown away. But I was wrong. A series of blind taste tests showed that a well-made copy was just as good as the real thing: aura was not a physical quality. The folk philosophy I had hoped to explain by a semiconscious reading of the indexical marks of past use was better explained as another fetishism. And in just a few months of fieldwork, my project lay dead. I was growing increasingly apprehensive of what I would say to the Wenner-Gren Foundation, whose money I was nonetheless spending.

This project, as it collapsed, bequeathed me an interest in the things that were made "on the left," that is, illicitly, at late-Soviet enterprises and smuggled home past the pass gate. These things were many and varied—from kayaks and sauerkraut buckets, to glass trinkets, tombstones, and knitting needles—and many were strikingly beautiful. They had first interested me as a sort of artisanally made and long-living antithesis to the disposable, and then I kept seeking them out for the heroic, funny, and often riveting stories people told me about their creation.

While finding and cataloging such things helped fend off the feeling of failure, the lack of a clearly planned project still left quite a bit of free time, and so I was happy to oblige a friend who asked whether I would go down to Kolpino, an industrial satellite town a few train stops south of St. Petersburg to pick up a bagful of apples from a friend of hers, who had been blessed with such a surplus that season that she had begun an online campaign to find them new homes: in organizations for children and retirees, with moonshine-makers, zoo keepers, stable-hands, and everyone in between. Dobrova—the woman who had too many apples—lived on the side of a stream about a kilometer away from the train station, in a neighborhood that is best described as a deindustrialized suburb of an industrial satellite city. In this neighborhood of gravel-paved streets, where the service-station served as the grocery store, retired factory workers lived in hardy single-story wood-heated houses, next to middle-class families in suburban-style houses with indoor plumbing, next to migrant laborers in shacks made from, and heated by, packing pallets. Dobrova's house was like that of the factory workers but with running water. She had lived in the neighborhood for about five years by the time we met. In 2006, when her mother died, she moved in to take care of her ninety-two-year-old grandmother. Then her grandmother died also, but Dobrova stayed on. And then, just before we met, she lost several jobs to the megacorporation Gazprom, which was extending its auspices further into ever new areas unrelated to the sale of natural gas, replacing employees with its own loyal cadres in every new realm it touched. So Dobrova also had quite a bit of free time. We quickly became friends and I moved in.

The house had a definite history. It was built, I was told, circa 1946 by Uncle Grisha, who received the plot of land as a decorated frontline fighter, and had managed to obtain building materials while working as foreman of a POW labor brigade. The labor brigade had been tasked with building a bridge over the river Izhora, and it is anyone's guess what materials went into building that bridge, but Uncle Grisha's house was definitely built out of larch: a rot-resistant timber, which hardens with age, does not grow in the area, could have hardly been bought in 1946, and which Uncle Grisha modestly masked with drab wooden siding.

Half a century later, and after Uncle Grisha's death, a local branch of the Azeri mob moved in with a setup for the production of bootleg liquor. And then Uncle Grisha's niece sold the house to one of her coworkers—to Dobrova's mother—cheap and as is.

Thus in 1994, Dobrova's mother organized an operation of the police special forces to seize what was legally her property, moved in, and began a new round of home improvement. The house's veranda was roofed with sheets of industrial aluminum, left by the evicted bootleggers in reparation; the fence was covered with paint bought from the foreman of a railroad maintenance crew; a new stovetop (figure 0.1) was cut to size from a sheet of titanium alloy intended for submarine armor and hauled off factory grounds by a plant locomotive driver named Sanya, the occasional romantic partner of Dobrova's ex-boyfriend, whom Dobrova's mother welcomed as family. In the early 2000s, a work crew laying fiber optic cable along the Moscow–St. Petersburg rail line was persuaded to chop a few coils from their countless reels, and a walk-in greenhouse was set up in the yard: polythene stretched over this skeleton of blue cable casing (figure 0.2). Most important, the house's communications were greatly improved. Dobrova's mother paid people from the water company to run a pipe to the house from the municipal pump, and she

FIGURE 0.1. Hairless cat asleep on a titanium alloy stove top. Image courtesy Elena Tipikina.

FIGURE 0.2. Walk-in greenhouse frame, made of fiber-optic cable casing. Image courtesy Elena Tipikina.

paid people from the electricity company to hook up another input line, bypassing the meter. By the time I moved in, Dobrova had managed to legalize both of these initially illegal actions of home improvement. But, excepting the new middle-class suburban-style houses, hers was still one of the few on the block with running water.

As is well expected of households (Polanyi [1944] 2001), Dobrova's ran not on measured exchange but on reciprocity. Indeed, for measured exchange there was not much resource. Dobrova's main source of cash income was from a room she rented out in St. Petersburg, and from small ghost-writing jobs, for which she was typically paid in bags of pet food; a friend of hers employed by an international pet food company wrote off the bags as promotional material, and Dobrova sold them to acquaintances at a significant discount. But while she rarely had cash, she often had stuff, which she shared quite easily. She shared water with Shura, the neighbor on the left—a retired factory worker whose only other access to water was at the municipal hand pump down the street; with Pavel, the neighbor on the right, who had a high managerial position at an enterprise separating oxygen for Kolpino's metal factory and paid for his house's running water on the meter; with the migrant workers across the street, who came over with buckets when the hand pump froze over or broke, as it frequently did. She shared horse manure, gotten in gratitude for acting as MC on a horse show, with anyone who wanted to come pick some up. She shared the rabies vaccine with the neighborhood cats, against their feline wills but with the consent of the owners. Favors and debts circled around the household and through it: domestic and semidomestic animals lived here and nearby, were brought for weekend stays, were born, and died; friends came by with bottles of wine and spent the night; neighbors came over to borrow some cash, return a favor or bring by a bottle of beer; acquaintances drove up to buy discounted pet food. Imported delicacies regularly graced the table, gleaned from work by a friend employed in the veterinary border patrol unit of the St. Petersburg port, through which they were shipped to the city. I distinctly remember shark fin, eel, and an entire head of semi-hard cheese, something like Jarlsberg. Former factory workers came over, as did future Gazprom middle managers, former KGB operatives and present-day businessmen, taxi drivers and foremen, ballettmeisters and accountants, botanists and stuntmen, veterinarians, dentists, and biologists working for the city's water works.

Talking to people in this Kolpino neighborhood about the personally useful things that they had managed to make "on the left" at work in Soviet times, two things became quickly apparent. The first is that the stories people told me about Soviet times often concerned transactions that happened well into the early 2000s: transactions, for example, by which the above greenhouse and stovetop were made. The second is that people often contrasted this Soviet era to the 2010s narrative present, in which, I was told, everything had been sold (*vse prodano*), and everything had been bought (*vse kupleno*). This buying and selling was not market exchange. It was dispossession and the shadowy usurpation of power: complaints about how everything had been sold pointed to communal resources being sold out to private interests; complaints about how everything had been bought pointed to the clandestine purchase of favor that was assumed to structure access to institutions, resources, and opportunities. Uniting these complaints into one recognizable discourse was the widely discussed image of corruption (*korruptsiia*), of "the abuse of public office for private gain," as the World Bank defines it, of officials using public infrastructure for their own selfish ends: organizing yacht trips with money that should have gone to fund hospitals, selling off public parks to private condo developments.

But the many informal transactions that I heard about, saw, and took part in while I lived with Dobrova in Kolpino were not said to be the result of corruption at all. They were said to be the result of good relations, neighborly help and people being decent. This, for example, was how Dobrova explained the house's electrical situation. The second input that had been jerry-rigged to circumvent the meter had started to smolder by the time Dobrova moved in. But when she disconnected it, she found that the house's legal two-kilowatt input was insufficient: if the water heater was running, the washing machine would cut the breakers; if the kettle was on, nothing else could be. So Dobrova went to the offices of the electricity company, asked for an official appointment, and showed the inspector two sets of bills. "Here are the bills my mother paid," she told me she told him, "And here are the ones I pay now. Notice that hers are for forty-five rubles, and mine are for four hundred. How do you think that worked? That's right—she was stealing electricity from your company. And I—for reasons of personal safety and convenience—I don't want to do that. But now tell me, how can I upgrade the electrical input to where I can run a washing machine and a boiler? I have a ninety-two-year-old war veteran to take care of." Officially upgrading the electrical input was prohibitively expensive: it required replanning the entire house, which cost thousands of dollars. But the inspector found a way to resolve the situation. He asked how recently Dobrova's mother had died, and whether the death was sudden. "Here's what you do," she told me he told her: "Go buy a six-kilowatt meter and order a routine meter-replacement, and I will tell the guys the story. They will run the line to your house and replace the old meter with the new one. And then a few days later an inspector will stop by and ask how come you have six kilowatts—and you will say: I have no idea, mother just died, and I don't know what she did with the documents."

Seen in these terms, the scheme by which the house got six kilowatts is not corrupt—not even by the World Bank definition. It is not corrupt because it is not privately motivated. The official did not sell off public infrastructure to build himself a yacht; he helped Dobrova navigate a bureaucratic system that had put her into an impossible position: into a situation in which her ability to take care of her elderly grandmother depended on jerry-rigged electrical wiring, which was not only illegal but also unsafe. I heard many such stories of grace, human decency, and neighborliness from my friends in St. Petersburg and Kolpino. And there is no shortage of similar stories in texts documenting informality, (post)socialist second economies, and other actually lived economic practices. But often, these stories are studied skeptically. Exemplary of such skepticism, Alena Ledeneva's influential *Russia's Economy of Favours* (1998) argues that "blat," the circumvention of formal distribution rules through informal social relationships, worked by a "'misrecognition game'—in which blat remains obscured by the rhetoric of friendship, etc. in one's own case, but could easily be recognised in the case of someone else" (Ledeneva 1998, 9). The analyst's skepticism of the speaker's "rhetoric of friendship" here rests on her certitude of actual motivation. What really drives people to circumvent the formal rules? Are speakers' actions really as friendly, selfless, and neighborly as they claim? This question—unanswerable by social science, best left to the omniscient readers of human souls—may be raised by theories of misrecognition because it is immediately sidestepped. Analysts know acquisitiveness and greed to lurk behind that rhetoric of friendship in which speakers misrecognize their own intentions. The analyst sees the specks that speakers cannot see in their own eyes, as well as the logs they recognize in the eyes of others. What *really* drives people to circumvent the rules, it is assumed, is private interest.

But if the rhetoric of friendship can thus be said to be an obfuscating mask, so can a rhetoric of private acquisitiveness. Setting aside impossible questions of true motivation, the more interesting question for social science may be how people recognize the ethical values for which they strive: how they position themselves as ethical actors, and how they imagine themselves to relate to the world. And in this, scholars of misrecognition are doubtlessly right: such ethical evaluation is a question of point of view, a value judgment in the eye of the beholder. A sympathetic person may explain a particular action as valiant, neighborly, and decent; an unsympathetic one may say that it was nothing more than selfish theft. What I find interesting about such descriptions is that I repeatedly heard the same values heralded: when talking about how they made and obtained things illicitly from their late-Soviet workplaces, people condemned acquisitive theft while celebrating maverick actions for the collective good. It was this ethical stance that speakers commonly associated with Soviet times, even when describing events that happened after the USSR had collapsed. And when I turned to historical documents, I was surprised to find that such associations were more than just nostalgia. They were historically sound: the ethical stance of mutual aid upon which I heard speakers draw in their descriptions of Soviet times helped Soviet enterprises meet their economic plans, despite endemic shortages, by framing irregular but necessary transactions as a social good. It was heralded by popular media texts, newspapers, films, and children's cartoons. And in some sense, it was the whole point: ideological statements, party policies, and legal codes all recognized that helping one's fellows do what needs to be done, and even going around the law to do so, was central to the project of building a truly communist society, in which state institutions would become unnecessary as people learned to live ethically, allowing the law to wither away. Underlying such theories of social self-management was a property regime that guaranteed specifically nonprivate ownership rights: that guaranteed citizens the right to "personal property."

This book tells the history of such personal ownership, and of the socialist household economy in which it functioned; of how this political, economic, and social formation ran, how it collapsed, and how I heard its history narrated two decades later, in the 2010s. The story begins, in chapter 1, with a distinction I heard repeatedly associated with Soviet times, the distinction between private greed and personal investment in collective projects. Chapter 2 traces this distinction to the legal definitions of personal and socialist property: the bedrock property regime upon which Stalin-era legal scholars legislated a modern industrial society that would function by the nonmarket logics of householding, whose members would be guaranteed personal stakes in the commonweal rather than private possessions. Chapter 3 then follows the logic of this property regime through the history and historiography of Nikita Khrushchev's reforms, which explicitly foregrounded collectivist ethics as the way to build stateless communism. Chapter 4 shows the tragic success of Mikhail Gorbachev's perestroika reforms, which unfurled the delicate tension upon which this property regime relied: the tension between individual collectivist interests and the interests of the socialist household economy in toto. A short conclusion takes this book back to its historical present: to the spring of 2022, when many of the people around me in St. Petersburg knew not to "talk about politics" but easily justified Russia's undeclared war on Ukraine by a particular historiographic narrative about the Soviet past.

A study of how the socialist household functioned, how it collapsed, and how it was remembered, this book is thus also about that spectral image that anchored twentieth-century liberalism as its nefarious antithesis; the image of the paternalist totalitarian state, whose jealous political control over the economy leads it to trample over all that which ought to be private. Underlying this nefarious image, and the "state phobia" it justified (Foucault 2008, 76), is the question of how individual interests ought to relate to the public good in a large modern society, which, it is assumed, cannot possibly function by the nonprivate logics of householding.

This book tells the story of a large modern society that did.

Corrupt Totalitarianism

I am certainly not the first to point out that actions may be corrupt from one point of view and perfectly ethical from another (Smart 1993; Gupta 1995). The definition of corruption is itself notoriously slippery. Anticorruption organizations like Transparency International define it as the "abuse of public office for private gain," or as "the abuse of entrusted power for private gain," or they choose to forgo definitions entirely. "The TI [Transparency International] chapter in Denmark," writes Steven Sampson, "has recently removed the definition of corruption from its statutes, concluding that it constituted an impediment to its work. Corruption is now whatever TI defines it to be" (Sampson 2005, 121). By some of its broadest definitions, as the usurpation of common resources for individual use, corruption can be said to be as old as politics itself: a "most dangerous threat to [the] political legitimacy" of all orders grounded on the notion of popular sovereignty, with its fragile fiction of citizens' equal political rights (Muir and Gupta 2018, S12). By other definitions, it is an explicitly modern problem. In his 1968 opus *Political Order in Changing Societies*, Samuel Huntington finds corruption especially prevalent in societies undergoing "rapid social and economic modernization," wherein the new expectations, demands, and possibilities of political and economic modernity come to be improperly aligned with traditional social entitlements and obligations (Huntington 2006, 59).

But the corruption that concerned Huntington and his mid-twentieth century colleagues is not the same as that which came to be incessantly discussed in the 2010s. For one thing, for Huntington, corruption was not a sign of structural moral failure. As traditional societies developed toward modernity (which in Huntington's text is the image of his own contemporary American greatness), corruption could actually be good. "A society which is relatively uncorrupt," he writes, "a traditional society for instance where traditional norms are still powerful, may find a certain amount of corruption a welcome lubricant easing the path to modernization" (Huntington 2006, 69). In the 2000s and 2010s, such statements were no longer acceptable. Around the world, corruption accusations were framed in reference to the anticorruption "industry" that, supported by organizations like Transparency International and the World Bank empowered "integrity warriors" to battle corruption in the name of good governance (Sampson 2005, 108). This "global morality discourse" of anticorruption gave analytic coherence to a plethora of disparate claims about bribery, nepotism, patron-client relationships, gifts, favors, and favoritism (Sampson 2005, 108). It provided people across many geographic locales with a discourse to narrate what was wrong, unethical, and untimely about their own societies. Its breadth spanned postcolonial and postsocialist locales (Hasty 2005; Smith 2018; Morris and Polese 2014), and reached into the very center of modernity itself: into the "heartlands of advanced capitalist democracy." Seen as the "greatest single threat to democracy" outside war, it was noted to haunt "modern politics and economics, threatening the legitimacy of states and markets while simultaneously animating repetitive, incomplete attempts to cleanse and legitimate the political economic order" (Haller and Shore 2005, 10; Muir and Gupta 2018, S5).

The haunting quality of this twenty-first-century image of corruption names the transgression of a critical but factually untenable category distinction: that between public and private realms. And while Huntington also defined corruption as "behavior of public officials which deviates from accepted norms in order to serve private ends" (Huntington [1968] 2006, 59), it was only after the end of the Cold War that such behavior became a haunting global concern. Studies of the global anticorruption industry often note the twenty-first-century image of corruption to be the incessant shadow of neoliberal governance, spurred by the very privatization and structural adjustment programs that claim to stamp it out, driven by moral claims to equality and "an 'audit culture' stressing accountability, openness, transparency and unambiguous indicators" (Sampson 2010, 275; Haller and Shore 2005). They trace the emergence of such anticorruption discourses to a series of resolutions adopted in the mid-1990s by institutions like the UN and the World Bank (Wedel 2012). And they repeatedly return to the question of why this global morality discourse emerged when it did: "what about the contemporary moment makes corruption such an obvious and concerning problem to so many people in such different contexts?" (Muir 2018).

One answer lies in the end of the Cold War, and in the central role a certain image of Soviet socialism played in neoliberal thought. On the most basic level, corruption fits nicely into the ideological void left ready for it in the liberal political imagination by that "unabashed victory of economic and political liberalism" (Fukuyama 1989, 3) that was widely celebrated for having defeated the totalitarian menace. To scholars of postsocialist Eastern Europe the alignment of corruption and totalitarianism will likely seem unsurprising. Post-Soviet states are not only noted to be the "birthplace of the anti-corruption industry" (Sampson 2010, 264) but are also often denounced for corruption in explicitly totalitarian terms. Investigations of Russia's "kleptocratic tribute system," for example, are not uncommonly prefaced by speculations about why it took "Western policy and academic communities so long to embrace this view of the Russian political system as a steel hand in an initially velvet glove? We may never know precisely when the current regime decided to do what they have clearly done, any more than we know on which day Stalin stopped being a pencil pusher and decided to imprison millions in the gulag, or even when Hitler hit on the idea of exterminating the Jewish population of Europe" (Dawisha 2014, 4).

Drawing a straight line between Vladimir Putin's Kleptocracy, the GULAG, and "the idea of exterminating the Jewish population of Europe" sounds wild. But it flies by unnoticed in texts like Karen Dawisha's well-received *Putin's Kleptocracy: Who Owns Russia?* Hitler, Stalin, and Putin easily flow together as representatives of that totalitarian, corrupt, barbaric, and improper modernity against which the liberal political imaginary struggles to define itself (Buck-Morss 2002). The fundamental pathology of this improper modernity lies in its mismanagement of the distinction between public policy and private interest. Today this purported mismanagement justifies the global moral governance of anticorruption. Throughout the Cold War, it justified liberal pundits in framing the world's recent history as that of "the desperate struggle of lovers of freedom prosperity and civilization against the rising tide of totalitarian barbarism" (Mises 1951, 13).

Totalitarianism, the "theoretical anchor of cold war discourse" (Pietz 1988, 55), was already a driving concern at the 1938 Walter Lippmann Colloquium, where the term "neoliberal" was adopted (Reinhoudt and Audier 2018).[1] It remained central to postwar popular and academic liberal thought, helping channel "the anti-Nazi energy of the wartime period into the postwar struggle with the Soviet Union" (Gleason 1995, 3; Adler and Paterson 1970). But the roots of totalitarianism run deeper: to the question of whether people in modern societies relate to their collectivities differently than do their nonmodern peers. This question preoccupied much nineteenth-century critical thought. It was a question of the one and the many, of progress gained and of paradise lost, of whether something had fundamentally altered for humankind when it slipped from socially embedded economies into publics, stranger sociality, and scientifically rational thought.

Early anthropology contributed to this discussion with ethnographic studies of "primitive" nonmarket economies (Pearson 2000; Elyachar 2020). And in this usage, the term "primitive" was not an expression of scale. It was an expression of radical alterity, marked as savage deficiency: complex economies were not built up of more primitive elements. Quite the opposite, Euro-American philosophers and ethnographers showed time and again that the social worlds of modern and primitive man differed radically. The differences were twofold. On the one hand, the modern condition was alienated, while the primitive was immediate. For better or worse, moderns understood things, beings, and relationships in relation to abstract universals, like commodity value (Marx [1867] 1976), standardized public goods (Heidegger [1927] 1962, 164), socially disembodied narrative forms (Benjamin [1968] 1936) and contractual systems of law (Maine 1906, 267). Primitives did without such abstractions: without abstract labor time, certainly, but also without abstracted standards of measurement, naming, and historical time (Malinowski [1922] 1984; Boas 1895; Evans-Pritchard 1940, 105). On the other hand, the modern condition depended on the acquisition of things, while "primitive man [expressed] an aversion to economic exchange" (Simmel [1907] 1971, 43–69) and instead preferred to focus on gifting things out (Mauss [1925] 1990).

The suggestion that acquisitive material trade was not the original economic relation captured the Euro-American public imagination well beyond the academy (Murnau 1931). But was such trade a necessary outcome of modern alienation? Must acquisitive trade and the mediation of abstract third terms go together? In his scathing 1920 denouncement of the Bolshevik Revolution, Ludwig von Mises famously claimed that they must. The relation between them, he argued, was the very basis of modern rationality and freedom: individuals' peaceful co-operation hinges on their ability to make rational choices about their production and consumption of things, and such choices are possible only when a system of competitive market price expresses the true value of every commodity. If we are to be rational moderns, our complex economies must therefore be based upon the market exchange of private property. An economy without such exchange would be ultimately irrational, and it would be inherently despotic: in the socialist claim to dispense with private property, Mises saw nothing less than a threat to civilization itself (Mises [1922] 1951, 511; [1920] 1935).[2]

The theories that have become known as neoliberal trace their own origins to this claim of the inherent irrationality—and consequent despotism—of nonmarket modernity. And so, although the real history of socialism's role in the rise of neoliberal theory and practice cannot be boiled down to this simple standoff between markets and planning (Bockman 2011; Sanchez-Sibony 2014), these mythic origins remain important precisely as myth: one that has justified neoliberal policies by insisting that only the headless mediation of a market economy can properly situate individuals in modern society. Against the terror of total control, wherein "economic planning would involve direction of almost the whole of our life" (Hayek [1944] 2007b, 127), the early neoliberals insisted that modern man lives in peace with his fellows only when each seeks his own individual good, with market price mediating such independent desires to the scarcity of desired goods. Moral and evolutionist, and often racist (Slobodian 2014), this narrative equated social progress with commercial relations; collectivism with moral failure; socialism with civilizational regression (Whyte 2019; Hayek [1979] 1998, 153–76). Fostering theories about how to govern social life by the competitive logics once thought reserved for the market (Foucault 2008; Brown 2015), it justified policies characterized by the privatization of objects to be used in this competitive game: not only formerly collective property, but also social relations not formerly thought to be property at all (Elyachar 2005).

This book is written at a moment of widespread disgruntlement with this particular version of liberalism; at a moment in which academic and publicist discourses across many languages, localities, and political party affiliations were searching for alternatives to the global morality regime of good neoliberal governance. I began ethnographic work on this project in the wake of the 2008 financial crisis, in which US banks foreclosed on private mortgages and the Federal Reserve bailed out the banks, stabilizing the financial sector but leaving its moral foundations shaky. I wrote it in an era when publicist, economic, and social science literature discussed the crisis of markets, liberalism, and the environment (Roitman 2013; Boyer 2016; Masco 2017); when anthropological literature increasingly commented on the duplicity of the 1990s "transitions to democracy" (Kalb 2009; Hickel 2015); when scholarly and publicist texts turned with renewed concern to questions of moral economy (Palomera and Vetta 2016; Rakopoulos and Knut 2018; Skidelsky 2014).

The concept of moral economy once allowed E. P. Thompson to show that eighteenth-century British food riots were rebellions "in defence of custom," driven not only by biological hunger but also by the demand for customary economic rights (Thompson [1991] 1993, 9). Time and again, crowds facing grain shortages and spiraling food prices did not simply loot the necessities that they could not buy. They seized stores of grain, sold it at the customary price and returned the proceeds of such sales to the owner. "It is not easy for us to conceive," Thompson wrote, "that there may have been a time, within a smaller and more integrated community, when it appeared to be 'unnatural' that any man should profit from the necessities of others, and when it was assumed that, in time of dearth, prices of 'necessities' should remain at a customary level, even though there might be less all round" ([1991] 1993, 252–53). In the 2010s Thompson's proposal was easier to fathom. As scholarly texts argued that "moral economies" had been made unthinkable under the specter of totalitarianism (Rogan 2017, 9) and that democracy itself was becoming unthinkable under the specter of neoliberal governance (Brown 2015), popular movements on both the right and the left challenged the separation of economic realms from social, political, and moral questions. It was not hard to imagine that the "deplorables" roiling against extractive transnational capital's refusal to put America First (Povinelli 2017) made demands similar to those of the eighteenth-century rioters, who stormed barges to keep grain on local markets (Thompson [1991] 1993, 295).

Similar to Thompson's illiberal crowds, many of the people I met in and around St. Petersburg in the 2010s wanted their state to provide fair distribution rather than transparent institutions. And thus at a time when the US media regularly accused Putin of being a "Threat to Liberal Democracy" (Diamond 2016), a common Russian complaint was that he was too (neo)liberal; that the state he headed did not do enough to provide its citizens with free healthcare, schooling, roads, train travel, and stable employment; that it, instead, allowed private profit to be made from the sale of its natural resources. This made corruption an easy topic of conversation, and one explicitly concerned with the acquisitive dispossession of common resources. Narratives of such dispossession often harked back to perestroika, when "all those thieves" who cared solely about their own pocketbooks, wrecked the Soviet Union and sold it off. And often, they condemned the law that allowed the commons to be thus legally dispossessed. In this moral discourse about the political economy, corruption was the existence of corporations like Gazprom—a private natural gas company in which the Russian state owned a majority share. While my political science colleagues at Harvard told me that Gazprom was not corrupt insofar as it contracted above board and paid taxes on its employee salaries, my Russian friends told me that it was the essence of corruption, precisely because it did so. That a private corporation selling the country's natural resources could pay its employees' astronomical salaries legitimately and fully taxed, while impossible tax rates forced small businesses to pay their employees in laundered unrecorded cash, made it the epitome of corruption; it proved that the laws were written in its favor.[3] Speakers often traced the origins of this corrupt Putinist state to the Soviet Union, and the perestroika (lit. "reconstruction") reforms that brought it down. Some insisted that the USSR had disintegrated when glasnost opened society's eyes to the regime's immoral violence; others insisted that it collapsed as a result of a plot to destroy the great military super-power; still others assumed that it had simply ground to halt, having run out of steam, money, and resources. But most everyone agreed that perestroika enabled wide-scale theft, and that this theft has profoundly structured Russia's political, legal, and economic landscape.

Economics and Households—and Property

The Soviet Union, as is well known, had little respect for private property. And the question this raised—the question of how a large, industrialized state could function without a market defined by privately motivated exchange—is one of the gnawing problems of twentieth-century political thought. For liberal theorists, this question raised the specter of totalitarianism; for their Soviet counterparts, it formulated a method by which the state would be made to "wither away" (Lenin [1918] 2014).

At heart, this liberal-socialist standoff was about the question of the one and the many, of how individual interests may be ensured in a modern society of strangers. We now know a good deal about the economic side of this historical conversation: how Soviet economists grappled with questions of value and planning, supply and demand (Barnett and Zweynert 2008; Boldyrev and Kirtchik 2017) and how neoliberalism developed in conversation with socialist economics (Bockman 2011; Rupprecht 2022). But the Soviet answer to the question of the one and the many—with its accusation of individual-crushing totalitarianism—has remained unexamined. And for a good reason: because its root claims baffle our scholarly optics. They mix morality, politics, and economics, those three aspects of life that should be kept separate in the analysis of industrial modern worlds.

This book is a historical ethnography of this dark side of the moon, of the *sotsialisticheskoe khoziaistvo*, the socialist household economy.

It sounds strange to describe the economy of a modern twentieth-century state as a household—because we typically think of the economy as something that explicitly excludes both the private sphere of the household and the political sphere of the state. But this definition is new. "As recently as the 1920s," writes Timothy Mitchell, "Palgrave's *Dictionary of Political Economy* contained no separate entry for or definition of the term economy. It used the word only to mean 'the principle of seeking to attain, or the method of attaining, a desired end with the least possible expenditure of means'" (1998, 85).[4] Mitchell traces the history of the notion of the economy to the emergence of econometrics, whose natural-science language allowed economic processes to be studied as objective facts removed from the social concerns they express. Drawing on Philip Mirowski (1989), he traces the rise of this mathematical language to the post-1870s shift in economic thought: from the classic economic theory that value derived from the labor cost of production to the marginal utility theory that derived value solely from consumers' subjective desire. If value expresses what the market's consumers are willing to pay, then the economy can be studied apart from substantive and political questions: it can be divorced from the private realm of the household and the political realm of the state. But while this new way of figuring economic transactions became central to both liberal and socialist economic thought (Steedman 1995; Bockman 2011), early Soviet leadership rejected it outright. The theory of marginal utility stood accused of being an *Economic Theory of the Leisure Class*, as Nikolai Bukharin ([1919] 1927) termed it, of being a theory that could only make sense from the perspective of the rentier, who takes no part in production, whose only interaction with society is based on his own acquisitive wants. And so from the 1920s on, marginalism in Russia was effectively banned (Allisson 2015, 173).

Bukharin was a leading Bolshevik revolutionary, and a head editor of the *Big Soviet Encyclopedia*, whose first volume (1926) includes a long critique of the Austrian school's marginal theory of value. His criticism formed part of a wider early Soviet discussion of bourgeois science, which stood accused of a twofold mistake: of studying social relations as motionless structures that do not implicate the scholar himself or

herself, and of studying individuals' relationships to these social structures as purely subjective psychological phenomena (Vološinov [1929]
1986; Arvatov [1925] 1997). Neither approach could grasp the true
nature of social life, Soviet critics argued, because neither took seriously
the generative relations of production that characterized society and
implicated the scholar within it. Predictably Marxist, the Soviet solution focused instead on the historically contingent and class-driven generation of things, meanings, and power (Kiaer 2005; Tret'iakov [1929]
2006). And the point was not just to study these material relations but
also to change them, to thereby eliminate the coercive superstuctru-
res they supported. These superstructures included morality and law
which, as the leading legal scholar Evgeny Pashukanis argued, would
both wither away in a communist society, in their very form (Pashukanis
[1924] 2002, 61). The social person of the future would be driven not
by abstract notions of duty or fear of criminal sanction, but by a joyful
collectivist striving: submerging his ego in the collective, he would find
"the greatest satisfaction and the meaning of life in this act."[5] A tool
used to create this "new, higher, more harmonious form of link between
the personality and the collective," early Soviet property law therefore
recognized private property only as a temporary concession, a relation
slated for extinction (Pashukanis [1924] 2002, 160).

But how would an economy work without private property? Mises
famously claimed that such an economy would be impossible—because
the state is too large to be run as a household. "Only under simple conditions," he writes, "can economics dispense with monetary calculation.
Within the narrow confines of household economy, for instance, where
the father can supervise the entire economic management, it is possible
to determine the significance of changes in the processes of production,
without such aids to the mind, and yet with more or less of accuracy"
(Mises [1920] 1935, 102). But a national economy would be impossible
to plan through use-values alone. Even if the goals of production could
be established, the steps needed to achieve those goals would be impossible to calculate without a functional value mechanism: "the human
mind cannot orientate itself properly among the bewildering mass of
intermediate products and potentialities of production without such
aid. It would simply stand perplexed before the problems of management and location" (Mises [1920] 1935, 103). In this reading, households delimit the sphere within which private economic interests may
be disrespected. On all greater, properly economic scales the subjection
of private interest to public policy would necessarily produce chaotic
results.

Following this liberal analytic, studies of the Soviet economy have often described it as a large corporate structure under centralized, top-down control—something like a countrywide factory (Sutela 1991, 7)—and have explained the fact that it did somehow manage to function by the illicit persistence of private interest; by the unplanned exchange, bargaining, and other actions of the "second economy" that prospered in the fertile shadows of command (Grossman 1963, 1977). An analogous argument has been made about the persistence of citizens' private lives despite ideological prohibition (Field 2007; Reid and Crowley 2002). Allowing that the concepts of public and private may be defined in particular and explicitly socialist ways, such approaches hold that the notions themselves are opposed and mutually exclusive. Susan Gal's pivotal work, for example, shows that state-socialist notions of public and private were defined in relational metaphors rather than spatial ones. But it assumes that the notions themselves were opposed: that socialist notions of public and private chart "a discursive opposition between the victimized 'us' and a newly powerful 'them' who ruled the state," whereby the citizens' "imperative to be honest and ethically responsible among those who counted as 'us' [is contrasted to the . . .] distrust and duplicity in dealings with 'them' and with the official world generally" (Gal 2002, 87). Attempts to overcome this binary logic often run into the problem of mutually exclusive terms; Yurchak's deterritorialized publics of *svoi* (our people) may be unstable, shifting, and not defined vis-à-vis state institutions (2008, 117–18), but they semantically imply a *chuzhie* (not-ours). If there is an inside, then there must be an outside. If there is an us, then there's also a them.[6]

This mutually exclusive oppositional quality is inherent to the concepts of public and private. But it occludes an important economic and ethical logic: that of Soviet citizens' constitutionally guaranteed rights to a personal share of the "growing wealth of the socialist homeland" (Rubinshtein 1936, 42–43). Definitively, this personal share was not private. It was not alienable from the greater socialist whole and could not be opposed to it, because it was one of its constitutive parts.

Sacred and Inviolable

By 1938, both Pashukanis and Bukharin were purged. With their deaths closed the era of Soviet legal and political thought that Western scholars typically find most theoretically promising—and the story of Soviet socialist household economy began. Its story is that of the

answer Stalinist legal scholars presented to the accusation of totalitarianism in the debate of the one and the many; of the *sotsialisticheskoe
khoziaistvo* they legislated; and of the collectivist logics that kept it functional despite its poor planning.

In Russian, the term *khoziaistvo* describes substantive economies of
all types, from the national economy (*narodnoe khoziaistvo*), to individual
households, and even individual playrooms. "Pick up your *khoziaistvo*"
one might say to a child upon walking into a room strewn with Legos.
Grammatically, the term implies a subject position: a *khoziain*, who takes
dominion over the *khoziaistvo*, a head of household. In some cases, this
subject position might remain indefinite. This was the case with the
narodnoe khoziaistvo, when it emerged in the nineteenth century as a
translation of concepts then popular in the "pan-European shift in economic thought, away from a conception of government and economy as
the management of sectors, goods, and territories (and, through these
categories, people) to a conception of government of people comprising
the economy" (Kotsonis 1999, 37). In these nineteenth-century discussions, writes Yanni Kotsonis, the proper role of the state in managing
this *khoziaistvo* was an open question. Some argued that *narodnoe khoziaistvo* existed only as a function of the state; others, that it "should
imply that 'a subject is absent' (*otsutstvuet sub"ekt*) and . . . should also
lack a sense of a 'single will' (*edinnaia volia*) embodied in the state, so
that the 'popular economy' might be 'regulated but not administered'
by the state" (Kotsonis 1999, 38). By contrast, *sotsialisticheskoe khoziaistvo*
had both a single will and a subject position, as well as a goal: it was led
by the party and strove for communism, that nonlegal order in which
the coercive state would be made to wither away.

Like all households, the *sotsialisticheskoe khoziaistvo* had a material base:
one theorized in direct contradistinction to the primitive accumulation
of capital. In the early 1930s, after fifteen years of "socialist accumulation" had violently dispossessed most owners of their private property for the benefit of the industrializing socialist state, an infamous
antitheft law was implemented. It punished all theft of collectivized
property, no matter how minor, with ten years' incarceration or death.
Stalin justified this socialist law against gleaning with explicit allusion
to the legal history of prior enclosure acts: socialism, he explained, must
"declare communal property sacred and inviolable" to overcome capitalism, just like capitalism had itself managed to break the preceding
feudal order by declaring private property sacred, and punishing in the
harshest way violators of its interests (Khlevniuk et al. 2001, 240–41).

Thus drawing its rationale from the prior criminalization of customary use-rights, the law also radically reinterpreted this legal history. Private enclosures destroy a collective's right to use property in favor of an individual's right to possess it. The decree of August 7, 1932 forbade illicit possession but said nothing of illicit use.

Foundational documents of the socialist household economy drew on key liberal tenets and tweaked them accordingly. Borrowing from the 1789 Declaration of the Rights of Man and of the Citizen the notion that citizens' right to property is "an inviolable and sacred right," the 1936 Stalin Constitution declared socialist property to be "the sacred and inviolable foundation of the Soviet system." Taking from liberal constitutions the insistence on individual citizens' private rights, it proclaimed individual rights to be personal. Along with the right to labor and rest, the right to vote, and the right to social security, the Constitution guaranteed citizens the right to own, use, and inherit personal property. And this idiosyncratic form of ownership posed no risk to the sacred wholeness of socialist property, because it was essentially usufruct; it was theorized as each individual citizen's stake in the inviolable commons.[7]

The propaganda maelstrom released in celebration of Stalin's Constitution heralded the co-constitutive nature of personal and socialist property as the basis of a truly democratic new social order: the answer to bourgeois-liberal fascism (Wimberg 1992, 315). Legal journals did also. At the urging of Prosecutor General Andrei Vyshinsky, Soviet legal scholars reiterated Stalin's rebuttals to liberal accusations of tyrannical irrationality, particularly his insistence that "collectivism, Socialism, does not deny, but combines individual interests with the interests of the collective. Socialism cannot abstract itself from individual interests" (Stalin 1934; Vyshinsky 1935).[8] Only socialism, they argued, could provide true support for individual citizens' flourishing, because only socialism seamlessly integrated the individual into the collective. "Personal property in the USSR cannot be counterposed to collective property," Vyshinsky explained to Soviet law students. "It does not conflict with the latter, the two are harmoniously congruent. The growth of collective property provides for the growth of citizens' personal property. In turn, the growth of personal property promotes the development of citizens' culturedness, industrial and social activity, which itself leads to the growth and strengthening of collective property" (Vyshinsky 1938, 189).

Little turned out as planned. But as they worked to formulate a new legal philosophy by which civil law would work without private ownership, Soviet legal scholars isolated the principle that did, in fact, hold the *sotsialisticheskoe khoziaistvo* together: a political morality of collectivist use-right. As in premodern European political imaginary, the socialist household was a moral entity whose members "had positive moral and ethical obligations to themselves, to others, and to the society as a whole" (Koziol 2011, 188), foremost, the obligation of mutual aid. In the face of endemic shortages, enterprise managers relied on their personal connections to secure their material inputs, and could therefore never take the position "that the laws are sacrosanct" (Berliner 1957, 222). Through the optics of private exchange, such unplanned redistribution looked like criminal misappropriation and shady dealings—and this is how liberal analysts have typically understood it.[9] But in their own stories, socialist managers described their informal transactions as friendly mutual aid and "rescue in time of need" (Berliner 1957, 187); they framed them as ethical neighborly actions, carried out for the greater good.

Mises was right in a sense: the corporate structure that was the planned Soviet economy was neither effective nor rational. But, to recall his formulation, households differ from factories, not only in size. They also differ in their organizational logics, in that factories are organized by rational relations while households are organized by ethical ones. Ideal factory workers carry out their tasks according to regulations, undistracted by personal obligations, while household members are committed to each other through unquantifiable ties of obligation and entitlement, care and well-being, commitment and confidence, communality and affection, honor and pride. These socially embedded relations typically fall to the wayside as regimes of private property replace traditional custom and use with possession and contract (Polanyi [1944] 2001, 57). But they were the spirit and lifeblood of the socialist household economy, whose enterprise managers were expected to act as *khoziaeva*, as usufruct owners who "show 'initiative' and take vigorous measures to safeguard [their] flow of materials" (Berliner 1957, 222; Rogers 2006; Schechter 2017).

The line between such conceptual categories—between the factory and the household, the formal and the ethical, the public and the private—is notoriously slippery. It is in the eye of the beholder, a question of ethical framing rather than of objectively verifiable fact. It is elusory, and it is constitutive. By framing certain relations as ostensibly personal, private, and noneconomic, it safeguards the rationality of that which is thereby said to be properly economic and public. For example, while the market obviously cannot function without its next generation of workers, the assumption that bearing and raising this next generation is a question of private familial intimacy produces the image of public economic spheres as free, fair, and universally accessible (Gal 2005; Bear et al. 2015). The Soviet Plan relied on a similar sleight of hand. It worked not by the iron laws of allocation but by "planning cum improvisation" (Powell 1977), and the latter depended on the personal ethical relations Soviet people formed with each other as members of the socialist household, striving for that household's ultimate communist aim—or, at least, for their local collectives' immediate goals.

Khoziaeva got their materials from other *khoziaeva*; the socialist household was comprised of a multiplicity of nestled households, all the way up to the ministries, and all the way down the work group. Successful Soviet managers maximized their allotments of socialist property, minimized required outputs, and stockpiled excesses whenever possible to create "intentional leftovers" (Bize 2020, 474) that could then be redistributed as need be for ostensibly upstanding ends: to resolve newly arising shortages, to help the members of other work-units resolve their shortages, or simply to make useful things—like kayaks and tombstones—for personal use.

Which Collective? Whose Common Good?

For the group of theorists who met in Paris in 1938 to discuss Walter Lippmann's *Good Society*—and for those who followed in the neoliberal tradition thereafter—substantive economies spelled the death knell of freedom precisely because they necessitate a *khoziain*: someone who chooses the ultimate aims for which all are then forced to strive. Beyond the bounds of the family household, such common aims were seen to be inherently despotic. "Collective action in the interest of all can only be made possible if all can be coerced into accepting as their common interest what those in power take it to be," writes Friedrich Hayek in an early essay on Nazi-Socialism. "At that point, coercion must extend to the individuals' ultimate aim and must attempt to bring everyone's *Weltanschauung* [worldview] into line with the ideas of the rulers" (Hayek [1933] 2007, 247).[10]

This question of ultimate aims also formed a central problem for academic historiography of the Soviet Union. Were Soviet subjects passive brainwashed cogs in a system that administered their lives from above? Were they materially interested cynics, perpetuating the system without caring much about its stated ideological aims? Or were they motivated also by a sincere belief in, as Stephen Kotkin put it, "Marxism-Leninism, the official ideology of the Soviet state . . . a powerful dream for salvation on earth, and one that spoke the language of science" (Kotkin 1995, 225)? In the mid-1990s, Kotkin's work kicked off a new historiographic interest in subjectivity.[11] Focused on the language in which one becomes a subject, these studies, as Sheila Fitzpatrick writes, understood ideology not as a body of canonical Marxist-Leninist texts but "more as *Weltanschauung*—something collectively constructed rather than imposed" (Fitzpatrick 2007, 87).

But what was the content of this Soviet *Weltanschauung*? For what ultimate aim did members of the socialist household strive? In this book, I answer this question by shifting its terms. Following Louis Althusser, I understand ideology as notions by which we make sense of our place in the world—by which we imagine not just our conditions of existence, but above all our "relation to those conditions of existence" (Althusser [1970] 2001, 164). To locate these notions, I turn to the material base: to these conditions of existence. In the Soviet Union, that material base was the planned economy, whose imperfect distribution system brought everybody together. Different Soviet collectives imagined their own common good differently—according to regional, ethnic, class, and gender differences, differences in personal taste, family history, and difference of epoch—but there was one ideal on which almost everybody agreed. Most everyone agreed on how a person ought to relate to this material base. Collectivism was not only the ultimate aim toward which the *sotsialisticheskoe khoziaistvo* formally strove, it was also the ideology that kept it functional in the face of its poorly planned economy. People drew on collectivist idioms of neighborly mutual aid to explain their formally irregular actions, which kept the socialist household (and their individual households) functional in the face of endemic material shortages. And the logic of socialist and personal property, therefore, created a certain harmony between the aims of the party and the plans of the people.

But this apparent harmony hinged on a delicate tension: on the idea that seeking the good for one's particular collective also furthers the cause of the socialist household itself. Soviet legal scholars addressed this tension with the notion of *khozraschet*, which, they argued, emerged in the 1930s as a specifically socialist principle. During the New Economic Policy era, state socialist enterprises were obligated to perform economic calculations—known as *khoziaistvennyi raschet*—when dealing with market actors. But in the early 1930s, party officials and legal scholars presented *khozraschet* as a fundamentally new dialectic unity of individual enterprises' material interests and the socialist plan that was specific to the planned economy, impossible for "a private entrepreneur, the bearer of private property, [who] is by nature individualistic and disorganized. He has 'his own plan.' We cannot speak of his planning, for in the conditions of the proletarian revolution, for him, in the end, there is only planned death" (Rubinshtein 1933, 52).

Party leaders called on the principle to "strengthen economic organizations' initiative and give them a certain amount of independence, while simultaneously establishing their definite responsibility for completing state tasks according to contract" (Molotov 1933, 16). And legal scholars explained this apparently double demand of obedience and independence with the specifically socialist nature of *khozraschet*: the fact that a "certain independence within the limits of a given whole" (Rubinshtein 1933, 52) was possible only within the planned socialist *khoziaistvo* based on socialist property.[12] Pointing to the socialist household's unresolvable tension, *khozraschet* never ceased to be theoretically murky. Managers tried for large-scale embezzlement sometimes turned to the principle in their defense—not always successfully (Cadiot 2018, 259)—and still in the late 1970s, civilists lamented that "the literature lacks a sufficiently clear and precise definition of the concept" (Rakhmilovich 1977, 19). In practice, it was a principle of semihard budget constraint that was called upon to keep managers from conducting their horizontal trade as pure barter. In the words of Prosecutor General Vyshinsky, *khozraschet* was to teach managers to "count money, teach them to value this money, to save this soviet ruble and soviet kopeck and thereby to learn to accumulate funds for socialist construction" (Vyshinsky 1931, 3). *Khozraschet* demanded that horizontal transactions between enterprises be calculated in money—but, of course, without market price.

And then it proved lethal. By the mid-1980s, the idea that markets automatically generate the most effective solutions had become a sort of international common sense, even within the Soviet Union. Betting on this commonsensical truth, Gorbachev's perestroika reformers proposed that fortifying *khozraschet* with market mechanisms would force Soviet people to take greater personal responsibility for acting as their enterprises' *khoziaeva*. They proposed, specifically, that forcing enterprises to acquire their own inputs through horizontal inter-enterprise trade, while allowing them to sell their deadened material stockpiles at the state-set price and for the benefit of their own work-collectives, would make people "face the necessity of feeling that they are the authentic *kho-ziaeva*" of the socialist enterprises that employed them (Abalkin 1987, 84). These reforms promised not only to perfect socialism and speed up the socialist household economy that had become stagnant. They also promised to de-Stalinize Soviet society; to liberate Soviet people from the irrational, oppressive, and wasteful bureaucratic rigidity of the "Stalinist administrative-command system" that tied managers' hands and crippled their mindsets, that got in the way of Soviet people's personal ethical, rational, collectivist actions.

And in a sense, they were successful. But what they sped up, in practice, were the customary use-rights that had been the planned economy's personal shadow. By encouraging people to sell their enterprises' ostensibly deadened stockpiles of socialist property for the good of their own particular collectives, perestroika unfurled the delicate tension upon which socialist property relations hinged; it placed the collectivist good of particular collectives into direct conflict with the good of the socialist household as a whole.

In the 2010s, when I asked people about their self-made Soviet things, I often heard narratives in which the terms Soviet and perestroika were used to describe actions that had actually happened well after the Soviet Union itself had collapsed and the perestroika reforms that had destroyed it were over. People used the term perestroika when talking about the era's widespread dispossession of collective infrastructures, and used the term Soviet when talking about the enterprise-based actions of personal reciprocity, collectivism, and mutual aid upon which they relied to make do in these economically hard times. The two terms described similar transactions from radically different points of view, two moral-economy views on the same era: perestroika referred to the dismantling of socialist infrastructure as seen in terms of private interest; Soviet referred to the same actions as seen in terms of personal, collectivist entitlements and obligations. But I rarely heard the term "perestroika" used to describe the economic reforms of Gorbachev's perestroika itself (1985–91). Across the board, people tended to associate Gorbachev's reforms with political, ideological, and ethical changes. And when asked specifically about the economic reforms of perestroika, they often talked about the properly neoliberal reforms of the 1990s, politicians like Egor Gaidar and Anatoly Chubais, and policies like currency deregulation and privatization vouchers. This was true of those who heralded perestroika as the collapse of the totalitarian state and of those who denounced it as a plot to sell out the Soviet Union to foreign interests.

By 1990, Gorbachev's reformers had broken up into bitterly opposed factions, which vigorously blamed perestroika's disastrous outcomes on each other's stalemating and indecision. But circa 1986–88, they were still very much in consensus. Gorbachev's speeches, texts of his leading economic advisers and of popular Soviet publicists, economists, politicians, and the texts of the 1987 and 1988 reform laws all worked around the same theory, the one that was laid down in 1986, at the 27th Party Congress. This theory is that if workers' material well-being were tied more directly to their enterprises' success at inter-enterprise trades, personal profit would become both stick and carrot: naturally punishing the lazy, rewarding the industrious, and making "the work collective genuinely interested in the best, the most effective use of the resources assigned to it" (Abalkin 1987, 86).

Introducing horizontal inter-enterprise trade with no intention of liberalizing prices or legislating private possession, this project seems contradictory from the standpoint of market economics. But the creation of a market economy was never its stated goal. Its goal, instead, was to perfect socialism. And the method by which the reformers proposed to do so seemed reasonable. Simply put, they proposed that liberating management from the unwieldy demands of central planning would create an ethically self-governing system: that requiring work-collectives to seek out their own trade partners would materially stimulate them to be assiduous with the socialist property they manage, to be resourceful with their own worktime, to be inventive, and to strive with more vigor for the greater social good.

Theorized in the collectivist logic of socialist property relations, this was an ethical project. Intending to liberate people from the planned economy's Stalinist micro-management, to stimulate workers' feelings of personal responsibility for socialist property, foster initiative, and make people "feel that they are the *khoziaeva*" (Gorbachev [1986] 1987, 84), it created conditions in which the collectivist personal use of socialist property sped up so profoundly that the state monopoly over socialist property collapsed. Economic historiography typically explains the Soviet collapse as the result of uncontrolled private interest: as the result of "Gorbachev's piecemeal reforms [in which], communist terror was removed, but market discipline was not established, [allowing] workers and managers [to rake] off enterprise income that used to go to government" (Sachs 1991), as "legal changes and declining supervision" allowed certain "well-connected individuals" to "pry assets from the grip of the Soviet state" (Barnes 2006, 43). But reading the perestroika reformers' texts through the prism of socialist property law suggests another explanation. It suggests that Gorbachev's reforms stalled the economy not by liberating private interest but by rousing personal ethics. By economically obligating people to personally manage socialist property for the greater collective good, perestroika took off the limits of how ethical one could be. Placing the ethical obligation to further collective interests into direct conflict with the dispossession of collective infrastructures, it ran afoul not of actors' private greed but of their personal obligations.

Thus, in a twist of poetic justice, collectivist social self-management did make the socialist state wither away; it fractured the socialist household into a myriad overlapping personally managed usufruct monopolies, which distributed the socialist property allotted to them for the benefit of their own particular socials (Humphrey 1991; Filtzer 1991; Burawoy and Krotov 1992). And what was left? A plethora of conspiracy theories about how Gorbachev had sold out the Soviet Union to foreign interests; a plethora of commonsensical explanations about a teratological marketless state succumbing finally to the natural market forces of history; and the common assumption that perestroika was a primarily political and ideological (and perhaps moral) reform project, whose economic side was haphazard, half-baked, and indecisive. This book's insistence that perestroika was both decisively implemented and thoroughly theorized begs the question of what the reformers were thinking. The idea that Soviet state socialism could be fixed simply by raising efficiency, changing mindsets, and cutting waste may seem ludicrous: a misguided attempt to raise the efficiency of an inherently flawed system, an attempt whose very failure proves the ultimate triumph of markets over totalitarianism. It is true that the market alternative also creates massive inequality, sectarian strife, and an environmental disaster that may soon kill us all. But, global policymakers assure us, this can be fixed with minor tweaks to the system. All that is needed is more technology, more efficiency and, finally, more morality, all of which may be profitably provided by the market system itself (Zizek 2009; Hickel and Khan 2012; Peebles 2018).

In this shadow of liberalism's own apparent speed up, this book reexamines the Soviet attempt to build a modern, self-governing, efficient, and democratic society. Starting with popular historiographies of "the Soviet," it tells a story of central planning and stateless government, civic morals and citizens' property rights, individual interests and the commonweal, as seen through the prism of collective interest.

Chapter Outline

Each of the four chapters that follow is framed by an ethnographic riddle: a question that came out of my fieldwork, and whose answer I found in the theory and history of socialist property law. The overall riddle is this: Why did people in Russia in the 2010s narrate the past in ways that were often at odds with the factual truth of chronology? The first chapter sets out this question, and the next three chapters trace its development through three major shifts of socialist property law—under Stalin, Khrushchev, and Gorbachev. Each shows how these developments created, altered, and then destroyed the socialist household economy. Throughout, the book remains anchored to the 2010s of its ethnographic present, driven by the question of what truth there is in the popular historiography of Soviet times. It finds this truth in the political morality upon which the socialist household was founded and by which it ran: on its particular political morality of collectivist use-right.

CHAPTER 1

The "Soviet" Things of Postsocialism

In 2011, Vera worked as a kindergarten teacher, although she also had a diploma in glass engineering. She graduated from the Leningrad Institute of Mechanics and Optics in 1990, and her graduating class, she told me, was the last of the lucky ones, the last that still had jobs waiting for them. When her husband graduated from the Builders' Technical College a year later, things were already breaking down, and there were no jobs to be had. But her cohort also did not hold onto their jobs very long. Her college girlfriends now are all here or there: working in school cafeterias, hair salons, and real estate. Not one of them has a specialist job, despite all their education and diplomas. It is unfathomable, she said, how all these people just got cut off. It's a tragedy. For those who were relatively young when it happened, like she was, things still worked out alright somehow. But many of the older people just broke down with actual heart attacks and strokes when they suddenly found themselves jobless, unable to feed their children—they just broke. In 1994, Vera went on maternity leave. And when she came back, the laboratory that had employed her was gone. So that was that.

The lab where she worked was part of Svetlana, a military-industrial lightbulb and transistor plant so large that one of its sides stretched the length of three tram stops. She had gotten the job because her mother had used her personal connections to get her out of Svetlana's dirty production sectors and into this lab that worked to develop new technologies for making and decorating consumer glass goods. Although, Vera said, the lab spent most of its time making gift orders.

> VERA: There were some glass plates available as products of mass consumption, but these ones that we made, I don't know that they were ever sold—at least I never saw them for sale. And as I understand it—how did we have it back then? An exchange. Those plates we used for exchange—you give me, I give you.
>
> XC: Exchange between your plant and other enterprises?
>
> VERA: With other enterprises . . . like, when you have to obtain something, have to hammer something out [vybit'] for our sector . . . it actually doesn't lend itself to any rational reason. You know, the laboratory is experimental—it's always trying new things, and so it generates a lot of waste, rejects. And waste—who needs waste?
>
> XC: Oh, I get it, so from the laboratory one could take out a lot of . . .
>
> VERA: Yes, well, not a lot, but you know, I worked there myself, with those little plates. And there is this saying: you have a part of what you work.

And at this point in our conversation, Vera opened the lower section of her bedroom cabinet and took out stacks and stacks and stacks of glass plates, which she had accumulated during her four years at Svetlana (figure 1.1). She had other things from her time at Svetlana as well: bowls, kitchen glasses, and a small bag full of the decals that she had applied to glasses and plates in the lab for hours at a time. "Sometimes you would just be sitting there all day gluing, gluing, gluing. If there was some holiday, New Year's, there would be a slew of orders. Everyone needs to help out." She later used some of the decals to decorate her kitchen.

When I asked people like Vera—my friends and neighbors, and the friends and neighbors of my friends and neighbors—about the useful things they had managed to make at their late Soviet workplaces and smuggle home, I was often frustrated by the fact that people told me stories about things that were not actually Soviet. Often, after having photographed some such thing from all sides and having discussed the details of how it was made, I would put the dates of its owners' work histories together in my head and realize that it was a thing made in

FIGURE 1.1.   Glass plates gleaned from a lightbulb and transistor plant, circa 1991–94.

the late 1980s and 1990s, after the perestroika reforms (1985–91) had taken hold or even after the USSR had collapsed. At the time, I found this categorical indeterminacy quite irritating, and I went to some lengths to track down those things that were properly Soviet. So Vera's plates were not really the things I was hoping to find. Since Vera had only started work at the factory in 1991, they could only barely be said to have been made in the Soviet Union. Moreover, they could only barely be said to have been self-made. These plates were not exactly "homers," in the sense of things made "for personal use on company time and with company materials or tools" (Anteby 2008, 4).[1] They were more like factory-produced things that had been made to order and then smuggled home off factory grounds.

But in Vera's narration, the plates were both self-made and Soviet. What characterized them as such was how they were made and obtained: by what means and for what ostensive ends. Vera stressed that she never sold them, just took them to have, to give away, for her children to use. She explained that the experimental laboratory's planned wastefulness left some wiggle room as to what happened with the rejected samples. And she stressed her personal involvement in the collective labor by which they were made. "We got shipments of flat glass disks. And in our small laboratory, we heat them up, bent them to form; each type of glass has a slightly different melting point . . . and then you put on the decal, you see whether it takes, find the ideal temperature regime. Only the head engineer did this of course, he had a great deal of experience . . . and the rest of us—we all just helped out."

I asked her whether the plates had themselves all been discarded, and she laughed: "Not necessarily! They might not have been discards." But they had all been carried out past the plant's pass gate in small batches, hidden under her shirt. Autumn coats made this easier.

> VERA: Because if you wanted to do it officially—well, that could only be if there was some big holiday, and only with your supervisor's permission, and you would be checked from all sides . . . it was practically impossible.
>
> It was as if . . . well, just imagine, you work there yourself, but you cannot bring anything home! It's not good to say this, I guess, but what could one do? They're your own work, things you made yourself. And in the meantime, of course, management would take boxfuls. Understandably, they have deals they need to put through, gifts . . . But really it's terrible, that corruption.
> XC: And the things that people made at the plant themselves?
> VERA: Couldn't take them out either.

It is my search for these things that people made at the plant themselves that had brought me to Vera's house. My friend Marina, who taught kindergarten with Vera in 2011, had mentioned my search for such artisanal self-made Soviet things, and Vera very graciously volunteered her glass flowers (figure 1.2).[2] Blown for her in a different sector of the same industrial transistor plant, the flowers are made from oxygen-free infrared optical glass and are startlingly beautiful—thick, with a bluish tint that glints dark in certain permutations of light. Vera had seen the flowers around, she told me, and one day she stopped by a friend's sector.

> I say to her, listen, Tat'ianka, I need to have some of those flowers.
> And she tells me—go inquire over there, our guys make them. She says, yeah, offer them a splash of alcohol. We had technical alcohol to wipe down all of our various instruments at my laboratory, and so I'd skim a little off the top, and a little more, and a little more . . . and by the end of the month, I brought it to them.

FIGURE 1.2. Decorative glass flower, made from infrared optical glass at a lightbulb and transistor plant, circa 1991–94.

The glass blowers made other things too: wine glasses, bowls, vases. Vera had ordered several of the latter, but they all came out sort of lopsided. She suspects that maybe she did not offer enough alcohol. Anyway, she told me, she does not know why she wanted the glass flowers so badly; it was just something, something nice.

As we talked, I kept trying to turn the discussion toward these self-made things that constituted my object of study. But listening again to the recording of our conversation, I am struck that no firm and fast line separates the plates from the flowers in Vera's narrative. The plates were also, in her words, "Your own work—things you made yourself." This self-made nature helped legitimize their existence in her bedroom cabinet.

Talking about the plates and the flowers, Vera and I had a long conversation about Soviet times. She talked about material scarcity and irrational industrial waste, but also about welfare and neighborly social relations, and what she called the "immaterial values" of collectivism and friendly help. On the whole, her description of the Soviet era was positive, spoken in a tone of nostalgia. "We had a great material base at Svetlana," she said.

> VERA: There was a medical center, a pool, sauna, circular shower, lunch hour aerobics. A polyclinic, a dentist—for free—everything was free then, all during working hours. You could just talk to your manager. Svetlana was great. And for women, they had all the conditions set up. You go to the diner, there are several tables; you can always eat comfortably, great variety, anything. And they had their own meringue-making sector—the meringues were phenomenal. You could not get them in the city, not that quality—people would ask me to buy them. There used to be such a terrible shortage of everything: even buying a box of candy—you'd have to "obtain" it.
>
> XC: And at the plant you could buy it?
>
> VERA: Well, not candy, no; but they did make their own meringues— white and pink, phenomenal. You could buy things. You could buy fresh meat. I never did because I didn't have a family. But yes, you could buy it—so a woman leaves Svetlana like she is coming out of a store. Theatre tickets you could get. They were also in deficit—to any theatre. And we had our own shoe repair station.

This description of Soviet times is, strictly speaking, not Soviet. It is a description of perestroika and the early postsocialist years (1991-94) when Vera worked at Svetlana. But in this same conversation Vera described perestroika in different terms. In her telling, perestroika was an era of social collapse and abandonment: of the rise of racist nationalism and the collapse of a system in which, in her words, "We lived like one big family." Recalling her older coworker, who had suffered a stroke when he found himself laid off with four kids, she told me that it makes her cry just to think back to that hopeless era.

Similar images of perestroika punctuated many of my other conversations about the Soviet past: people described it as a time when collective infrastructures were stolen, dismembered, and sold abroad for a pittance, when everything fell apart. But most often, this image of perestroika narrated events that happened during the 1990s rather than during Gorbachev's perestroika itself (1985-91). So there was this apparent category mistake in my interview data: to many of the people with whom I spoke, the significance of the terms "Soviet" and "perestroika" did not derive from the state formations they named. People often used

the term "Soviet" to describe events all the way through the 1998 financial crisis. And many of the people who did so were well aware of the
historical facts; they could talk in great detail about when property laws
changed, and new types of ventures were legalized, when particular sales
contracts were signed, and when shipments were shipped. In such usage,
the term "Soviet" indexed a particular political and moral economy
rather than a state formation. "The prices were Soviet," an entrepreneur
named Ivan told me, describing how he had produced titanium climbing gear for the international market from 1993 to 2000: "The price
of metal did not include energy." A lot has changed since Soviet times,
Oleg, an artisanal leatherworker, told me,

> OLEG: First of all, in the Soviet Union, I could not just come to
> the factory and buy leather. They just didn't sell to individuals.
> Only to organizations. I tricked them though—back when the
> Radishchev [leather] factory was on the Kozhevennaya line, one
> of my former directors was the director of [the 5-star restaurant]
> Astoria. And through Astoria we bought the leather.
> XC: But why would Astoria need leather?
> OLEG: Oh, no one asked. It's just a piece of paper that goes through.
> Maybe to reupholster their chairs or something.
> XC: Was this in the 1980s?
> OLEG: This was 1992, 1994 . . . the Soviet Union had already col-
> lapsed, but the factory was still state-based.
> XC: That's the most interesting time . . .
> OLEG: It was the most horrible. The most horrible time.

In this most interesting, most horrible time, the "Soviet" did not
peter out slowly. It intensified: when I asked people about the things
they had made at Soviet factories, I was often told about things made
between 1988 and the mid-to-late 1990s. People had certainly made
such things earlier too, and I almost never heard speakers make categorical distinctions between things made during different Soviet periods.
But as I was collecting such stories, there just seemed to be more of
them from the time of the Soviet Union's factual collapse. Cemeteries of
industrial towns provide a good illustration. In the 2010s, the Kolpino
city cemetery was full of self-made stainless steel tombstones. Many are
decorated by this tree ring design you see in figure 1.3. It is left by an
industrial polishing machine. And the tombstones' inscribed dates of
death mean that they can themselves all be dated, like the shiny metal
tree rings of history. In my search for the authentically Soviet, I found

FIGURE 1.3. Stainless steel tombstones at the Kolpino cemetery. One is decorated with an ortho-
dox cross, another with a communist star. All three are inlaid with photos of the deceased.

that the first people to be commemorated by a stainless steel tombstone
in the Kolpino cemetery died in the early 1960s. But most dates of death
range from the late 1980s to the mid-to-late 1990s.

The Riddle and the Method

My attempts to catalog self-made Soviet things thus ran up against
the classic ethnographic question of what it was exactly that I was
studying. In the stories I heard, the "Soviet" was a category that could
stretch over more than three decades—from the 1960s to the 1990s.
It could classify things made at the height of the Cold War together
with things made after the Soviet Union had completely collapsed.
What were the conceptual boundaries of this Soviet era, which could
sometimes temporally overlap with its perestroika opposite? What did
it mean to say that a thing was self-made and Soviet? This is the riddle
that guides the present chapter. Its answer lies neither in the things

themselves nor in the actions that made them, but in the way that the stories about them were told.

My search for such things began with my friends and neighbors in Kolpino, and then branched out into several directions: former factory workers, outdoor enthusiasts, hobby collectors. I quickly gathered about a hundred objects, documented with stories and photographs. These things covered a very wide breadth of usefulness: from flasks and knitting needles, to kayaks and tombstones. Their owners and makers hailed from a wide breadth of class backgrounds, from manual workers to high-level managers and engineers. But there was a common thread running through the stories I heard about their creation, in that they were all happy stories of some successful action, of something done well. Some thing, after all, had been gotten. This is why there was a story to tell. Partially, this happiness had to do with the fact that people generally like to tell wild stories about all the stuff they managed to get away with (Cherkaev 2017). Partially, it was a factor of time. Kept around since the "Soviet" era, these things were now heirlooms in their own right, and even if some of my interviews began with people wondering why the hell anyone would care about them, they typically ended with them hoping that their self-made Soviet things would, by being recorded, enter history. There was also another important factor to these happy narratives, in that when I went over my recordings to figure out what exactly people were proud of, I found that they were proud of similar feats.

People of different class positions and professional backgrounds told me stories about having made and gotten different things in different ways, and these stories were united by similar notions of goodness, similar ideas about which ends people should seek (Taylor 1985; Robbins 2013). This was a delicate commonality, that of how people described what they did, how they represented "their relation to [their real] conditions of existence" (Althusser [1970] 2001, 109). Evaluation of particular actions sometimes varied, because questions of valor are inherently subjective. When I retold the story of Vera's plates to people in Dobrova's neighborhood, my interlocutors did not believe it. Those little plates, I was told, were a hot commodity around 1990, just before the advent of microwaves, in which their gold-plated border explodes into tiny glass splinters. In this telling, the plates were an example of the endemic theft and resale that characterized perestroika, rather than of Soviet self-making, collective labor, and ethical obtaining. But the virtues expounded by the speakers who doubted Vera's ethical claims were legibly similar to the ones she aspired to in her story; they doubted whether her particular actions were ethical, not her ethical framework itself.

The people I talked with agreed on this ethical framework, and they presented their actions in its favorable light. No one told me stories about having ripped off his entire work collective, and stolen things for his own selfish greed while leaving everyone stranded. This does not mean that such things never happened, of course. But it does suggest that such actions are not seen as something to be proud of. People generally like to recount their lives in ways that make them look good, and none of my interlocutors chose to brag about selfish theft as the way to do so. But they were happy to tell me about having broken the law in ways that were selfless and essentially victimless. They condemned acquisitive theft but celebrated maverick actions for the collective good. They told stories of solidarity, personal responsibility, and neighborly help. They talked about the material stockpiles that were not being used, anyway. And they associated these stories with Soviet times, even when describing events that happened long after the USSR had collapsed.[3]

Historical epochs cannot be analyzed solely through memoirs. Memory is subjective, and speakers' present assumptions are bound to color their narratives of the past. But these happy stories I heard about Soviet things gave me a thread to trace into the historical archive. Making me attend to the virtues for which people narrated their felicitous Soviet striving, they forced me to radically reconsider the "second," "shadow," and "favor" economy literatures' focus on factually illegal and emically immoral actions (Grossman 1977, 1982; Ledeneva 1998).[4] Starting with Grossman's classic studies, this literature is concerned with everything Soviet people ought not to have done, including "much of the perfectly legal private activity which [was] possible in the USSR" (Grossman 1977, 25). Uniting under one category "all production and exchange activity that fulfills at least one of the two following tests: a) being directly for private gain; b) being in some significant respect in knowing contravention of existing laws" (Grossman 1977, 25), it usefully tells us that Soviet people ought not have broken the law or acted acquisitively. But it does not tell us what people ought to have done. What ultimate ends should they have been seeking? Liberal historians have often sidestepped this question by assuming that people everywhere strive for the same privately driven ends. The joyful narratives collected in this chapter open a space to radically rethink these assumptions. They present us with the curious fact that, twenty years after the Soviet Union collapsed, people associated their properly Soviet actions with a particular form of ethical striving.

The Archive of Things

Among the oldest self-made things in my collection are the steel and titanium hooks depicted in figure 1.4. Such hooks were used for clipping onto rope-tow lifts, of which there were about a dozen up on the hills around Leningrad after the late 1950s and early 1960s. The lift-tows were put up by various institutes, and their cables often differed in diameter. Hook designs also varied: some were specific to a particular diameter, but others were universal, allowing them to be used on any number of lifts. These particular hooks were made in the 1960s for a man who, at the time of our 2012 interview, headed a laboratory working with satellite-based navigation systems. I asked him how the lift tows were maintained, and he told me it was a community effort.

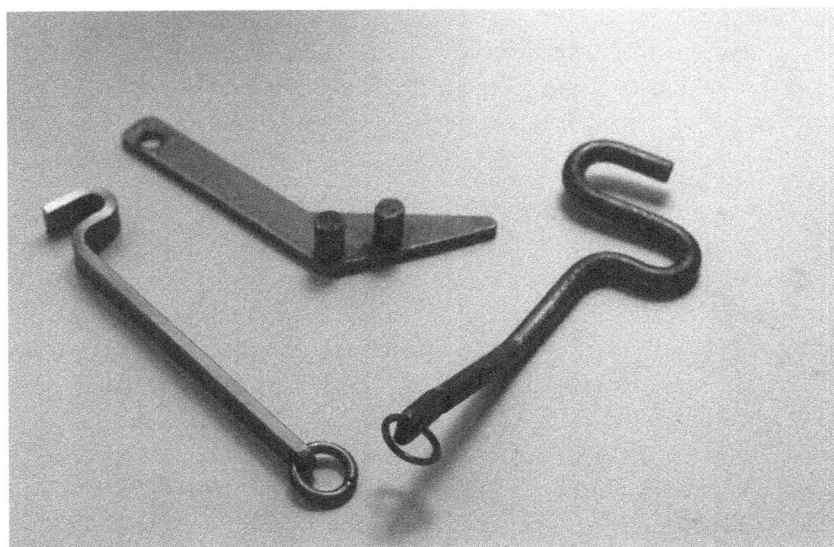

FIGURE 1.4. Three steel and titanium hooks, a rope-tow ski lift accessory. Gleaned from a classified institute in Leningrad in the 1960s.

XC: Who maintained the lifts?

A: Those lifts that institute collectives used, the institutes would support them, paid for the electricity, you know, we did everything ourselves, tuned everything up, changed out the cables, did it all ourselves—it was not a state thing.

XC: Were there private ones? Like if a group of friends, just decided . . .

A: Of course they were!

XC: But that must have required large investment . . .

A: None at all—the [lifts'] motors were stolen, what investment? . . . Well, no, of course, they were not private. The electricity was the institute's, they would find some money for the electricians . . . but generally speaking, this was all community organized [na obshestvennykh nachalakh].

The specific enterprise supporting this community-organized ski lift was a nameless classified institute—known only by its PO Box—at which the lift hooks were themselves also made.

A: You would just bring some alcohol—about 150 milliliter—to the guy who could guillotine off a bit of titanium for you, and about as much for the welder. And I got 15 liters of distilled alcohol a month for the lab. I could gild any worker!

XC: Was carrying them out a problem?

A: I would just have them in my briefcase, they never checked. Oh, you could take out carloads. It all depended on who and how. Everyone had his own pass gate guard—you could take out anything.

This description of the infrastructure of outdoor sport as a communally organized affair rather than a state thing, was generally held to be true. Late Soviet mountaineers, skiers, kayakers, and climbers made a wide array of gear for their hobby activities: from "disembodiment" (razchlenenka) dry bags, made by cutting up chemical-protection suits; to smokers and camping ovens made from medical sterilizers; to bolts, ice-axes, belay devices and parkas made from variously obtained industrial materials. The production of this gear was not a state thing, because it was done through personal channels, and often in circumvention of some laws, regulations, and rules. But it was neither outside of nor opposed to the state. These lift hooks that were made from titanium gleaned from one sector of a highly classified enterprise in exchange for some alcohol gleaned from another sector were smuggled out past the pass gate to be used on the rope-tow lift officially supported by that same classified institute itself, as part of its affiliates' officially registered ski club.

Narrative focus on the community means that these self-made things fail the first of Grossman's "second economy" tests: they are not made for private gain. They also often fail the second test: they were not necessarily made in knowing contravention to rules, regulations, and laws. Notorious for generating material shortages, the centrally planned Soviet economy understandably drove actors to hoard materials, and such hoarding itself exacerbated shortage (Kornai 1980; Verdery 1996, 20–29). But hoarding also created largely useless material stockpiles, which could be put to various uses. A lot of metal gear in Leningrad, for example, was made out of titanium (and duralumin), obtained at the city's many large military-industrial enterprises. Ivan, the climbing gear entrepreneur quoted above, explained that,

> There were norms: this much titanium has to be used in the construction of this ship. There is some leftover, but they report that it was all used. And it lies in the warehouse. And everyone tried to raise the norms, because that's the way the Soviet system worked; how much will they give you next year? As much as this year, plus you could ask for a little more. And if you did not eat everything, next year they would give you less. So everyone tried to take a little more, and it all accumulated, accumulated . . .

Hoarding whenever possible left enterprises with an unaccounted surplus, which individuals could often put to personal use in legal ways. Ivan recalled that when he needed a down jacket for high-altitude climbing, he happened to be working on a construction site near a feather-and-down factory,

> So I went in to talk to the head engineer, who scratched his head and said, listen—the best would be if you find a way to take our eider down. We have an untouchable reserve of it from the Ministry of Defense that's expired—but, since it's considered group "A" material, like precious metals and stones—we need permission from the Ministry for its realization. It had already expired, but it's group "A," so they cannot realize it. Well, what to do?
>
> Write, the guy tells me, to the vice minister of meat and milk production. And I wrote that we were such heroes, we were going up this very difficult mountain, that we will bring glory to our

country and to the city of Leningrad, and therefore we ask you to please give us, for cash payment, so many kilos of down. And it worked! I had the first down jacket like that, and then, with my help it took off . . . we consumed tons of eider down!

That's how it all worked . . . or it would have rotted.

The shells for these down jackets had to be made of cauterized nylon, which was terribly difficult to get. But a friend of Ivan's happened to have a girlfriend working in an out-of-the-way railway station, which happened to have yellow cauterized nylon curtains in their offices.

So he thought fast about it, came to me, and we scratched our heads and went to see the station manager. Listen—we tell her—why don't you let us make you real curtains: with frills, with folds, they'll be awesome. We'll take these down, and give you new ones. We need this thing, and you'll get some nice curtains. And along the way we learned that the railroad had cauterized nylon in all the station offices on this line. The nylon was originally intended for military use—not parachutes, because it breathed too well, but something else, I don't know what. It was new, so maybe it had also expired and had to be utilized, I don't know. The railroad, for me and my friends, our nylon came from there. Other *touristy* [trekkers] got it from other sources, but we never had to seek those out because we had enough.

The down jackets for Ivan's entire climber collective were thus constructed from legally obtained industrial materials: the curtains were fairly exchanged for better ones, and the eider down was purchased from the factory, at state price, and by permission of the minister of meat and milk production.

But the materials for these jackets were also obtained irregularly: in circumvention of the planned economy's quota-based distribution, through the interpersonal relationships in which people worked together to redistribute their enterprises' material allotments. Such relationships generate indeterminate personal debt between the people who made the transaction possible (in this case, the train station manager and the feather and down company director who had helped the guys out); and this debt could often be settled in mutually beneficial material exchanges, whereby all the parties involved helped their respective collectives, organizations, or enterprises. Thus Dobrova, whom we met in this book's introduction, recalled wandering aimlessly around a trolleybus yard once as a teenager, waiting for a friend of hers, whose dad worked there. Dobrova and her friend were both members of their town's youth horse-riding section, and so they were both concerned with getting and making tack.

> Exploring around the place out of idle curiosity, I came across a store of nylon webbing. The yard is supposed to receive two rolls a year. They don't need it, but they take it, because otherwise they might not get it the next year. And so they wind up with an entire storage room full, floor to ceiling. The webbing is for pulling the trolleybus' reins back on the wires, should they come off—but it is allocated as if the drivers spent their days doing nothing but pulling the reins on and off.
>
> So we came up with a brilliant racket—he gave us these rolls, two or three carloads, and in return, we provided sleigh rides to the upstanding trolley park employees and their children. They were completely happy to have fulfilled their programs of weekend Family Relaxation and the Culture of Sport, and we were completely happy to have 500 meters of webbing, which we instantly started sewing into quality halters and reins, so that our horses no longer had to be dressed in the shitty products of Soviet mass production.

While most of the self-made things I was told about had been made from material obtained in "some knowing contravention of existing laws" (Grossman 1977, 25), stories did not differentiate categorically between legal and illegal transactions. In both cases, narrative stress fell on striving for the greater communal good and on effectively tapping unused stockpiles. Recognizably illegal actions were typically framed in these stories as necessary and victimless acts, whose illegality is overshadowed by the greater social good. "I could provide happiness [oschastlivit'] to myself, to my friends. It was amazing happiness!" a mathematics professor told me, recalling that he could easily swipe technical alcohol from work in Leningrad in the 1980s, and that he once bartered some for brand new industrial nylon air-filters, from which climbers sewed mountaineering backpacks. The swap happened at the factory at night, and he left up over the roof and down the fire escape to avoid plant security, elated.

Scholarship on the "economies of favors" is decidedly skeptical of such claims of obtaining for friends. But the amazing happiness of the mathematician's narrative is a strongly positive emotion, a heroic feeling of indeterminable social greatness attained by bringing great value to a community. It is hardly the sheepish attempt to disguise mercantile interest "by altruistic motives of friendly help" (Ledeneva 1998, 42). The mathematician's joy of bringing happiness to his collective is also hard to write off as the mere misrecognition of motives because the value of the heist depends on subsequent friendly personal collectivist relations. A bag full of industrial nylon air filters is useless to someone without polyurethane—a material intended for sound isolation in tractors and tanks, slabs of which were cut in half lengthwise with an electrified wire and used in backpack construction. It is useless without technical skills and the knowledge of how to make such a backpack. And it is most obviously useless without a team of fellow mountaineers, with whom to go into the mountains. "We did all of this very seriously," Ivan explained,

> Because we had nowhere to realize our potential, but we had quite a bit of free time. Working for the state took only a little bit of energy, and for the rest, you had to realize yourself somewhere. I had a friend who calculated food rations. And that's important, there have to be enough calories, minerals, and water to keep the organism sustained while you are working hard at high altitudes. And so a person sat down and went into the literature, he counted it all out; we had 450 grams of dry ration per person per day—but it had everything. You wouldn't be full, but it could keep you going for ten days. So some person counted all of this out, and someone else, like me, went into metal. I, for example, never counted food. I trusted the guy to do it. Others sewed.

Necessitating many different and hard to get materials and skill sets, the construction of gear was typically narrated as a communal affair. Figure 1.5 shows one of the kayaks that were made around Leningrad in the 1970s and 1980s. This boat's carcass, which folds up into a backpack for easy transportation, is made of duralumin tubes. And getting the duralumin "was an actual criminal operation," explained a kayaker who, at the time of our 2011 interview co-owned an outdoor goods store. "There was a guy who, over the course of about five years spent his nights at the metal warehouse base by Rybatskoe [an industrial suburb of St. Petersburg]—he would go over there, swipe the pipes, and only certain kinds of duralumin worked—sometimes he'd stash them somewhere and come back for them later." Other people, who had themselves heisted, offered friendlier firsthand accounts: "the pipes we would heist

FIGURE 1.5. Kayak made from gleaned industrial materials, shown on the rapids nearby St. Petersburg. Image courtesy Anton Voronov.

from sprawling, poorly guarded warehouse lots around the city's outskirts. Four kids would climb into the lot after dark—it was guarded by a guy and a dog, but they are either sleeping or watching TV—and haul the pipes to some deserted place, from where we'd sort and bundle them and take them home on public transportation."

The duralumin tubes are fixed together into the kayak's carcass with snaps, made by boiling down Polyethylene. And this carcass is then lined with polystyrene foam (*penoplast*), which most gear constructors remember sourcing at the Kirovsk plant, where it was intended to be used for sound isolation for tractors and tanks. "We just took it from the warehouses, did not strip any live tanks or anything like that," explains the mathematician whose feelings of amazing happiness are described above. The polystyrene-lined carcass is then covered with a skin made from a TransAvto long-haul truck tarp, which gear constructors recall buying from truckers for a bottle or small cash, or just cutting off the trucks. The hydrodynamics of the kayak shown in figure 1.5 were calculated in the Ioffe Physics Institute, which was also the source of tetrahydrofuran, a chemical used to glue sections of truck tarp together into the kayak's outer membrane.

It is not accidental that many boats were made in this general fashion: quality base models for kayaks, and for many other types of outdoor gear, were outlined in officially published DIY guides. Illustrated with diagrams, these guides provide detailed instructions for making everything from parkas to hang gliders, and openly advocate using hard to get materials, like duralumin.[5] Instructions for kayak construction in Petr Lukoyanov's *Self-Made Touring Gear*, for example, note that "for carcass construction, it's best to use duralumin tubes D16T or D1T, with 1-millimeter thick walls and the diameters: keelson—25, stem—22" (Lukoyanov 1986, 85). The instructions are accompanied by a detailed diagram.

In the summer of 2012, I met with an inventor who had authored several belay devices described in the book *Alpine Touring Gear* (Direktor 1987). Boris was part of a large gear-developing community and had many examples of equipment made by other people and sent to him for advice and comparison as examples of new innovations. Some were signed with the artisan's name or marked with an identifying sign, like the etched tulip in figure 1.6; others were clearly made from scrap metal intended for industrial instrument panels (figure 1.7). I asked Boris whether *Alpine Touring Gear* was ever condemned for advocating the illegal appropriation of resources. But the question surprised him.

> Why would it be condemned? Well, if you get caught, you might get a talking to . . . but they would not take you to court for a book! And if you made it at the plant, well depends on which plant, whether it is a classified enterprise . . . Look, it did not interest or disturb anyone that you made mountaineering gear. But misappropriating socialist property, there was an article [of the legal code] about that. See, you have to distinguish between what was prohibited and what was not. It was not forbidden to publish anything, but how you'll manage to make it, that's your problem. Maybe someone knows how to, himself—maybe I have a lathe bench at home.

Much of the gear that was made thus by communal effort, at work, or from materials obtained at work was used within state institutions to further officially recognized goals. Kayakers passed merit divisions of the highly regimented Soviet sport in boats made out of stolen duralumin tubes and swaths of truck tarp, and took these boats on state-financed trips. The climbing gear that Boris and others manufactured was used in state-financed base camps—to which subsidized tickets were distributed through the climbing sections of institutes, universities, and enterprises. Thinking of people going into the mountains by

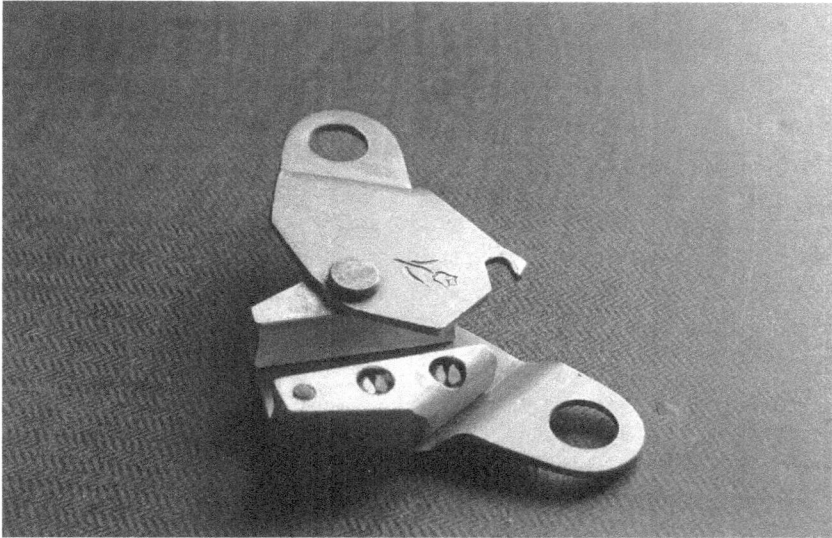

FIGURE 1.6. Gear, signed by an artisan author.

FIGURE 1.7. Gear made from metal stamped 100 kHz.

themselves, Boris turned to his wife and started laughing: "I see now," he laughed: "over there [in the United States] they have their own ideas—they think that we could just buy climbing gear and go into the mountains. It was not like that with us. Mountains are very dangerous. This is why everything was regulated. Rules, preparation, various norms. A very well-developed system."[6]

It is well known that people in Soviet-style economies lived around the state's rules, and studies of late socialism have provided a series of concepts for understanding such practices, like Grossman's command and second economy (1977), or Gal's language ideology of the public "them" and "extensionalized, imagined assembly of 'us'" who engage in horizontal relations (Gal 2005, 32). Alexei Yurchak (2006) points out that informal late Soviet social collectives were unstable in regard to their membership and deterritorialized in regard to state institutions, and I am generally sympathetic to this approach. But I want to suggest that we reformulate the question with attention to ethical motivation, starting with two contemporary Russian terms: rules (*pravila*) and understandings (*poniatiia*), with the latter employed similarly to how English speakers might use the notion of communal standards or ethical norms. "In the 1970s we lived more by understandings [*po poniatiiam*] . . ." a great storyteller once told me, a man with several criminal convictions and several successful firms, "and blatant commercialism, it somehow was not OK: it made you a *baryga* [a peddler, a hustler]." In this usage, rules refers to any definite obligation, whether required by law or by plan, while normative understandings refer to the tacit obligations people have toward each other.[7] But while understandings are beside the rules, they do not necessitate breaking them. The two are not counterposed, but distinguished by differing obligations: rules demand obligation to the issuing agency, and understandings demand obligation to an undetermined group of people to whom one is personally bound. These obligations are not categorically opposed to each other: actions can be said to abide by both rules and understandings, by one of them only, or by neither.

The ethical stance that emerges from narratives of self-made Soviet things is a question of understandings, largely unconcerned with the rules. But the objects produced by these actions were often openly and proudly displayed, as cemetery memorials, for example. When I lived with Dobrova in Kolpino, our next-door neighbor Shura was a retiree from the metal plants, who had spent her working life as a sheet metal worker. I stopped by one day when she was out grilling with her friend

Tamara, who had been in charge of a tool-making sector. It was a nice spring day to be drinking outside, and for my benefit they swapped stories about who swiped what and got what made at the plants. I asked them about the cemetery memorials. "I talked to Valentina," Shura said of the fencing that surrounds her family's plot, "and she ordered it from the guys."

SHURA: Would've been shitty driving it out, but Lekha tossed it over the fence . . . oh, their sector was right by the fence anyway—they've got barbed wire, but he tossed it over, and a car came by to pick up. Valentina had it ordered like scrap. The pipes are really long—she ordered them as scrap.

TAMARA: Of course, they made memorials at the plant! You come up, ask: guys, you got stainless, yea? What will it cost [*skol'ko stoit na lapu*]? They'll make it for you, they'll carry it out. You come up, say: guys, I need a still, I need a stainless tank—you know, we didn't have anything.

XC: Tamara, it was easy for you—you worked at the plant, you were section manager. But for other people? Was there a black market where you could buy everything?

TAMARA: Oh, just by friendship! Someone comes to me, asks: Would it be possible to make this? Sure, I say.
—And how . . . ?
Oh, I would say, go talk to Van'ka over there . . . and you would go to one of the guys. Like when I moved to my apartment here, and I needed flower boxes made, I went to fill out the paperwork, and the administration just hassled me and hassled me . . . so I went to the guys working on ventilation, brought the drafts.
—Guys, will you make them?
—No problem!
—How much will you take?
—Half a liter.
I still have the boxes up on my balcony.

Such stories present the circumvention of rules as a victimless action that overcomes the difficulties posed by shortages, work plans, and regulations while causing no harm to one's fellow workers.

Describing how they obtained something, or how they provided something for others, my neighbors' stories stressed solidarity, collective responsibility, and mutual aid. This is as true for stories of personally useful things, like cemetery memorials, as it is for stories of things that

FIGURE 1.8. Vise, made at a metal plant by a lathe machinist for work-related needs, early 1980s. Image courtesy Elena Tipikina.

people made specifically for work-related purposes. Narratives of useful self-made things rarely distinguish between things' usefulness at work and their usefulness at home. Figure 1.8 shows a vise made in the early 1980s by Shura's late husband, a lathe machinist named Borya. It is one of the few instruments in his extensive toolkit to have survived to this day. Shura explained that,

> When he got retired on disability, and I was working at the ventilation plants, the lathe machinists would come up saying, Shura—I don't have this . . . I don't have that . . . bring everything you got, we will buy it all. So I sold all the instruments to their boss, and he gave them out to the workers. I remember I asked Borya—how come you sold them so cheaply? And he said, well, I can't very well can I . . . ? [seeing as] I know them all . . .

> > XC: Why did Borya make his own tools? Couldn't he buy them?
> > SHURA: Oh, that was thirty years ago—of course he couldn't buy them. Tools, you know, I come up to the boss at the factory: I need a caliper, where can I find one? It's now they make them—now you can buy them at the store, but before you couldn't find them. And I needed a large caliper, over a meter, to draft. Well yeah, and if there isn't one, you go

borrow it from somebody who has one. What else can you do if there isn't one? It's nowadays you can buy everything.

Using his time and materials at work, Borya made tools for working, at work and at home; and he also made other useful things, for himself and for others. Shown in figure 1.9 is a pan with a stainless steel handle he had soldered on, replacing the original one that heated up inconveniently.

XC: Where would he get the stainless steel?
SHURA: Well now, do you really think . . . He worked at the metal fittings factory, and he made everything there, he made the dies. They would give him a sketch, and he would make the die—like they gave him a sketch for the Zenit [the local soccer team] pin. No one had them, only the coaches and team members. Well, do you really think that he wouldn't keep one for himself?

"Shura," I teased her: "did you swipe stainless at the plant?" "No," she laughed, "we took it." Many of Shura's everyday things are made from materials that had thus been taken. Her roofing: they had to take the backroads to dodge the cops, and Borya painted the metal panels a nondescript brown before she put them up on the roof. The stainless steel heat isolation between her chimney and ceiling. Her sauerkraut bucket (figure 1.10): stainless steel, she got the metal from the Krupskaya candy factory when she was down there for a job, installing radiators, and a guy at work argon-soldered it. Her collection of brass nozzles for connecting a tap to a garden hose: Borya spent half his shift making each one, she says, they made great gifts (figure 1.11). Her kitchen knives (figure 1.12): the ventilation plant where she worked was not a military enterprise, so they were laxer on the pass gate. She would get tool steel and give it to Borya to take into his plant, to make the knives on his workbench.

XC: Didn't they wonder why he was bringing steel in?
SHURA: Nooo, no one cared what you brought in! The hard part was taking it out.

Collections of useful tools for use at work and at home are common among people who had worked with metal, or whose personal relations included close ties to people who did. "We had mechanical workshops at the institute," explained a physicist who had worked at the Ioffe Physics Institute in the 1970s, describing the crochet hook depicted in

FIGURE 1.9. Store-bought pan with a new stainless steel handle attached at a metal plant. Image courtesy Elena Tipikina.

FIGURE 1.10. Sauerkraut tub made from stainless steel gleaned from a ventilation plant. Image courtesy Elena Tipikina.

FIGURE 1.11. Brass nozzle, made by a lathe machinist at work. Image courtesy Elena Tipikina.

FIGURE 1.12. Kitchen knives made at work. Tool steel blades, clear ebonite handles. Image courtesy Elena Tipikina.

figure 1.13. "There was a wonderful guy there—you would come and say, Vasia, I need a crochet hook, could you find a little hollow pipe, about yay thick—and then at the tip, solder on a bit of copper, but really make the transition smooth, so that it does not catch the thread . . . we made everything, I even knew how to work the bench myself, made everything for skiing too."

The physicist was a member of the Red Crochet Hook, a sewing circle established in 1962 by several young women who had become mothers and needed to knit for their children. In 2012, the group was still going strong with about fifteen members. I made my way to one of their Thursday night meetings to ask about self-made ski gear and found that everyone at the table had a story. About ski boots, for example:

> We covered boots with epoxy and fiberglass, which we had on hand for the compressors at the gas-turbine station. See, for natural gas to make it to the consumer, you need compressors and turbines to drive it, and we made them. We had epoxy to glue gages onto the compressors, so we would take that epoxy and cover the boots with it to make them hard. I made them for myself, my boyfriend, my boyfriends' friends . . .
>
> [Another voice at the table:] What! You can't say that! That's classified!!
>
> [General laughter.]

The members explained that the Red Crochet Hook is much more than a sewing circle; it is a circle for information exchange.

> How can you survive in Russia? You've got to know places: where to get tickets, where to get this or that . . . and through the crochet hook you could get everything—from cars to knitting needles. We are all different—look, Liusia is a geologist, Marina and I are from Phystech, Svetlana has a degree in economics, Ira from Politech, Lialia worked with the sovkhoz, Katia finished the German school, and then she worked for the railroads, Irka graduated from the University . . . And then we all had hobbies; we were volleyball team captains, skiers.

There were crocket hooks for sale in Soviet stores, but not as nice as the one shown in figure 1.13, not as long, not as small. And there were knitting needles—but not as thick and convenient as the ones made from ebonite at the Ioffe Physics Institute.

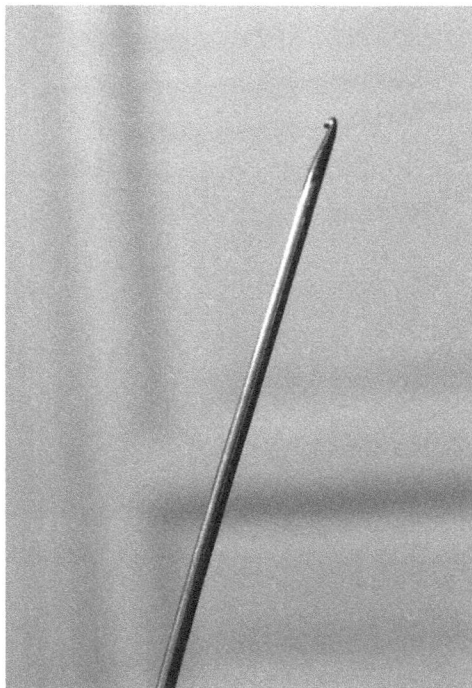

FIGURE 1.13.   Crocket hook made at the Leningrad's Ioffe Physics Institute. Stainless steel pipe, copper.

Members of the Red Crochet Hook are unique in how explicitly they narrated the goals of informational and material exchange. But nearly everyone I talked to told me stories of how relationships with family and friends had been mobilized for, and solidified through, the making and obtaining of things. The creation and gifting of these things often spanned generations, and many such things have since become family heirlooms. The ergonomic flask pictured in figure 1.14, for example, was made in the experimental sector of the military ship-building factory Znamya Oktyabrya (Flag of October). It was made on a computer-operated lathe bench for the section manager, who had it made as a gift for his son-in-law, Volodia, when the latter was sent to work at a mayonnaise plant in Alma-Ata as a young engineer. The flask was used to carry out refined (odorless) sunflower oil, and it was a gift for Olga, Volodia's wife and the section manager's daughter, who used

Figure 1.14. Flask. Made on a computer-operated lathe bench. Stainless steel. Leningrad, circa 1970s. Image courtesy Elena Tipikina.

FIGURE 1.15. Four screw-top adjustable knitting needles. Made on a computer-operated lathe bench. Stainless steel, brass, fishing wire. Leningrad, circa 1970s. Image courtesy Elena Tipikina.

the oil for baking and cooking. "It's now that shirts are worn loose," Olga explained,

> Back then, everything was tucked in: men wore suits and ties. And this [flask] is nothing! Another guy at the factory had a three-liter flask. He would suck in his stomach, put in the flask, put on a white shirt over the top, a tie, a suit: buttoned up and ready to go home!
>
>> XC: How much could a flask like that have cost?
>> Olga: Oh, it wasn't for money, people just made them help out their own [dlia svoikh]. Made them at the plants, just for friendship.

The section manager also had other gifts made on the computerized lathe bench, like the delicate screw-top knitting needles depicted in figure 1.15, connected to an adjustable length of fishing line, which Olga still uses. Similar trans-generational gifts include candleholders, glass trinkets, carafes, glasses, and many kitchen implements. Knives, choppers, axes, and carving tools are by far the most common articles in my archive of self-made things. They range from simple (figure 1.16) to extremely elaborate (figure 1.17). Handles are typically made either of black or clear ebonite, often put down over some colorful printed fabric or tin foil; or else they are made of bits of colored plastic, cut up and reassembled into a colorful pattern. Blades are typically made out of tool steel.

Self-made things typically had to be smuggled out past enterprise pass gates. But they were also typically made from materials that were said to be widely available. Shown in figure 1.18 is a questionably Soviet hedgehog, a glass trinket made at an optical plant where its owner, a man named Sergei, worked during 1987–92. The place was large, Sergei said: "We even had a stadium. But for some reason nobody played there. And so the stadium was piled up with metal ingots. Aluminum, copper, brass. These huge ingots. There was a sea of metal. Stainless, everything. Everything was just lying there, and you could just take what you needed, so long as it was just for yourself . . . Although of course you couldn't carry anything out." Sergei himself was a metalworker. So he did not make the hedgehog himself. He bought it, for a small sum of money through friends at this same factory. "Because the territory was huge, it was not possible to know everybody personally. So it all worked through acquaintances." He had bought some other things too: a glass carafe with a blown deer inside, a glass crocodile, a pen holder that looks

FIGURE 1.16. Knives and forks with simple black-ebonite handles, affixed at work. Top two knives are steel blades. Middle two: stainless steel self-made blades. Bottom: store-bought knife blade. Factory town near Leningrad, circa 1960s–1970s.

FIGURE 1.17. Knife with elaborate clear ebonite handle, made at work. Leningrad, circa 1960s–1970s. Image courtesy Elena Tipikina.

FIGURE 1.18.   A barely Soviet hedgehog. Blown glass. Made at the LOMO Leningrad Optical plant, circa 1987–92.

like a devil. And many other things he made himself. He welded together spare bolts and parts to make candlesticks, he repurposed projector engines to make drills and, like most everyone else who had access to a workbench, he made knives. The blades of his knives are made out of tool steel, the handles are decorated with colorful fabric, fixed under a strip of clear ebonite.

> SERGEI: We'd just get sheets of it [ebonite]—large sheets, and there would always be scrap leftover.
> XC: What was it used for?
> SERGEI: I don't know—to make handles, transparent control panels . . . there were always leftover scraps.

Ethics and Enterprises

Stockpiles are most obvious when they take up whole stadiums. But stories of how people gleaned socialist property also extend to stockpiles of monetary value. In these stories, commendable actions are also distinguished from condemnable crimes by the assumed motivation behind the act: commendable acts are explained as serving solidarity and furthering collective interests, and condemnable ones are explained as selfish greed. The exchange of money makes ethical obtaining somewhat more problematic but not impossible. As we have seen throughout this chapter, "small cash or a bottle" is recognized as an acceptable token of gratitude for the person who helped one obtain something.[8] The irregular exchange of larger sums could also be ethically upstanding, even in cases of criminal economic schemes, so long as such exchange is narrated in terms of the collective good. In 2012, I talked with Georgii, who ran an antique store in downtown St. Petersburg. He said that around 1972, when he was working in a used bookstore in downtown Leningrad, the library of the Siberian Branch of the Academy of Sciences was being expanded, and "their money was limitless."

> Their people came in, dug through our stacks, picked out books— we had them packed and shipped, and they paid us with a cashless transfer. They would have one person in town for a week, then he would leave, and the next person would come in. And since this concerned me professionally, I looked through stack after stack, and quickly caught on to the idea—there were no novels, no magazines; they needed serious things, especially concerning the Far East. And then I would spend my day off digging through the other used bookstores and buying the books that I thought they would find interesting. I changed the price, made it [laughs] appropriate—creative labor.
>
> The director of acquisitions would ask me—now, who is going to pay seventy-five rubles for this? People made ninety a month in those times. And I would say, seventy-five is the minimum! If they don't buy it, I will. But I almost never missed. I caught onto their idea very well.
>
> XC: How did it work, exactly?
> GEORGII: I set the prices, asked my friends to bring the books in to sell, because I obviously could not use my own passport. But I had a lot of friends, and a lot of girlfriends. We set up a row of shelves in the basement, where we put the books that might interest them. They didn't ask us for this, but were grateful for it later.
> XC: And all of this was officially done through the store?
> GEORGII: Yes, yes, and afterward they sent two thank-you letters, extending special gratitude to the bookstore on Gercen Street, which has books that one cannot even find in the public

library—one letter was sent to LenKniga, and the other, which was especially valuable, to the Party's GorKom [city council].

As Georgii told it, this scheme was virtuous even while it defrauded the Soviet state of large sums of money. Like Shura's and Olga's stories about getting tombstones and flowerboxes, the story is victimless and helps everybody involved: the Siberian library's employees save time, the bookstore on Gercen street earns thank you letters and overfulfills its sales plan—and the Academy of Sciences' money was limitless, anyway. Georgii, too, through his friends who helped him put the books up for sale, earned quite a bit of money: the difference between the price he initially paid for the book and the price at which he resold it. But when I asked him whether he had his own parallel trade while employed at the bookstore, he stalled uncomfortably. And then he said, "I will not deny it. Yes—but not a substantial one. Besides, as they say in the investigator's offices, off the record, salaries were not very high, and sometimes one wanted to earn some money; and sometimes, yes, I bought certain things, not for my own collection, but with the intent of earning something." Georgii's hesitation around the question of monetary self-interest is common in narratives of self-made things, and I often heard the ethical practices by which these things were made contrasted to the narrative present, in which things were said to be only done and gotten for money.

Tamara and Shura talked easily about getting metal and making personally useful things at the plants, but they were also harshly critical of theft. "People talk now about the GULAG, about unfair imprisonment in the Soviet era," Tamara said, "Well, maybe people did get sent to prison, but maybe they deserved it, maybe most of them did." And, she said, what she would propose to do now is to take all those thieves, all those who wrecked the country, who sold it off, who care solely about what's in their pockets—take them all and put them into a GULAG: "we can build more than one White Sea Channel today if we round up all the thieves."

DOBROVA: But Toma, they will take us all—we are all thieves.
TAMARA: Oh, what kind of thief are you? What do you steal?
DOBROVA: It's just that I don't work. When I worked, sure I stole . . .
    I stole paper.
SHURA'S SON VALERA: I steal all kinds of cheap Chinese shit.
DOBROVA: Speaking of which, why don't you swipe me a new saucepan with handles?

Dobrova's and Valera's aside is funny because it shifts registers. The theft of cheap Chinese saucepans is not the practice at which Tamara aimed her image of catastrophically widespread thievery. Nor was this image associated simply with falling social mores. It was, instead, part of a recognizable historiographic narrative about perestroika: a social catastrophe during which the material foundations of social and economic life were ferreted away.

No one even thought about stealing in Soviet times, Tamara said. Working was interesting—it was always about inventing something new. But by 1994,

> I was working at the railroad plants [*zhelezka*]. Before, our director was a Class-A guy, took the commuter rail to work with us, a stand-up guy. But perestroika began, and they replaced him with this new jackass. Stopped paying our salaries, while he kept buying himself new cars. Good thing I lived with my son, either he would get paid, or I would; we did alright. But I saw how they made money: we would get new wagons, and they would make the guys cut them up. Sold them for scrap metal, and kept using the old ones. I saw this all with my own eyes, the guys almost crying; they had just overhauled the wagons, and here perestroika began.
>
> It was utter destruction. The people will never forget it. 1917 will come again, my son keeps saying. People will get together, they see how unjust it all is. No unions, no laws.

Her son sold metal too. "The guys see their bosses taking out wagon loads, well they aren't dumb either." They would take copper ingots, one by one, out over the fence. Sold them to Estonia, Tamara said, bandits drove around in those days, buying up nonferrous metal.

I opened this chapter by suggesting that oral histories of irregular exchange often use the term "Soviet" to define a form of a political and moral economy rather than a state formation. This is an economy centered around labor collectives and enterprises, and narrated in explicitly ethical terms. I often heard people marvel at the irrationality and wastefulness of centralized distribution—about stadiums of scrap metal and about educated engineers who spent their workdays gluing decals. And I heard them denounce this system's unfair distribution of privilege—with old Party members lying in elite hospitals amid vases of fresh fruit, while sick children are placed into overcrowded facilities without basic medical supplies. But in these same stories, the Soviet era was often associated with the ethical actions by which people helped each other overcome these unfair, irrational, and wasteful deficiencies of planning. And these actions, in turn, were often associated with the sheltering function of work collectives and enterprises. Nadezhda Kuzmenichna, whose husband made the no-frills practical kitchen knives shown in figure 1.16, had spent her working life at a large metalworking plant near Leningrad. She retired as the head of a sector. In 2012 when we spoke, she told me that she still identified as a "real Soviet person." And then she elaborated:

> Behind the railroad tracks, that's where the plant is. Was. Now it's all been stolen away [*razvorovali*]. Before, that is where they made high-powered electrical machines, 4,000–5,000 kilowatts, turbo-generators, hydro-generators, and now there is just one sector left, making some kind of small machines. Some small construction bureau left.

> XC: And the apartment?
> NADEZHDA KUZMENICHNA: That's all the plant. We got it all for free. The plant gave it to us.
> XC: Did it come furnished?
> NADEZHDA KUZMENICHNA: Well no, the furniture is ours . . .
> XC: So how did it work—you were told that you would be moving and you bought furniture?
> NADEZHDA KUZMENICHNA: Well, first they gave me a room. Here, not far away. In a two-bedroom apartment, I had a room, eleven meters.
> XC: Also from the plant?
> NADEZHDA KUZMENICHNA: From the plant.
> XC: And then you moved here?
> NADEZHDA KUZMENICHNA: And then the children were born, we had a family. And they gave us an apartment. And that is all. The plant built all of this. And then, besides the plant, there was also the "furnace," they made high-frequency electro-furnaces there. And a research institute of equipment development.

It is against such narratives that we must understand Tamara's insistence that in Soviet times "no one even thought of stealing." Self-made tombstones and stainless steel buckets are not stolen but gotten through acts of friendly reciprocity between people trying to make do despite material scarcity, while stealing—in Tamara's narrative as in the narrative of the retired engineer above—is not just an action that takes what does not belong. It is an action that dismantles the very material base of the social. "The whole truck park sold off to new owners who sold it off for scrap metal," a former truck mechanic told me, describing the horror of perestroika: "Working Kamaz, Maz, and Zil trucks, sold as scrap metal to Sweden and Britain." They brought in a portable presser, he said, and cut the trucks up right there, in the park, cut them right through their metal carcasses, pressed them into blocks, loaded them into other trucks, and took them straight to the port on Vasilievskii Island, to load into shipping containers. Fifteen trucks a day. This image of ravenous greed and selfish destruction is widely associated with perestroika: "greedy, cynical, unprincipled and unprofessional," summarized the mathematician whose story of "amazing happiness" is related above, explaining that at his institute's Communist Youth League he "got a good look at these kids who are now running this country."

In subsequent chapters, we will see how the deregulatory reforms of perestroika factually sped up Soviet ethics, at the same time as they stalled the planned Soviet economy by encouraging actors to make use of ostensibly stockpiled materials for the greater collective good, and thus placing the ethical obligation to further collective interest into direct conflict with the unethical dispossession of collective infrastructures. But for the purposes of this chapter, I want to point out that people often use the terms "Soviet" and "perestroika" to explain potentially coterminous politico-economic relations. Stories of perestroika tend to focus on the dispossession of collective infrastructure. Stories of Soviet times tend to focus on the relations of personal reciprocity that helped people get around challenges, shortages, and regulations for the greater social good: striving to provide for one's own collectives, enterprises, affiliates, family, and friends.[9] These are two common ways of narratively framing the types of material relations that became prominent with Gorbachev's economic reforms: either as actions of personal reciprocity to keep social worlds, work collectives, and entire enterprises functional despite material and regulatory difficulties; or as actions of greedy, cynical, and unprincipled thieves who sell off the communal implements of labor for scrap, and thereby dismantle the infrastructure of ethical action itself. Sometimes, these ostensibly successive historical epochs factually overlap in one and the same narrative.

CHAPTER 2

Gleaning for the Common Good

As I asked people about their self-made Soviet things, I often heard explanations of how the Soviet system worked. These narratives typically circled around themes of interconnectivity and top-down control, and they often seemed formulaic. If told by people who thought that the Soviet Union was bad, they focused on irrational wastefulness and lack of freedom. If told by people who thought it was good, they focused on safety and welfare. As fieldwork data, they seemed pretty useless, until I looked at them again through the prism of socialist property law. When I did, I saw that these stories held an answer to the riddle posed by the self-made Soviet things people had shown me, many of which had been made years after the Soviet Union collapsed. Less a description of the Soviet political economy than an expression of socialist ethics, these narratives, I came to realize, testified to the fact that the Soviet was not only a political state but also an ethical one. Their point was less in what they described than in how they described it.

Uniting such stories was a particular subject position, a first-person plural: a *we* who "had everything under Soviet rule [*vlast'*]," or a *we* who "had nothing." "In Soviet times," explained Nadezhda Kuzmenichna, whose narrative of endemic perestroika-era theft closes the previous chapter:

> All the factories used to be interconnected, so that everyone knew what everyone else was doing and how much of what was needed. Back when everything worked, before this new regime [*vlast'*] came and destroyed everything. And let me tell you, Soviet rule [*vlast'*], it raised me, everything I have, I got because of that system. If you had a head on your shoulders, you could get ahead. Study, work hard, and get ahead. We had everything under Soviet rule, and what we had was good.
>
> Caviar! Right after the war there was caviar, sure, five rubles a kilo, and they sold it, I still remember, in white enamel basins. Not like now! Ha, no, not like now when one thief sits atop the next, accusing the other of thievery! And there was none of this *tuneiadstvo* [unemployment, lit. "eating in vain"]—we/they made them work![1]
>
> There was one, lived a floor above, a boy named Sasha, who just did not want to work. We/they put him away—not long, maybe just a year or two—and when we/they let him out on mandatory labor, we/they gave him a month to find a job. And, every evening, at nine o'clock, I would hear footsteps on the stairs—*zok, zok, zok,* up the staircase—and I would say, oh! that's the neighborhood cop going to check whether Sasha is home or if he's off running around somewhere.

The "we" animating these stories of Soviet times marks some collective with whom the speaker expressed solidarity: some group of people who helped the speaker do this or that. It could be a family, a work collective, or a group of friends, could be patriotic or dissident, law-abiding or criminal. And of course, this is what the pronoun we means—a collective subject. But the "we" of these narratives also has a particular history; it was a "we" with particular entitlements and obligations, a "we" of a particular property regime, whose history may be traced to the origins of the socialist state.

The Private and the Personal

The Soviet "we" starts to come into judicial being in 1918, with the first Constitution of the Russian Soviet Federative Socialist Republic

(RSFSR). As Mikhail Reisner, one of the authors of that Constitution, explains in the pamphlet *What Is Soviet Rule?*, the main tenets of Soviet rule hinge on offering "true equality" to the "laboring brotherhood" by explicitly denying equal rights to those who live by exploiting others. "But this does not mean that we forbid them from entering our common laboring family. Let them abandon their unjust power, their *tunei-adstvo*, their property and their capitals, let them set aside their pride and their disdain for the workers, let them take up 'productive and socially-useful labor' (art. 64) and the deal is done. Then, as equals, we will take them into our Socialist republic, in which a great rule is established: 'he who does not work, neither shall he eat' (art. 18)" (Reisner 1918, 12–13).

Thus in 1918, the subject of Soviet rule was explicitly defined against the exploitative classes who were not us, not part of our common laboring family. These excluded not-us were nevertheless recognized as Soviet citizens; they were denied political and civic rights, but with the view that such rights could be reinstated through socially useful labor (Alexopoulos 2003, 32). "The Soviet Constitution of July 1918 provided that the 'nonlaboring' elements of the population would be deprived of the right to vote," explains Yanni Kotsonis, "and the accompanying regulations subjected them to additional tax rates. But the law and the regulations on the disenfranchised still referred to them as citizens and did not make provisions for stripping people of citizenship; there was, indeed, no category of noncitizen. . . . All of this suggests an interplay of particularism and universalism that was amply reflected in early Soviet fiscal policy, manifest in the simultaneous emphasis on class struggle and universal civic enlistment" (Kotsonis 2004, 562). This split—between class struggle and universal citizenship—defines the idiosyncratic structure of early Soviet property law.

Juridically, the early-Soviet civil codices of 1922 and 1926 recognized three types of property ownership—state, cooperative, and private (*chastnaia*).[2] They protected the private rights of all Soviet citizens, whether of the amorphous laboring brotherhood or of the exploitative classes, and they recognized all citizens as private individuals. But these citizens' private rights were not absolute; they were defined as a temporary right, a property relation meant for extinction, a necessary concession in the process of building socialism. "Soviet law acknowledges and guarantees the property rights of private citizens," early Soviet textbooks explain, "but it takes measures to ensure that the use of these rights not contradict those aims for the sake of which they are granted [the construction of socialism], and does not see an independent value in such rights" (Magerovsky 1927, 151). This nonabsolute nature of private rights led early-Soviet legal scholars to argue that the three types of property recognized by the Civil Codex—state, cooperative, and private—were in actuality so different from one another that they could hardly be theorized in the same category (Magerovsky 1927, 161; Stuchka 1931, 17). State property "is not simply the state's right to private property," explained Pyotr Stuchka, chairman of the Supreme Court of the RSFSR, in 1931.[3] "Quite the opposite, as a class concept, it is the direct antithesis to the right of private property, it comprises, in the juridical sense, a single inviolable fund that is inalienable and that enjoys a series of legal entitlements for its protection" (Stuchka 1931, 25). Put simply: state rights were absolute, private rights were not. Private rights were recognized only insofar as this recognition did not hinder the socialist project.

Stuchka argues that this fundamentally unequal relationship between state and private property fruitfully implodes the basic tenets of civil law, which had regulated Russian property relations since the mid-nineteenth century. The Russian Imperial *Digest of Laws* drew on Roman legal categories to define full and complete ownership as a familiar cluster of rights: to manage (*usus*), benefit from (*fructus*), and dispose of (*abusus*). This tripartite definition of full and complete ownership rights was inherited by the young Soviet republics.[4] But "*abusus* [*vladenie*] is disappearing entirely from the Soviet codex as superfluous concept," notes Stuchka, "as it has already disappeared from the Land codex, where it is naturally replaced by the concept of *usus* [*pol'zovanie*]" (1931, 22). Following Stuchka's reasoning, we can say that the property regime that was being constructed in the young socialist republic was that of usufruct: a regime in which the right to use and benefit from property could be extended without the third term that completes ownership rights, without the absolute right to dispose of that property at will.

But while this process was underway, while *abusus* was in the process of "disappearing entirely from the Soviet codex," the law still recognized Soviet citizens as private individuals, endowed with private rights. And as private citizens, Soviet people still needed to buy and consume to sustain themselves—they needed food, clothing, stuff. This meant that private property remained inescapably prevalent and inescapably problematic. Still in 1933, civilists defined retail trade as

A simple purchase-sale contract . . . concluded by two parties, of which one is usually a state store, a cooperative store, or a kolkhoz (bearers of collective, socialist property), the other is an individual citizen, a private individual.

What happens to the property rights over the thing about which these two parties conclude their contract? Apparently, the right of ownership of such a thing transfers from the hands of a socialist enterprise to the hands of a private individual. We seemingly see here the transition of a thing from socialist material property into private property. (Zagviazinskii 1933, 252)

Through the early 1930s, there was not much that legal scholars could write in justification of this practice, except to point out that most such transactions were conducted by private citizens who were fully embedded into the Soviet economy; and that, in the communist future, the institution of private property would be abolished (Zagviazinskii 1933, 252). To the early-Soviet tripartite definition of ownership, the fact of private consumption was inherently problematic.

And then the problem was solved. It was solved because a fundamentally new property regime was established. By 1936, legal scholars happily note that "the overwhelming mass of the population is now tied to the social [*obshchestvennym*] (state, kholkhoz, cooperative) *khoziaistvo*" (Rubinshtein 1936, 14–15).[5] And that, based on such social unity, a new regime may be established to resolve the awkward early Soviet triad of state, cooperative and private property rights, by declaring "state socialist property" to be one unified front against private possession. Before 1936, legal scholars proposed dual legislation: a civil codex [*grazhdanskoe pravo*] regulating private ownership and merchant trade, and a separate codex called *khozaistvennoe pravo* regulating the centrally planned part of the economy: the socialist firms' exchange and procurement of goods (Campeanu 1988, 38). In 1936, the two codices were decreed to be indivisible (Rubinshtein 1936, 23).[6] The basis of their indivisible unity was a new property relation, one named the basis of the socialist order, sacred and inviolable.

This sacred, inviolable property was first called into being by the notorious decree of August 7, 1932, which made any and all theft of this sacred property—no matter how small—punishable by death or by ten years of hard labor, and declared all those engaged in such theft the enemies of the people. In 1932, the term "socialist property" had not yet solidified, and this draconian law protected "collective (socialist) property." Legal scholars celebrated it as the origin of a new theoretical and political era. In a 1933 article, Leonid Ginzburg wrote: "The decree from

August 7, 1932 concerning the fortification of collective (socialist) property is one link in a glorious chain of nationalization laws . . . Declaring socialist property to be 'the basis of the Soviet order,' it raises the entire question of socialist property to unprecedented theoretical and political heights. The decree of August 7 gives direction to the entire theory of Soviet law" (Ginzburg 1933, 9).[7]

Ginzburg proved right. The 1936 Stalin Constitution, which restored voting rights to the formerly disenfranchised (Fitzpatrick 1993, 758), repeats a phrase from the 1932 law almost verbatim, with collective property now called socialist. It obligates "every citizen of the USSR to safeguard and strengthen socialist property, as the sacred and inviolable basis of the Soviet order, as the source of the wealth and might of the Motherland, the source of the prosperous and cultured life of all laborers." And it declares "those encroaching upon collective socialist property [to be] enemies of the people."

In twenty-first century Russia, the 1932 law is commonly known as the law about "three stalks of grain." I am unable to trace this etymology. But it is notable that, in his 1881 commentary to the Book of Ruth, the Rev. James Morison, citing the seventeenth-century Hebraist Johann Benedikt Carpzov, writes that "the later Jews had a set of fantastic bylaws concerning gleaning, detailed by Maimonides. One of them was, that if only one or two stalks fell from the sickle or hand of the reaper, these should be left lying for the gleaners; but if three stalks fell, then the whole of them belonged to the proprietor" (Morison 1881, 30). In the 1932 Soviet version, the state set no lower threshold. Any theft of socialist property (a bit of coal, a handful of grain, a nail taken home from the plant) was to be punished by death or ten years' incarceration. The "sacred and inviolable basis" of the Soviet order originates with this unconditional and unreserved violence against all private threats to the state's monopoly. Socialist property, writes Ginzburg in 1933, must capture "not only the leading role but the absolutely prevailing position." The question of "who gets whom" must be decided in both city and countryside (Ginzburg 1933, 5). No private claims to take back what had been dispossessed, to chip away at the socialist whole were to be tolerated.

The early 1930s was a time of widespread famine: a direct consequence of the forced collectivization of peasants. It was also a time during which the state coffers swelled with Soviet citizens' gold. Between 1931 and 1935, the Soviet foreign currency store Torgsin accumulated an estimated 100 tons of pure gold, mostly in the form of everyday gold items that people brought in to trade for basic foodstuffs (Osokina 2006). The accumulation of gold and the collectivization of peasants, and the famine that draws them together, were part of one ravenous process known as "socialist accumulation": a process of massive dispossession that wrung out all available sources of value for the benefit of the industrializing socialist state (Goldman 2022). "In order that industrialization may go forward," Stalin explained in 1926, "old factory equipment must be renovated and new factories built. . . . But, comrades, in order to renovate our industry on the basis of new technical equipment, we need considerable, very considerable, amounts of capital. And we are very short of capital, as you all know" (Stalin 1926). The proposed solution drew on all available resources while "carefully plug[ging] up all those channels and orifices through which part of the surpluses from accumulation in the country flow into the pockets of private capitalists to the detriment of socialist accumulation" (Stalin 1926). Nationalization played a critical role in this process (Osokina 2018), as did terror, collectivization, and forced labor policies motivating obeisance while providing the fortifying socialist economy with cheap labor (Harris 1997; Baron 2001). "On the one hand, fearing the fates of their repressed neighbors, peasants ground their teeth and entered the hated collective farms," Oleg Khlevniuk explains. "On the other hand, the property confiscated from the repressed was, by the calculation of the Stalinist leadership, to form the collective farms' material base" (Khlevniuk 2010, 36).

This violent process of dispossession created the material basis for a new regime of socialist property. In many ways, the process resembled the primitive accumulation of capital. It "had the same content as the capitalist model, expropriation; it employed the same basic instrument, violence; and in principle it embraced the same object, the producers" (Campeanu 1988, 116). But, as Pavel Campeanu notes, it also differed critically in that it was neither market nor class based (1988, 116). Socialist accumulation did not dispossess one class for the benefit of another. It dispossessed everyone for the benefit of those who successfully joined the new state-led economy. And in 1936, based on such complete dispossession, the new Stalin Constitution granted all Soviet citizens personal rights to those common grounds. Along with the right to labor and rest, the right to vote, and the right to social security, the Constitution guaranteed citizens the right to personal property: to own, use, and inherit stuff.[8]

Sometimes assumed to be "a legitimizing cover for the acquisition of property that was private in all but name" (Siegelbaum 2006, 6), the institution of personal property was actually a very particular form of ownership based on an explicitly nonprivate logic. Unlike the definitively distinct and opposing notions of private and public, the personal and the socialist cannot be opposed because they co-constitute one another. In the words of Prosecutor General Vyshinsky's 1938 legal textbook:

> Personal property in the USSR cannot be counterposed to collective property. It does not conflict with the latter, the two are harmoniously congruent. The growth of collective property provides for the growth of citizens' personal property. In turn, the growth of personal property promotes the development of citizens' culturedness, industrial and social activity, which itself leads to the growth and strengthening of collective property. Socialism truly harmonizes the interests of singular persons and of the entire society. In our system, the development of a person's material well-being happens through the development of the material well-being of the entire collective, quite unlike the dog-eats-dog law of exploitative, capitalist societies, in which the strong gobble the weak. Comrade Stalin said: "collectivism, socialism, does not deny individual interests, it combines them with the interests of the collective. Socialism cannot turn away from individual interests. Only a socialist society can give the fullest satisfaction to these personal interests." (Vyshinsky 1938, 189)

Theorized as each Soviet citizen's right to a share of the "growing wealth of the socialist homeland" (Rubinshtein 1936, 43), personal property was the right to a stake in the sacred commons, to a place in the socialist household.

The Socialist Household, *khoziaistvo*, and Its *khoziaeva*, Its Usufruct Owners

At our table, no one is unwanted
by his own deeds everyone's rewarded
with gilded letters we write out
Stalin's All-People's Law.

These words' grandness and their glory
no years' passing will efface:
a person always is entitled
to education, labor and to rest.

These stanzas are missing from the theme song of the 1936 film *Circus* (Aleksandrov 1936); they were added in 1937, a year after the film was released (Dem'ianov 1937). But their meaning fully saturates this popular musical comedy. *Circus* opens in the American South with a scene of a young white woman escaping an angry mob with a baby in her arms. Chased by the mob, she jumps onto a moving train and into the arms of a circus director, who subjects her to domestic abuse and makes her perform in the ring—an acrobatic act in which she is shot out of a canon—and who keeps her in line by threatening to expose her past. The circus tours Moscow, where the American woman falls in love with a dashing Soviet stunt man and, after a brief comedy of errors, succeeds in leaving her jealous abusive manager and staying in the Soviet Union. In the final scene, as the American woman and Soviet man are performing a more glamorous socialist version of the cannon act, her former manager breaks into the ring and exposes her awful secret: that her child is black. But the Soviet crowd thinks nothing of it. We like all children here, the Soviet circus director explains, have as many as you like: black ones, red ones, dappled ones. The audience members pick up the adorable toddler and pass him around, keeping him out of the hands of the abusive racist and singing to him, each in his own language. Throughout the film, these happy inhabitants of the socialist household sing a catchy song about the Motherland:

> From Moscow to the farthest borders
> from the southern mountains to the sea
> a person walks along as a *khoziain*
> of his vast expansive Motherland.

The violence that created this "great family's" sacred commons also found reflection in popular Soviet texts, colored with the cheery aesthetics of socialist realism.[9] Also released in 1936, the film *Convicts* is a comedy about the notorious Beltbaltlag labor camp that built the White Sea Canal (Cherviakov 1936). In real life, this building site was the first large project on which the Soviet state formally acknowledged using forced labor. "We did this before, we are doing it presently, and we will continue to do so," explained Vyacheslav Molotov in his report to the 1931 All-Union Congress. "It is profitable for society. This is useful for the culprits, whom it habituates to labor and makes into useful members of society" (1931, 2). The prisoners, he added, live lives of which the impoverished free citizens of other countries could only dream. A myriad of popular publications developed Molotov's celebratory image of forced labor, painting a cheerful picture of the horrendous conditions in which hundreds of thousands of people labored and died. Central to these publications was the authoritative narrative forged by a team of Soviet writers, who had been invited on a luxurious tour of the White Sea Canal for this expressed purpose. Among those invited was Nikolai Pogodin, screenwriter of *Convicts* (Klein 1995).

Convicts' protagonists hail from two distinct pasts: hardened criminals and declassed intelligentsia. The peasants who made up most of the GULAG population are absent from the film, and the prison camp itself is depicted as a sort of a northern sanatorium, where forced labor appears largely voluntary. It is this voluntary nature of labor that provides the narrative drama: initially, neither the criminals nor the intellectuals want to work, but then both are won over and swept up in the process of socialist construction. The main protagonist, an authoritative criminal, named Captain Kostya, comes around when the wise police boss running the camp shows Kostya that he believes in him; he gives Kostya a gun and puts him in charge of a timber-harvesting expedition. At first, Kostya's men are incredulous. But Kostya tells them not to argue: "There's no one above us, I alone am the *khoziain* of this operation. Do you trust me? Get on board."

The lead female character is also a hardened criminal, thief, and murderess, and she also becomes an exemplary worker. She is beautiful, but she is not Kostya's love interest. Instead, Kostya courts Margharita Ivanovna, a member of the declassed intelligentsia who, incarcerated for some unstated reason, performs administrative work in the camp's office and goes around reciting the effete poetry of the Silver Age. In recognition of his timber operation success, the police boss gifts Kostya a button accordion, and with this accordion Kostya serenades Margharita Ivanovna.[10] Margharita Ivanovna is smitten. Kostya tells her that he used to be a pilot. They flirt and kiss, and when his accordion breaks due to its shoddy workmanship, she invites him to come to see her at work for some glue with which to fix it. But when she later finds out that Kostya had been a thief, not a pilot, she refuses to have anything to do with him. "We haven't enough for our own needs," she tells him when he comes asking for glue. "We're not in Moscow," another office worker chimes in. "You can't buy anything here, can't steal it." Incensed, Kostya storms off and then comes back to seek retribution on the man who told Margharita Ivanovna of his shady past. "I'm a bandit," he says, breaking into the man's office, "I'm not someone you could just gift a drop of glue to. But I know how to steal, and I've come to rob, and I will maim decent young men." He frightens the office worker and lets him go, and throws up his hands: "Oh, mademoiselle, why did you have to be such a petty bitch?" When armed guards rush in to apprehend him, Kostya escapes and runs straight to the police boss to plead his case. The latter hears him out and issues the following orders: release Kostya from punishment, return to him his accordion, give him some glue, sentence Margharita Ivanovna to fifteen days' administrative arrest. Back at the worksite, the guys forgive Kostya for skipping out on work to seek vengeance, voting unanimously to "treat our comrade humanely."

It is my contention that this drop of glue, which Kostya sought and which Margharita Ivanovna first promised and then denied him, held together the *sotsialisticheskoe khoziaistvo*: the socialist household economy, built on the sacred foundation of socialist property, owned and managed by its *khoziaeva*, its usufruct owners.

To grasp this particular logic of ownership, it helps to compare three contemporary Russian ownership terms: *vladelets*, which stresses possession; *sobstevnnik*, which stresses property; and *khoziain*, which stresses management. A dog, for example, can be said to have a *khoziain,* a master with whom it is bound in relationships of authority and obligation. And it can also have a *vladelets*, a registered owner who has the right to sell it, or to lease it for breeding. Or, if the dog belongs to a puppy mill, it might have a *vladelets* but no proper *khoziain*. The term *sobstevnnik* can technically replace *vladelets* in this example, but it sounds somewhat pompous to say that one is a *sobstevnnik* of a dog. Typically, the term *sobstevnnik* is reserved for larger property claims, like puppy mills.[11] And, like the ownership-as-management rights of a *khoziain* may be contrasted to ownership-as-possession rights of a proprietor, so may an economy as *khoziaistvo* be contrasted to an economy as a formal system of possessions exchanged. Most broadly, *khoziaistvo* refers to stuff over which a *khoziain* has dominion: even a man's private parts are, somewhat lewdly, said to be his *khoziaistvo*. The usurpation of a *khoziain*'s dominion over his *khoziaistvo* by someone acting as a *khoziain* without formal rights to do so is described by the verb *khoziainichat'*: "I hope you don't mind that I am *khoziainichaiu* here," a mother-in-law might say as she barges into your kitchen and starts reorganizing your pantry. *Khoziaistvo*, explains Stephen Collier, "as a noun, can refer to a farm, a household, or virtually any nexus of production and need fulfillment—that is, to almost any unit of substantive economy. But *khoziaistvo* can *not* imply the formal meaning of 'economic'" (Collier 2011, 81).

The critical distinction between an *ekonomika* and a *khoziaistvo* lies in their subject positions. An *ekonomika*—a formal economy—may be a headless space of circulation, in which a multitude of actors trade, each seeking his own benefit. But a *khoziaistvo* must necessarily have a *khoziain*, a master who manages it. Soviet civilists were very aware of this distinction in the mid-1930s, as the term *sotsialisticheskoe khoziaistvo* was emerging alongside the institution of socialist property. As the 1936 textbook of Civil Law explains, citing Lazar Kaganovich's speech at the 17th Party Congress:

> Capitalism is not interested in, did not and does not know the question of how to organize the country's economy [*ekonomika*] as one integral whole, for this contradicts the very nature of capitalism. In the Soviet country [by contrast,] the question of how to manage each of the household economy's links [*zveno khoziaistva*], each of its branches, is an organic part of the question of how the entire *sotsialisticheskoe khoziaistvo* is organized. Leading the entire process of socialist construction—that is, the political and economic [*khoziaistvennoi*] reconstruction of society—necessarily demands a unified political and economic leadership, concentrated in the hands of the Soviet state [*gosudarstva*] and aiming to construct a classless socialist society, to develop and strengthen the socialist order. (Rubinshtein 1936, 13–14)

This socialist order was formally comprised of hierarchically nestled units; all of them were allocated predetermined shares of socialist property according to quota (called a "limit") and responsible for fulfilling a certain predetermined quota of labor and sociopolitical obligations (called a "plan").[12] But the mechanism of central planning that allocated shares of socialist property in this economy was highly imperfect; endemic material shortages frequently left socialist enterprises unable to secure that property to which they had use-rights, and for whose management they were responsible. Such conditions of uncertainty drove actors to maximize their material inputs and stockpile whenever possible because, as Joseph Berliner puts it in his 1957 classic study of the ethics of Soviet management, "a ton in the warehouse [was] worth ten tons on paper" (Berliner 1957, 109). Berliner notes that the hustle to secure the allotted materials was itself publicly recognized as one of the tasks of good management. "There is," he writes, "a positive exhortation to the manager to show 'initiative' and to take vigorous measures to safeguard his flow of materials. The manager who is content to submit his statement of requirements and then sit back is considered to be 'bureaucratic' and to lack energy" (Berliner 1957, 222). And he notes that one way for managers to thus show "initiative" was through exchange, negotiation, and trading. "The surest way of securing the supply needs of the enterprise is through direct negotiations, and thus the exchange of materials became an institutionalized way of meeting supply problems in the prewar period. The very fact of the widespread acceptance of trading encouraged enterprises to hoard materials they did not need, since they could be used for trading in exchange for needed commodities" (Berliner 1957, 109).

Most subsequent economic analyses have tended to see this situation as Berliner did: as an exchange of property. But socialist managers themselves—in my own interviews, no less than in the oral histories collected in the mid-twentieth century—tend to explain their own redistributive actions differently: as explicitly noneconomic, ethical actions of neighborly help.

I often heard people talk of this personal redistribution of socialist property as exemplary of the ways in which everything had worked in Soviet times. Sergei—whose barely-Soviet glass hedgehog we saw in chapter 1—explained that in Soviet times "everything hinged on the plan. You had to fulfill the plan, and slightly overfulfill it." And your ability to do so, he said, hinged on the "human factor." So when he worked as a brigadier at the optical plant, his duties included chatting with the warehouse clerks and drinking tea. "I come back to the sector and they ask me where I had been, while they were all working. Well, actually, I was working too: if the warehouse clerk doesn't give us material, we won't overfulfill the plan, and no one's going to get a bonus." Similarly, in the hundreds of interviews that Harvard collected with Soviet defectors and refugees shortly after World War II these two themes keep repeating: fear of brutal and unpredictable policing and the ethic of "good relations."[13] Speakers recall that "people have to help each other. . . . We all worked together to falsify the reports"; that "those who drink vodka together are good friends and in their working relationship they are much more lenient towards one another;" that "often workers would come and beg for bread and I would give it to them and write it off under the name of waste, in Russian *brak*."[14]

People often recall that a space of indeterminacy sometimes appeared between the quota of socialist property to which one was entitled, and the practical ways in which this entitlement came to be filled. They often recall that this indeterminate space could be personally managed. And that such personal actions were the very essence of good Soviet management. Scholars of the ethics of socialist management also note the personal obligation to use one's own good relations to meet the quota-determined obligations of the plan as critical to the very logic of being a *khoziain*, an owner-manager, who takes personal responsibility for the success of his *khoziaistvo* by securing needed resources through formal and informal means (Rogers 2006). Not only were all Soviet people welcomed to "walk along as a *khoziain* of their vast expansive motherland," but directors were said to be the *khoziaeva* of their enterprises (Rogers 2006; Collier 2011, 119–22; Cadiot 2018), commanders were said to be *khoziaeva* of their military regiments (Schechter 2017), and Stalin was said to be the *khoziain* of the country (Khlevniuk 2010). In the ownership terms of civil law, we can say that each such *khoziain* managed a householding unit that was entitled to a quota of *usus*—the right to manage socialist property—and was obligated to use that use-right appropriately. So Captain Kostya's insistence that "there's no one above us. I alone am the *khoziain* of this operation" is rather misleading. The statement belies the nestled nature of the socialist household, in which there was always another *khoziain* above. In the fictional example from *Convicts*, we can say that Captain Kostya's particular *khoziaistvo* was allotted certain entitlements (expendable human lives to be savagely broken felling timber, primitive tools with which to work, basic foodstuffs to keep the labor force alive, etc.), and obligated to perform a certain, predetermined amount of work (measured in timber harvested).

This was a usufruct economy, like Stuchka theorized. It was an economy of managers, who all used and enjoyed socialist property, which none of them could completely possess. With *abusus*, the right of absolute possession, bracketed by the sacred monopoly over socialist property, only *usus* and *fructus* remained. And in that indeterminate space between the quota and its fulfillment, between the amount of socialist property to which a work unit was entitled and the practical ways by which that entitlement came to be fulfilled, lay the critical ideological principle of this socialist household economy: the personal obligation to transgress *usus* for *fructus*, to circumvent the rules of use for the good of the collective benefit. This personal obligation was not just a coping mechanism that helped people get by in the shortage-ridden economy. It was formally recognized. Indeed, even celebrated. It is Margharita Ivanovna whom the police boss imprisons for refusing to give Kostya the socialist-enterprise glue, not Kostya, who threatens to maim the man who led her to refuse him.[15]

Gleaners and Hoarders

Striking in its unprecedented cruelty, the August 7, 1932 decree about "The Protection of Socialist Property" follows a long tradition of laws against gleaning. Historically, the erection of modern industrial states has relied on the codification of property ownership: on laws that enclosed common lands, restructuring "'rights' (held in common) into 'property,' or 'capital' (held in particular)" (Ditton 1977, 41), rationalizing variegate, flexible customs into definite property relations (Davis 1988; Thompson 1991; Linebaugh 1991), transforming "qualitative and particular entitlements and commitments . . . [into] quantitative and abstract rights and responsibilities" (Kockelman 2007, 170).[16] The 1932 decree was explicitly conceived with reference to these preceding enclosure acts. Stalin explained,

> Capitalism could not have destroyed feudalism, could not have developed and fortified, had it not declared the principle of private property the basis of the capitalist order, had it not made private property sacred property, had it not strictly punished the violation of this property's interests and created its own state for this property's protection. Socialism will not be able to finish off and bury capitalist elements and the individualist self-seeking habits and traditions that serve as the basis for stealing . . . if does not declare communal property (cooperative, kolkhoz, state) sacred and inviolable . . . if it does not protect [that property] with all its forces. (Khlevniuk et al. 2001, 240–41)[17]

But the 1932 decree "about three stalks of grain" also differs profoundly from the enclosure acts that ground private property. Rationalizing and simplifying the rights of ownership, private enclosure laws establish owners' exclusive rights to possess property and criminalize nonowners' rights to use what had previously been known to be common. In pre-Soviet Russia, this process began in earnest with the reforms of Catherine the Great. It differed from other European enclosure acts in that the right to private property was established by royal decree and never extended to all the estates.[18] But the main thrust of this process was similar to other enclosure acts; it also replaced customarily defined use rights in a territory with definitely determined possession rights of a territory.[19] The 1932 decree is different. It outlaws not illicit use but possession. The law protects "communal property" (*obshchestvennoe immushchestvo*) from "embezzlers" (*raskhititeli*) and other "antisocial elements"; calls such embezzlers the "enemies of the people"; decrees their execution to be the "highest level of social protection." But it elides the question of proper possession rights. Communal property appears to be collectively held. The law's preamble frames the protection of collective property as a demand of the people themselves. It cites "an increased number of complaints from workers and collective farmers about cargo theft from railway and river transport, as well as theft of property belonging to cooperative societies and collective farms, perpetrated by hoodlums and antisocial elements." The 1932 decree is legible as an enclosure act, but it is peculiar in that it protects communal use from illicit possession instead of protecting private possession from illicit use.

Understanding the different logics of enclosure that produced private and socialist property helps us dodge the temptation of theorizing one property regime as a deficient version of the other: of theorizing socialist property as a regime of "incomplete" property rights (Campeanu 1988) in which only Stalin alone could be said to be the true owner of everything (Gorlizki 2016). Socialist property does seem incomplete and teratological when seen through the prism of possession, without which private property makes little sense. But attention to these regimes' historical origins shows private property to be no more natural than its socialist counterpart; both are based on the legislation of certain forms of ownership and the violent denial of others. Instead of starting with the primacy of private property, I suggest that we start with the sacred origins of socialist property itself, with an enclosure act that protects communal use from illicit possession. Attending to communal use, we will see that socialist property relied on that ownership relation that the enclosure of private property systematically eliminates: customary use-rights. Such use-rights did not pass through the enclosure of socialist property unscathed. Outlawing gleaning under the penalty of death, the 1932 decree was meant to crush customary material practices as well as ethical norms.[20] But if we take seriously socialist managers' ethical claims, we will see that this cruel enclosure law also legislated into existence a new Soviet order, which relied on its own form of gleaning.

Gleaning—the right to take scraps—invokes an assumption that the remainders of some operations must not be losslessly reincorporated into cycles of profit but set aside for nonowners (Bize 2020). Leviticus not only entitles the poor to glean after the reapers, but obligates field owners to "not reap to the edge" of their fields or go back for the gleanings, to leave for "the poor and the foreign" (Leviticus 19:9–10). Positing the right of the excluded in terms of the leftover, gleaning presupposes a world in which remainders are qualities that do not easily become quantities of surplus value: in which the production and replacement of use-values take precedence over the circulation of exchange-values.[21] The socialist household was one such economy. Lacking free market prices, it was structured by the planned creation and distribution of material things. It also depended on these material things' explicitly demarcated remainders: it relied on its *khoziaeva* to take it upon themselves to glean leftover scraps of socialist property for the good of the socialist household, and it celebrated the gleaners who did so.

In the 1932 film *Counterplan*, for example, the Leningrad turbine factory's work collective struggles to meet the counterplan it has elected to keep, over and above formal requirements it was tasked with (Ermler and Yutkevich 1932).[22] From the very title, we are in the realm of custom and extras. Nothing compels the workers to complete this counterplan except their honor, which they feel depends on it. At stake is a new turbine, constructed by one of the plant's engineers to surpass the British model previously built at the plant. The work collective builds this new turbine in record time, but it fails to launch. Worse, after the first failed launch, the foundation cracked beneath the factory's machinery. Everyone blames the lathe machinist: an old-regime factory worker who had been drinking on the job (although the real culprit is another engineer at this same plant, a committed wrecker who, driven by his spite and hatred of everything Soviet, intentionally factors a mistake of .003 percent into his calculations). The counterplan seems doomed. But the party organizer refuses to give up hope; he turns to the lathe machinist and his old guard factory comrades, who recall an old machine stored away on factory grounds, "in the old abandoned workshop, where time and rain ate away at the machines that had served their time." They fire up the machine, jerry-rig some new parts (while, in the meantime, the engineers figure out how to solve the .003 percent miscalculation), and the new turbine runs. The unplanned counterplan is met with the enthusiasm of the labor collective, who work overtime to maintain their honor, and with left-over machinery, rescued from the grasp of rust and time.

These poorly warehoused leftover machines and materials had troubled Soviet politicians and planners from the earliest days of the Soviet order. But the planners' complaints were more about the improper warehousing of stockpiles than the fact of stockpiling itself. The problem, as Malenkov put it was that

In many enterprises equipment, raw materials, processed materials, tools, things for which our industry has a desperate need,
are piled up wherever they happen to fall, spoil, rust, become
useless . . . In Plant 61 in Lipetsk on January 14, 1941, 70 good
machines were accidentally discovered lying in the snow under the
open sky among the junk. But in the enterprise there is a director,
there is a Party organization, and finally, in Lipetsk there is a City
Party Committee. Just what were they looking after? Where is the
concern for the preservation of equipment? (1941, 2)

The poor management of stockpiles testified to the fact that these stockpiled materials lacked a proper *khoziain*. But the existence of stockpiles
was not, in and of itself, necessarily a bad thing. Indeed, those leftover
scraps that could be heroically mobilized to meet the unplanned counterplan (or at least to not fall too short of the planned plan), where did they
come from? They came from the prudent actions of good *khoziaeva*, who
set them aside as *nelikvidy* (lit. "illiquid assets" that fell from circulation).[23]
Scholars of shortage economies often note that soft budget constraints
and perpetual shortages led economic actors to safeguard their ventures
by maximizing the resources allotted to them, minimizing required outputs, and stockpiling whenever possible (Kornai 1980; Verdery 1996). Former socialist managers recall this process as well. "Enterprises put in their
orders for raw materials with a large margin," recalls Valentin Anisimov,
a man who had spent his working life as an acquisitions manager at the
Leningrad shipbuilding plant, "because they knew that only part of what
was requested would be granted. But sometimes everything was granted,
in which case the excesses accumulated in warehouses" (Anisimov 2003,
200). But socialist managers also recall something else, to which scholars
of shortage economies have paid little attention: they frame their narrated recollections in a particular ethical stance that condemns private
acquisitive theft while commending actions that break regulations and
rules for worthy collectivist social causes.

   This ethical stance matters. Functionally critical to the Soviet economy, it was also central to the ownership logic upon which this socialist
household was grounded; to the logic by which the *khoziaeva* of socialist
property were at once its owners and gleaners. The Old Testament injunc-
tions concerning gleaning assume a household economy in which social
justice is premised upon insurmountable inequality. They instruct field
owners not reap to the edges, nor go back for the gleanings, nor pick up
fallen grapes, but to leave all such scraps for the unfortunate—for the

poor and the foreign, for the orphan and for the widow. It is exceptional that Boaz takes Ruth in marriage, elevating her to the position of owner, precisely because gleaners as a class are never destined to own the fields, to be the owners' equals. But the socialist household economy was based on a different logic of ownership; on the sacred basis of socialist property, a commons over which all Soviet people were expected to walk along as a *khoziain*. And this household economy relied on its own form of gleaning. It relied on its prudent owners to glean illiquid remainders from the plan of distribution, and to personally redistribute these leftovers for some greater collectivist good.

Soviet procurement—the job of getting materials delivered to the enterprises that need them—depended on personal relationships formed between people in positions of distribution. And socialist managers often recall that these personal relationships generated personal benefits. But they tend to describe these personal benefits in socially embedded terms. Many people told me stories of how other people stole and got rich by illegal redistribution, and many told me how they enjoyed social status, success, and glory from such redistributive actions. But very few people claimed to have themselves gotten illegally, privately rich by their distribution of socialist property. Anisimov, for example, stresses in his spoken memoir that he never gave bribes, broke criminal law, or lied in a way that would hurt anyone—even as he recalls the personal bonuses upon which the business of Soviet procurement relied. Once, when his enterprise failed to receive the fittings they had been allotted, he was commandeered to the supplying factory with instructions to fill the allotment within ten days. The factory was near his home village, so he bought some seedlings for his mother and asked permission to stop off at home should he manage to get the parts sooner.

> For some reason, the factory did not make enough parts. There were a lot of procurement officers there from various enterprises. They used to call them "pushers" [*tolkachi*]. I walked into the factory, to the director's waiting room, sat near the secretary, and waited my turn. I had a magazine in my hands. Bright flowers on the cover. The secretary noticed the magazine, and we started talking. Torzhok is a small town with houses with yards, lots of flowers, and I guess she enjoyed them. I offered to give her the magazine, the bulbs, and the seedlings I had bought for my mother, and asked her to help me with getting the parts. And that is when I realized what power the director's secretary has. She took me

down to the sector, where they just loaded the fittings we needed, even though they were intended for a different client. I called my section manager, told him the order number, and spent the remaining days at home in my village. (Anisimov 2003, 198–99)

This story, as it is told, is not a story of bribery, of a secretary whose avaricious desire for seedlings leads her to break regulations and rules. It is a story of two people who, having become friends through their shared interest in flowers, become ethically bound to a collective good that may be sought within that unplanned, indeterminate space between the quota and its fulfillment. Since it matters little to the secretary's enterprise which particular allotment is filled that day, why not direct it to help a guy spend a few days with his mother?

Personal relations generate personal bonuses. But the delicate narrative balance that keeps the irregular but commendable circumvention of *usus* from collapsing into criminal and condemnable misappropriation of socialist property hinges on appropriate *fructus*, on such actions striving for the greater collective good. Customs, indeed, are not laws. Unlike the rationalized clarity that came to define possession rights, "agrarian custom," writes E. P. Thompson, "was never fact. It was ambience . . . Disputes over common right in such contexts were not exceptional. They were normal. Already in the thirteenth century common rights were exercised according to 'time hallowed custom,' but they were also being disputed in time-hallowed ways" (Thompson [1991] 1993, 102–4). The question of how much could be gleaned was nowhere clearly defined, and disputes over the matter could end up in court (Allen and Barzel 2009, 548). Leviticus does not, after all, specify how much to leave at the edges. It depends on the field and on the field owner's conscience. An ownership system of customary use-rights cannot be disaggregated from ethical judgment, which is always and necessarily in the eye of the beholder, open to conflicting interpretations. As with Vera's plates in chapter 1, different people may describe one and the same action differently.

I know a woman who spent most of her Soviet working life as a director of restaurants on the Moscow-Leningrad railroad (after which she became a real-estate mogul). Her son was a friend of mine. He told me that she doubtlessly never stole; he is sure of that. But that she did, of course, use the privileges her position afforded.

Do you know what getting a railway ticket was in those days? People would spend all day and night at the Moscow station, forty-five days in advance, in hopes of getting a ticket south—and I know people who just did not travel, for this precise reason. And with her, she would just tell you to go to kiosk number something-or-other and say that she sent you. Of course, for personal friends this wasn't even a problem: a phone call, Naden'ka, help! For others, who were not so close, it was implied that there would be some return gift. A phone call: hello, this is the director of the downtown bookstore speaking . . . and nothing was made official, certainly no money changed hands, but when three months later a Monet monograph came in, he would call. . . . She would still buy the things at state price—it's just that she could get whatever she wanted, clothes, caviar, always.

Another friend of mine, who also knew this railroad restaurant director, was less sympathetic: "Ha! She didn't sell! The hell she didn't. She would get, oh, let us suppose, a kilo of caviar as a thank you gift, and she would turn around and sell it to an acquaintance who sold it down the black market. Besides, she was director of restaurants, of course she sold! Do you have any idea how much wiggle room you have in a railroad restaurant?" (This latter friend recalls seeing cans of caviar stockpiled in the son's apartment.)

An insuperable line runs through such conflicting narratives: between personal redistribution for one's own private acquisitive interest and for others' collective good, between condemnable selfish theft and the commendable redistributive actions of a good *khoziain*. This distinction was functionally critical to the Soviet order, whose planned economy factually depended upon unplanned irregular exchange for its functional continuation. It was sacralized by Stalin's violent enclosure act. It came alive as the collectivist ethic upon which the shortage-ridden Soviet economy de facto relied: while endemic distribution problems drove managers to stockpile whenever possible, the difference that this insuperable line traced between private and personal motivation allowed them to ethically redistribute their hoards.[24] And it is this same distinction between the personal and the private that traces the contours of that particular collective subject with which this chapter began: the particular Soviet "we" that routinely came up in nostalgic recollections of Soviet times. My neighbor Tamara told me,

We had relations, everyone knew me, they would come when their motors broke down. Someone's drill broke, someone else's washing machine—Tamara, will you fix it?—Well, it's not hard for me. I would take the price of a bottle, only I didn't take bottles.

Or refrigerator-wagons; had a driver stop in once with a broken reel. The guy came to me in tears: Tamara, help me out. Well I did, of course, didn't charge him. He had a wagon full of meat in there . . .

Writing of eighteenth-century England, Thompson notes that customary consciousness asserts rights "as 'ours' rather than as mine or thine," but not in some kind of generous and universalistic communist spirit. "The communal economy was parochial and exclusive: if Weldon's rights were 'ours,' then Brigstock men and women must be kept out. But for those who 'belonged' to the parish, there remained some sense that they 'owned' it and had a voice in its regulation" ([1991] 1993, 179). In the socialist household, in theory, collectivist use-rights reached as far and wide as the socialist commons itself—a "vast expansive motherland" over which Soviet people were welcomed to walk along as a *khoziain*. But in practice every claim was particular: specific to time, place, and collective, and haunted, therefore, by the question cui bono?

Who benefits? Who is to say which actions truly intend the greater social good, and which only serve the individual interests of the actor and his or her immediate friends and family? It is this question that could not be asked in this economy of managers, who all used and enjoyed what none of them could possess. Asking it would cast doubt over whether the *khoziaeva* of each particular *khoziaistvo* were the *khoziaeva* of the socialist household itself. It would cast doubt over whether the socialist collectives all strove for the same aim. And it was this assumption of unified striving, of the universality of *fructus*, that justified the necessary transgression of rules upon which the planned economy de facto relied.

This unspoken, unspeakable question—cui bono?—haunts the demarcating line between the personal and the private, between the Soviet "we" (who had everything, or had nothing, under Soviet rule) and the perestroika "they" (who stole everything and "took the country apart by the screws"). And its haunting helps solve the previous chapter's riddle of why people showed me Soviet things that had been made in the mid-to-late 1990s, and told me stories of perestroika while describing events that took place well after perestroika had ended and the Soviet Union collapsed. They did so, because their narratives recalled Soviet times that were less about property law than about customary use-rights, less about the command-based economy than about the solidarity that made this economy function, despite its deficiencies. Because they drew the conceptual limits of the category Soviet around neither a span of historical time nor an expanse of a state formation but around the personal ethical logic of socialist property.

CHAPTER 3

Songs of Stalin and Khrushchev

By 2013, I had twined my life into Dobrova's. In my 2015 dissertation, I thanked her as the George Hunt of my *Kwakiutl Ethnography*, but she was much more. She was my informant and coauthor, my guide and my distraction, my editor and my audience, my reviewer, critic, mentor, and student. She was Dersu Uzala, Walter Benjamin, and Muchona the Hornet. She bent before neither law nor social derision, although she feared both. In years past, she and I might have been called traveling companions. We did travel together a lot. And most everywhere we went there was someone nearby who knew of Dobrova or was keen to meet her; people recognized her by her dog, which was large and black, and of a particularly imposing breed that lately had fallen from fashion. A few years before I met her, Dobrova had started an internet forum devoted to the Riesenschnauzer. Aficionados of this breed now welcomed us everywhere, and people who knew nothing about it still turned to look when Dobrova walked through their town with her dog. They sometimes asked her about it, and this was typically all she needed to learn about everything else. Dobrova could talk to anybody. In this way, we spent August 2013 in the Republic of Georgia, visiting a Georgian friend and her large black dog, talking to everyone.

Among the many memorable places we saw that summer was Gori, Stalin's natal town. There, a large museum of Stalin's life, times, and greatness greeted the visitor with his prediction: "Man is not eternal. And I will die. How will people and history judge me? There were many mistakes, but were not there also achievements? They will, naturally, attribute the mistakes to me. They will pile garbage on my grave; but the day will come, and the wind of history will mercilessly scatter it."

The Stalin Museum has been open since 1954. But, museum workers told us, this opening quote was added sometime around 2010. The quote comes from two memoirs describing the events of the 1940s but composed after 1970 and published after 1990.[1] So it is uncertain whether Stalin himself had uttered these words. But his specter most certainly embodied them; in the 2000s and 2010s, Stalin was everywhere. He came in a close third in the 2008 national TV contest *Name of Russia* to determine the most notable Russian historical figure, trailing Alexander Nevsky and Peter the Great. Hundreds of books were devoted to him: *The Occult Stalin*, *The Forbidden Stalin*, *Stalin's Dinner Toasts*, *Stalin the Foodie*, *Why Did Stalin Create Israel?*, *Stalin: Russia's Last Emperor*, *Why Was Stalin Killed?*, *Stalin, Hitler and Us*. Of course, this does not imply that Russians were universally Stalinists. Far from it. A good many of them were vehement anti-Stalinists. But in the 2010s Russia, Stalin somehow profoundly mattered. Flame fights about Stalin's legacy punctuated and animated public discourse: right-wing hooligans posted Stalin's images online (or ran a "Stalin-o-Bus" around town), offended members of decent liberal society retaliated with condemnations of the Bloody Regime, accused the right-wing hooligans of being its spiritual and physical heirs. The right-wing retaliated with accusations of treason and Fifth Column meddling. Both sides accused the other of rewriting history.

But there was one point on which most everybody agreed, a historical truth commonly shared across this flame war divide: everyone agreed that Khrushchev de-Stalinized Soviet society. This assumption seemed to be everywhere. My liberal-minded friends in St. Petersburg shared it, as did my illiberal retired factory-worker neighbors in Kolpino, as did my Anglophone colleagues. I shared it too. In the first draft of my dissertation I also noted that Khrushchev's denouncement of Stalin's cult of personality had led to the almost immediate release and rehabilitation of millions people who had been imprisoned in labor camps and forced-work settlements. The ease with which I had written those words is striking because they are false. It was not Khrushchev's 1956 denouncement of Stalin's personality cult that led to the release of millions of people. Those people—just under 1.2 million, about half of the incarcerated population—had already been released on amnesty in 1953.

Major reforms of punitive, judicial, and economic institutions were also begun in 1953, months after Stalin's death. These changes were visible even to foreign observers. In a 1953 article for the *International Journal*, Isaac Deutscher noted that

> A fairly comprehensive amnesty was decreed. The frame-up of the Kremlin doctors was declared null and void. The inquisitorial methods of the political police were bluntly condemned. The rule of law was proclaimed. Strong emphasis was placed on the constitutional rights of the citizen. Newspapers asked almost openly for the abolition of censorship and official control. . . . [T]he government ordered a revision of the targets of the current economic plans. Consumer industries were to raise their output . . . A new spirit made itself felt in the conduct of foreign affairs. (Deutscher 1953, 227–28)

All these reforms were put forth not by Khrushchev but by Lavrentiy Beria, the minister of internal affairs. In July 1953, Beria was accused of spying for Great Britain. By the end of the year, he was executed (Naumov and Sigachev 1999).

Yet most everybody I knew was committed to the idea that it was Khrushchev who liberated Soviet society from Stalinism. This popular historiography of de-Stalinization was not a disinterested one: Khrushchev was not simply a historical actor or a curiosity, he was something of a dividing line. Dobrova and I were once at a bathhouse with friends on March 5, the anniversary of Stalin's death. Our friends proposed a toast to the death of Stalin, and another for the soul of Khrushchev. When Dobrova refused the second toast, saying that she hopes Stalin and Khrushchev fry together in hell on the same skillet, several of the women witnesses to this situation assumed that she was a clandestine Stalinist. This situation was all the more striking because one of Dobrova's accusers had herself been suspected of Stalinist sympathies several years prior, when she worked on a TV documentary about Beria.

Accusations of lurking Stalinism always seemed near at hand in conversations about Soviet history. A bit after the bathhouse incident, I wrote a review essay critiquing a recent cycle of academic publications that run roughshod over historical facts and theoretical arguments to maintain the image of Khrushchev as liberator (Cherkaev 2014). The journal where my piece was published offered the author a chance to respond, which he did, writing that "I am fairly interested in the institutional history of the GULAG or historiography of Stalin, and I look forward to seeing what Cherkaev will tell us that is new and original about these subjects in her own work. I can only hope that her story will not be another attempt to explain the functional achievements of the GULAG and the patriotic wisdom of its creators" (Etkind 2014, 387). In Russian and English, in bathhouses and academic seminar rooms, in many of the conversations to which I was a party, there seemed to be something distinctly sacred about Khrushchev. Khrushchev, in this historiography, appeared as the obvious answer to Stalin. If you were not with one, then you must have been with the other.

But these flame wars that raged over Stalin's image were not really about him. They had much more to do with the events of the more recent past, events of which speakers had personal experience: with the popular historiography of Soviet times and perestroika, with present-day politics. Opposing sides of the flame war assigned Khrushchev and Stalin different moral values but maintained the sacred opposition between them. Exemplary of the illiberal Stalinist side is the position of Nikolai Starikov, a popular patriotic-historian publicist whose texts warn that "a negative attitude toward Stalin is quietly being created . . . Those who intend to rewrite Russian history have [for example] rewritten the memoirs of Marshal Georgy Zhukov. You and I, we did not even notice. I am guilty too. I have read Zhukov's memoirs, of course. But I could not have imagined that the proponents of perestroika [*perestroishchiki*] would completely have warped their meaning" (Starikov 2013, 145). Perestroika appears in this passage because the textual revisions in question concern discrepancies between the 1969 and 1989 editions of Zhukov's book. It also appears because throughout his oeuvre Starikov accuses the proponents of perestroika of destroying the Soviet Union, intentionally rewriting Russian history, and selling the country to foreign interests. Perestroika, liberalism, and foreign meddling are all but synonymous in this historical narrative: the Soviet Union fell to a secret plot, hatched by nefarious powers, their brainwashed agents acting in concert with greedy traitors to sell out the country.[2] It was betrayed first by Khrushchev, then by Gorbachev. And as the Soviet Union fell then, so may the Russian Federation fall also. Dmitry Belyaev, one of Starikov's acolytes, explains:

> Having come to power after the murder of Stalin, Khrushchev used the world's oldest trick—clearing his own name by smearing another's personality . . . The situation was monitored not only by Soviet people, it was also monitored by our old geopolitical

competitors. Khrushchev's hysteria about Stalin played right
into their game. The CIA and other special forces constantly
studied the Soviet Union, searched for its weak points. As it often
happens, the "weakest link" turned out to be the human factor.
They enacted a traditional scheme: bringing your own person
to power. In the early 1980s, M.S. Gorbachev quickly began rising through the ranks, already in 1984, he flew to meet Marga-
ret Thatcher in London, where he told her many Soviet secrets.
(Belyaev 2014, 58, 61)

Myself, I also believed in this opposition of Khrushchev and Stalin.
I believed in it as commonsense, as something I never thought doubt-
able. I began doubting only in 2013, and only because Dobrova's dog
cannot fly. Because she could not fly, we had to go to Georgia by boat,
and because we had to go by boat, we got stuck in Sochi on our way
back, waiting for the next train out to St. Petersburg. We rented a shack
in a kindly old woman's yard—I mean "shack" quite literally: a tiny
room built into a storage shed, clean and musty, the size of a walk-in
closet and packed with those lingering cast-offs of prior decades that
are usually stored in attics and basements—and we lounged around for
days there, with absolutely nothing to do. It was there that, flipping
through the junk books that were stashed in our room, I was surprised
to notice the complete absence of Stalin in Brezhnev-era history books.
If one believes the high school history textbook of 1977, no one called
Stalin ever did anything worth knowing about. I was amazed by this
absence, and by my own blindness, amazed that it had never occurred
to me to ask about the late Soviet status of Stalin. Clearly, Khrushchev's
de-Stalinization was more complicated than it might appear.

I spent the next several years looking for Beria, Stalin, and Khrushchev
in Soviet history books and post-Soviet commonsense. My excitement
about the historiographic omission I had found grew into disgust with
those of my contemporaries who kept perpetuating it. I wrote the above-
mentioned review essay, denouncing some popular academic writers'
disregard for historical fact. I raged against this historiography to anyone who would listen. And then I came to see that, like the Soviet things
of postsocialism, the folk historiography of de-Stalinization was itself
a critical ethnographic fact. Centered on the opposition of Khrushchev
and Stalin, it took up the whole Soviet past into a game of epochal hop-
scotch: the player hopped liberal through Lenin, Khrushchev, and Gorbachev; came back Stalinist over Stalin and Brezhnev—and, sometimes,

over Putin as well. Sometimes this hopscotching game reached as far back as Imperial Russia: Nicholas I and Alexander III aligned with Putin and Stalin in one smoothly recurring historical cycle (Sokolov 2017). But most often it was a game about perestroika: whatever historical epochs were discussed, the punch line often hovered over these reforms that had liberated—or had destroyed—Soviet society. And whichever direction one hopped, Stalin's thirty-year absence from official Soviet histories remained off-field and out of the picture.

Now You See Him, Now You Don't

I returned to the library stacks that fall semester after we got back from Georgia and had no trouble establishing when exactly Stalin went missing. In 1955, schoolbooks explained that "On March 5, 1953, the Soviet people and the workers of the entire world suffered a heavy, irreparable, loss. Lenin's student and the successor of his work, the great Stalin, died on the seventy-fourth year of his life. The death of Stalin, who had given his entire life to serving the people, was the heaviest loss. The bright memory of Stalin will eternally live in the hearts of the workers of the world. After the death of Stalin, our people gathered ever tighter around the Communist Party and the Soviet government" (Shestakov 1955, 282). But the 1957 editions do not mention his death at all. That year's high school history textbook mentions Stalin only twice: once as a supporter of Lenin's 1917 decision to begin the armed October rebellion (Pankratova 1957, 96) and once as the author of *The Foundations of Leninism*, a book that "played a significant role in the conceptual defeat of Trotskyism" (Pankratova 1957, 96, 193). In passages concerning World War II, the textbook replaces J. V. Stalin, commander in chief (*verkhovnyi glavnokomanduiushchii*) with an indefinite and nameless chief command (*verkhovnoe glavnokomandovanie*) (Pankratova 1957, 236).

So the explanation of Stalin's absence from official late Soviet histories seemed simple. Stalin disappeared, virtually overnight, because Khrushchev demanded it in 1956, in his famous speech at the 20th Party Congress, "Against the Cult of Personality and Its Consequences."

Firmly rooted in Lenin's theories of *State and Revolution* (1918), Khrushchev's speech mobilizes a particular historical narrative to argue that socialism was built by the enthusiastic labor of Soviet people, rather than by violent dispossession. Lenin insists that the creation of communism is a two-step process: first the proletariat must violently seize state power, after which the state itself will gradually become unnecessary and wither away. Following this logic, early Soviet revolutionary violence and mass terror were both necessary to defeat class enemies while socialism was being constructed, but they should have been overcome in favor of collectivist government in the 1930s, after socialism had been built. But this violent stage was not overcome, Khrushchev argued, due to Stalin's blinding egotism and "unbelievable suspicion [which] was cleverly taken advantage of by the abject provocateur and vile enemy, Beria, who had murdered thousands of Communists and loyal Soviet people" (Khrushchev 1956, S46). Such unjustified violence made Soviet people fear "their own shadows and to show less initiative in work" (Khrushchev 1957, S57). Socialism, urged Khrushchev in 1956, should now be returned to its Leninist principles—to collective leadership and socialist democracy, legality, self-criticism, and personal modesty. But quietly. "We should, in all seriousness, consider the question of the cult of personality. We cannot let this matter get out of the party, especially not to the press. It is for this reason that we are considering it here at a closed Congress session. We should know the limits; we should not give ammunition to the enemy; we should not wash our dirty linen before their eyes" (Khrushchev 1957, S57).[3] The speech was heard by the 1,400 delegates of the 20th Party Congress, and by employees at enterprises all over the Soviet Union, to whom it was read aloud at specially arranged meetings (Schattenberg 2006). Then it was classified.

And so, right after the Congress and all the way until glasnost, Stalin's name was carefully excised from public mention, removed from cities and enterprises, from history books, and from the National Anthem, which for the next twenty years was performed without words.[4] This omission of Stalin was instant and radical. It left that void that I noticed in Soviet textbooks in 2013.

But in 2013, I was surprised to discover the history of this historiography. I knew that Khrushchev de-Stalinized Soviet society, but had not stopped to ask what exactly this de-Stalinization had meant. Considering the late Soviet historiographic void left by Stalin, this question now pointed to an apparent disjuncture of terms: the events of the past did not fit neatly into the categories of the present. *Destalinizatsiia* is a loan word in Russian—the endemic construction would be *raz-stalinizatsiia* or *obez-stalinizatsiia*—and, unsurprisingly, it was not used when its English analog had first appeared in the 1950s and 1960s (Jones 2006, 2). At a time when mention of Stalin quietly disappeared from the names of places and factories, when the National Anthem was performed without words and when history textbooks explained that the "cult of personality belittled the role of the party and the masses, disparaged the significance of the party's collective leadership, and not uncommonly led to serious oversights in work" without explaining whose personality had been was the subject of that cult (Pankratova 1957, 270), the party's major reform program was also, of course, not associated with Stalin's name. The term did not gain traction in the Soviet Union until the late 1980s, when Russophone publicist texts explained that *"destalinizatsiya* is liberation from the legacy of Stalin and Stalinism," and saw in this process both the "origin [and the] difficulties of perestroika" (Gefter 1989, 394).

With perestroika, *destalinizatsiia* became the new party line. And as with many crucial turning points in Soviet history, this authoritative turn anchored to a general secretary's keynote address: to Gorbachev's 1987 speech "October and Perestroika: The Revolution Continues." Tracing the roots of late Soviet economic stagnation to the Stalinist past, the speech largely repeated the historiographic tenets laid down by Khrushchev, but named the very thing that Khrushchev had occluded: it returned Stalin's name to official discussions. Like Khrushchev, Gorbachev also insisted that socialism was built by the liberated labor of Soviet people, and that harsh top-down control was laudable while socialism was being built, but should have been surmounted right after. It had not been surmounted because Soviet society was caught in the sway of Stalin's personality, and the results gave root to stagnation: unjust political repressions and certain excesses in the work of collectivization negatively impacted morale. Stalin's death then enlivened society with newfound enthusiasm, Gorbachev claimed, but the reforms were curtailed. Although "it required no small courage of the party and its leadership, headed by Nikita Khrushchev, to criticize the personality cult and its consequences and to reestablish socialist legality" (Gorbachev 1987, 27), the mechanism of stagnation was not overcome and Stalinist command-style governance lingered even into the 1980s. By cleansing Soviet society of these Stalinist vestiges, promised Gorbachev in 1987, perestroika will speed up the socialist household economy and bring Soviet socialism back to its Leninist roots.

In the wake of Gorbachev's speech, countless publicist texts and personal memoirs fleshed out these newly canonical claims, casting a quick tie between Gorbachev, Khrushchev, and Lenin to legitimate perestroika as the ultimate battle for de-Stalinization. This historiographic narrative resounded throughout the Soviet media sphere, was picked up by Anglophone sympathizers on the other side of the Cold War border, and resounded back into the Russophone public sphere as into an echo chamber. It quickly assumed the status of commonsensical, historical fact. "The anti-Stalinist movement born under Khrushchev eventually grew, after many years of bitter political defeat and agony, into the perestroika movement led by Gorbachev in the 1980s," explain Stephen Cohen and Katrina Vanden Heuvel in 1989, translating the reformers' own origin myth into a neat chronological explanation for Western readers (Cohen and Vanden Heuvel 1989, 19).

Careful scholars will be skeptical of such commonsense histories. It is as difficult to argue that Stalin's personality cult was an unfortunate coincidence of Soviet industrialization, rather than the driving factor thereof, as it is to trace the origin of de-Stalinization to Khrushchev's 1956 speech rather than Beria's 1953 institutional reforms. Beria's reforms did, after all, release over 1,180,000 people (roughly 46.7 percent of the incarcerated population) on amnesty. They also radically restructured the GULAG's enterprises, closing the most expensive construction sites and distributing jurisdiction over the others among the different ministries. They overturned several loud political cases, like that of the "Kremlin Doctors." But in the 2010s, despite the many published historical studies of Beria's reforms, popular historical narratives still credited Khrushchev with having defeated Stalinism.[5]

The persistence of this popular historiography suggests that there is an important historical truth to Khrushchev's de-Stalinization as well, one that surpasses the emptying of labor camps and ending juridical terror. Born of perestroika, the image of Khrushchev's *destalinizatsiia* was not only about Khrushchev and Stalin. It was much more about the subsequent thirty years; about the late Soviet past of which speakers had direct personal experience. Gorbachev's mythical denouncement of Stalinism said something profoundly exciting to its own historical moment, something that no dry analysis of his headline speeches can justly describe. "There was suddenly this amazing freedom," one of my friends told me, describing glasnost, reiterating a sentiment I had heard related before, "to publicly say what everyone had known—about what shit it all was." Words, concepts, historiographies do not stay stable. They are constantly recreated, turned into texts that stand out from the flow of everyday life, made into recognizable solidities, and invested with authority vis-à-vis other truth claims. The perestroika concepts of Stalin and Stalinism were no exception. They were concepts of the 1980s; for their contemporary speakers, they signified an array of meanings whose significance derived from the pragmatics of their own usage and silence. Nearly everyone I knew in the 2010s assumed that, for better or worse, Khrushchev had unmade something that Stalin had made: that Khrushchev de-Stalinized Soviet society, whatever that meant. And whatever it meant, it seemed to mean more than restructuring punitive institutions and releasing prisoners. It was a question not of institutions but of spirit; of something at once more ineffable and more holistic, more a question of morals than laws. Looking at it through the history of socialist property law, I saw that it was also, at heart, a question of the *khoziain*.

Khrushchev's Collectivist Ethics

Khrushchev's Thaw is justly famous for more than his postmortem denouncement of Stalin. It is famous for having created that softer late Soviet era that is known for friendship rather than violence, for lives built within state institutions but with little regard for the formal demands of state ideology (Yurchak 2006), for faith in the truth and morality of science but little regard for the party's political slogans (Vail and Genis [1988] 1998). "At that time, there was a breakthrough—a revelation, a revolution," Khrushchev's daughter Rada Adzhubei explained in a 2009 interview, when asked about the wild popularity of the journal *Science and Life*, which she edited.

> And this was revolution on a wide front: new journals—*Youth*, *International Literature*, *Week*, the weekly *Beyond Our Borders*, the *Contemporary* theater. Poets read their texts to thousand-strong crowds, gathered in Mayakovsky Square and in the large auditorium of the Polytechnical Museum—Akhmadulina, Okudzhava, Voznesensky, Rozhdestvensky. Their fame stems from those times—and so does the popularity of *Science and Life* [Nauka i Zhizn']. And that time has a name—the Thaw, the era of hopes. Unfortunately, unrealized. (Adzhubei 2009)

I often heard and read about the Thaw described along these lines. But I almost never heard about the juridical reforms that were its basis and precondition. These reforms included a new approach to policing, leisure and media, and a new underlying philosophy of socialist property law. They were developed in 1956 and fully adopted in 1961, at the 22nd Party Congress, as the Third Party Platform. I did not hear the Third Party Platform discussed in everyday chatter, I rarely saw it mentioned in print, and I myself came to study it quite accidentally, by way of the fact that, when I finished my dissertation and tried to revise it as a book manuscript, I suddenly found that I had nothing to say.[6] To justify my existence, I picked up a series of projects: about stolen late Soviet penguins (2017), personally owned Stalin-era military dogs (Cherkaev and Tipikina 2018), about the concept of dignity as a juridical notion (2018b). And this last study threw me headlong into the study of Soviet civil law when I noticed that, along with that inherent human dignity that is equal in us all, late Soviet jurisprudence also protected the dignity of Soviet citizens in a different sense. It protected personal dignity in the sense of that subjectively experienced ethical state that may be said to define personhood (Taylor 1985), as one of the qualities by which people evaluate whether someone has acted like an undignified schmuck. The *Foundations of Civil Jurisprudence*, adopted in 1961 as a keystone part of the Third Party Platform, protected such personal ethical qualities by the logic of property law.

The Third Party Platform brought ethics thus into civil law to solve a problem as old as the Soviet project itself: the problem of how to build communism, a nonexploitative social order that has no need for the state and the law. In *State and Revolution* Lenin theorized the creation of communism as a two-stepped process: first, the proletariat must seize state power and nationalize the means of production, abolishing class distinctions and gradually making repressive state institutions unnecessary until, Lenin cites Friedrich Engels, "State interference in social relations becomes, in one domain after another, superfluous, and then dies down of itself. The government of persons is replaced by the administration of things, and by the conduct of processes of production. The state is not 'abolished.' *It withers away*" (Lenin [1918] 2014, 52). Following this line of thought, early Soviet jurists—most famously Evgeny Pashukanis and Petr Stuchka—theorized that law, morality, family, and state administration were forms of bourgeois superstructure: ideological constructs whose existence is maintained by an exploitative system based on private property. Such superstructural forms were expected to wither away when this exploitative system's material base was abolished, and early Soviet property law was therefore theorized to be as temporary as the private property rights it protected. The law, wrote Pashukanis, cannot be simply filled with a new socialist content. It must wither away in its very form. Morality, too, was another bourgeois superstructural form. "The proletariat may well have to utilise these forms, but that in no way implies that they could be developed further or be permeated by a socialist content. These forms are incapable of absorbing this content and must wither away in an inverse ratio with the extent to which this content becomes reality" (Pashukanis [1924] 2002, 160). Thus throughout the 1920s, legal scholars theorized a dual-sectored approach to socialist property law: a civil codex (*grazhdanskoe parvo*) that was to die off eventually as relations of private ownership did, and a separate codex called *khozaistvennoe pravo* that regulated material relations between socialist enterprises.

But positive law and morality did not wither away as intended. Instead, when the 1936 Stalin Constitution established the institution of socialist property, it adjudicated "the wholesale restoration of these 'bourgeois' institutions [of money, property, the family, criminal sanctions, the state, law] on a new 'socialist' basis" (Berman 1948, 235–36). Socialism was proclaimed to be both legal and moral (and branded aesthetically bougie), and the prominent legal theorists of the 1920s were denounced by those who replaced them for their "legal nihilism": for theorizing personal property as nothing more than private rights to the means of consumption, often expressed as "private (personal) property" (Amfiteatrov 1937, 42). In the aftermath of the 1936 Constitution, this was more than a theoretical error. Jurists advocating the dual-sectored approach were not just denounced for their theoretical mistakes, they were condemned for slandering the Soviet order: for portraying it as its totalitarian-minded accusers did, as a system that crushes its citizens' private spheres and individual wills.[7] "The rotten and deceitful conception of *khozaistvennoe pravo* that is based on Pashukanis's harmful theories . . . is a horrendous distortion of our legal reality," explains the 1937 article "Against wreckers' perversions in the theory of Soviet civil law" (Pavlov 1937, 55).

> It is well known that the enemies of socialism have always tried to present socialist society as an order that crushes human personalities, denies individual interest, chokes personal freedom—in a word, as a giant soulless machine that leaves no room for live human beings with their human needs and aspirations. It is also well known that . . . socialism does not deny individual interests but rather combines them with the interests of the collective, that, in the words of comrade Stalin, "socialist society embodies the only firm guarantee of the protection of personal interests." . . . This two-volume textbook [*Sovetskoe Khozaistvennoe Pravo* (1935)] presents personal property as a variation and a modified form of private property: . . . Here, personal property originates not in the

socialist order, labor and production, not in socialist property, but in private property." (Pavlov 1937, 55–56)

In light of the Stalin Constitution's new socialist legal philosophy, such theories were judged inexcusable. Civil law was no longer about private interests, and it was no longer expected to wither away. By the logic of socialist property, personal interests and rights were now to derive from and co-constitute the greater socialist whole. And civil law, therefore, was to express "the unity of collective [*obshetsvennykh*] and personal interests in the regulation of socialist society's property relations and of workers' civil rights" (Amfiteatrov 1937, 45). Private property was gone, so that personal rights could flourish.

And so when Khrushchev returned, two decades later, to this ultimate communist problem of making the state wither away, he reframed it as personal flourishing. The state, he explained in his keynote address to the 21st Party Congress, would wither away into fullness rather than lack; it would not leave an emptiness as that left between tree branches that are stripped of their leaves, but would be "the development of socialist statehood into communist social self-management" (1959, 102). Such fecundity did not require the elimination of law. It required, instead, cybernetics and ethics (and in practice, it was also helped along by the sale of petroleum.)[8] Cybernetics would automate economic planning so that "the government of persons is replaced by the administration of things," as Engels foretold.[9] Ethics would make Soviet people take greater personal responsibility for the collective good, stepping in to take up the slack wherever socialist state institutions fell short. Enacted as the Third Party Platform, this approach promised to build stateless communism by giving people more room to personally manage society—allowing society to outgrow the socialist state's institutions and rules. By this logic, the law was not wrong—just inadequate.

Morality was no longer expected to wither away. Quite the opposite. The Third Party Platform insists that "in the course of transition to communism, the moral principles of society become increasingly important; the sphere of action of the moral factor expands and the importance of the administrative control of human relations diminishes accordingly" (CPSU 1961, 108). Morality would not wither away like the law but would come to replace it; it would guide Soviet people as they collectively learned how to manage society.

In 1959, Khrushchev claimed (falsely) that political crimes were no longer committed in the Soviet Union, and that this "unprecedented unity of the entire population's political convictions" (Khrushchev 1959, 103) evinced a society ready to take over the state's administrative tasks: from the organization of medical care and physical education to the prevention of crime.[10] The Third Party Platform implemented his call in a series of quasi-juridical institutions, in which social collectives of the "so-called Soviet public (*obshchestvennost'*)" (Kozlov, Fitzpatrick, and Mironenko 2011, 44) took responsibility for everyday public order. Ostensibly voluntary social organizations were tasked with patrolling the safety of streets, judging minor infractions in "comrades' courts," initiating cases in real court, and supervising those found guilty in suretyship.[11] Soviet people were called upon to personally judge each other's "workplace performance, behavior at home, in everyday life, in the collective" (Ioffe 1962, 65) and in all such cases, their judgment was to be guided by ethical standards rather than legal statutes.

Morality became the guiding principle of "communist social self-management," and it thereby became an object of socialist property law: the 1961 *Foundations of Civil Jurisprudence* extended the juridical definitions of personal property to include personal ethical states. "The method of Soviet civil law is determined by its primary object—socialist property relations, appearing in value form," explained Olympiad Solomonovich Ioffe, renowned scholar of civil law.[12] "Having appeared, this method also became suitable for regulating those immaterial relations that directly relate to relations of property [like authorship rights]. Subsequently, it also became applicable to immaterial relations that are independent [of property relations]" (Ioffe 1962, 63). These independent immaterial relations included personal honor and dignity, which civil law now protected like all other personal property.

The law protected these personal ethical states, but it did not "regulate" them (Ioffe 1962, 62). It left ethical status an indeterminate question to be decided, on a case-by-case basis, by the social collectives themselves. Scholars of the new property law argued that citizens could have their honor and dignity protected only as members of a social collective. "The feeling of honor, like the feeling of duty, can only grow and fortify within a collective, by accomplishing socially important tasks," explained *Marxist Ethics* textbooks (Shishkin 1961, 56). And this indeterminacy made things lively. Ethical judgment cannot be rationalized without being squashed; it hinges on the question of appropriate motivation, which is always in the eye of the beholder. Leaving ethical judgment to be carried out by the collective, the law incorporated socialist ethics as indeterminate custom: an indeterminacy legal scholars

heralded for its ubiquity and its effectiveness. Enveloping "the perpetra-
tor in an atmosphere of condemnation," the collective's derision was to
make the legal decision a "continuously acting measure," whose enforcement is both necessary and unavoidable (Ioffe 1962, 69). It was to extend
social control beyond the reach of the law, to discern, as Khrushchev
proposed, "a violator not only after he has already committed an offense
or a crime, but when [others notice] deviations from communal norms
that could lead him to commit antisocial acts" (Khrushchev 1959, 104).

Much skeptical commentary has ridiculed the ideological, heavy-
handed nature of these late-Soviet moral demands, particularly
because, as George Kline justly points out, Karl Marx himself "had
asserted that you cannot legislate men into being good, since the foundations of morality, like the foundations of law, are economic" (Kline 1963,
26). But in some ways, it worked. My wager is that it worked, and that
it formed the basis of Khrushchev's liberalizing Thaw, the reason that
his reforms are renowned for de-Stalinization. The adjudication of
ethics worked for two reasons. It worked because it protected ethical
states without regulating them, and because the communist morality
it mandated was indeed based on economic foundations: because the
demands of the Moral Codex largely boiled down to that collectivist
relation upon which the shortage-ridden economy depended, to comradely mutual aid.

Adopted in 1961 as part of the Third Party Platform, the *Moral Codex
of the Builder of Communism* provided the guidelines by which Soviet people were mandated to ethically judge each other. Its demands, insists
Ioffe, must be placed above the law; they "must become the fundamental
law for Soviet people in their relationships with each other, with the
state and with society" (Ioffe 1962, 71). And in practice, this fundamental law was largely that of collectivism, humanism, and mutual aid. As
the 1963 *Agitator's Handbook* explains,

> The ethical standards of the new society, its ethical command-
> ments, are set forth in the *Moral Codex of the Builder of Communism*,
> which is sewn through with the ideas of collectivism and human-
> ism: man is to man—a friend, a comrade, a brother! That makes
> sense. Collective consciousness is begotten by the very nature of
> the socialist order, which provides a firm economic and social
> base for collectivism . . . Collective consciousness finds its expres-
> sion in people's fundamental awareness of their social duty, in
> each person's feeling of personal responsibility for the fate of the

collective and society as a whole, in selfless comradely mutual aid. (Morozov 1963, 144–45)

The social collectives in which such relations of mutual aid flourished were ostensibly mapped to the production units of the socialist household economy, but in practice they also surpassed them. The 1961 textbook of *Marxist Ethics* gives examples of collectives united by employment, by their members' shared obligation to manage socialist property at the "factory, enterprise, collective farm, military regiment" (Shishkin 1961, 56). It explains that "the Soviet person, regardless of the specific position he occupies, is always a member of some certain collective" and strives to help that collective "accomplish the tasks with which it is faced in a commendable way" (Shishkin 1961, 56). Defined by an "internal system of relations of comradely cooperation and socialist mutual help" that arises between people working together to achieve a socialist goal (Kharkhordin 1999, 89n47), such collectives were understood to unite people striving to better society, in their formal employment positions and in their personal lives. They could include members of one's work unit, hobby collective, circle of family and friends—or simply any two or more people who enter into relations of reciprocity. "Communist society is a society of collectivists," insisted Khrushchev. "Therefore we must foster in people the unity of personal and societal interests from childhood onward, must cultivate comradeship, readiness of mutual aid" (Khrushchev 1959, 242). This imagined "mega-kollektiv called the Soviet people" was comprised not only of formal, enterprise-based collectives, but also of informal collectives within those formal collectives, and of "informal collectives outside the official terrain altogether" (Kharkhordin 1999, 303).

Such collectives subjected people to unregulated social pressure. But they also bound people together in ethical reciprocity, whereby the formal demand to apply social pressure and moral derision could itself become subject to personal collectivist obligations of mutual aid. In relation to the latter, the former became rules that could be circumvented in the name of collectivism and the greater social good. Serving as *komsorg* (communist youth leader) was not a big deal, Sergei told me, it was just something one had to do.[13]

> Well, you had to give the impression of busyness—make it look like there was party work happening in the sector. There were some reports we had to write, often we could do without having actual meetings, but someone always had to be shamed, picked apart,

and sometimes we agreed who it would be ahead of time. Bad workers would be picked apart at the meetings, exposed to collective reprimand, sometimes wives would write into work, and then the sector would pick apart [the worker's] relationship with his wife . . . But people almost never got fired because where would he go? All the bums got rounded up and shipped out to a kolkhoz past the 101st kilometer.[14]

Late Soviet media—called upon by the Third Party Platform to "be a source of joy and inspiration to millions of people, . . . to enrich them ideologically and educate them morally" (CPSU 1961, 119)—presented this incongruity between personal interests and official demands as sometimes funny, but not morally repugnant. Examples abound in *The Fuse* comic shorts that, premiering in 1962, aimed to expose society's moral failures and educate righteousness. (They screened in cinemas before the main feature, often starred famous actors and were often hilarious.) The 1964 episode "Cards Don't Lie" (Rapoport 1964) opens in a modern-furnished apartment where a card-reading clairvoyant (played by the renowned Faina Ranevskaya) appears to be swindling a young woman, whom she drives to tears by telling her that her husband is planning to run off with his secretary. She charges the young woman ten rubles for the reading, and then—seeing more money in her purse—offers to return her husband through a "scientific method" for another fifty rubles, plus a ten-ruble guarantee. She takes out a machine with light bulbs, warns the young woman to be careful of sparks, talks about bio-currents, asks where the husband works, does something with her machine, and then reassures the young woman that now her husband will be virtually glued to her side. And after the young woman leaves, it turns out that she has not been swindled after all! The power of personal feminine solidarity works not against the socialist state's bureaucracy but through it, and Ranevskaya's diviner has her ways of manipulating invisible forces. She telephones the party organization at her client's husband's place of work, informs them that he is planning to leave his wife, to ruin the Soviet family, and asks them to please remind him of our Moral Codex. And thus along with a new codex of Soviet morality, people also got lucid instructions on how to use that new codex in their personal lives, because such personal use does not contradict the overarching communist-building goals of the *Moral Codex of the Builder of Communism*. It furthers them.

In real life, too, the new policy of shifting social control from the criminal justice system to the less defined pressure social derision and prophylactic police intimidation often made social control a matter of collectivist, personal interests. Thus infamously, in 1974, the literary critic Efim Etkind was dismissed from his job, stripped of his academic titles, and expelled from the Union of Writers. Several years later, he thus explained his trial "by means of 'public opinion'":

> I had not been acting illegally. To prove that would call for solid legal evidence. Had I kept a copy of *The Gulag Archipelago*? Had I "aided and abetted" the author? Perhaps. But the prosecution is obliged to provide evidence. There was no search; this copy was neither found nor seen by anyone . . . The only positive evidence is provided by my private letters. But all they tell is about my opinions, not my actions. Indeed the police did not deal with me themselves, they preferred to act through the professors and writers. Neither the professors nor the writers, however, either demanded or obtained any proof—they simply took the word of the police investigators. (Etkind 1978, 80–81)

The professors and writers who voted unanimously to expel him had acted in their capacity as members of professional collectives—of the Institute's Academic Council and of the Union of Soviet Writers—not as members of a jury in a court of law. Why did they vote? None of them, Etkind suggests, particularly cared about the accusation—which, in any case, had not been investigated. Like Sergei's recollection of communist youth meetings, where "someone always had to be shamed, picked apart, and sometimes we agreed who it would be ahead of time," Etkind suggests that his peers attended the meeting because it was just something one does "to get on with life" and have a career. He imagines these actions justified by collectivist rhetoric: "He couldn't leave his comrades in the lurch so he overcame his old age and his bad health and didn't even worry about the stupid things that the Western press was bound to say about him—after all, what does it matter if you're called an executioner or an assistant executioner once or twice, it doesn't stick and you'll have helped your side and not let them down at a difficult time" (Etkind 1978, 64–65). And when Etkind did reluctantly agree to leave the Soviet Union, his decision to do so was also motivated by collectivist selfless ideals.

> In the end, one of my friends, who had been close to me and my family for several decades, said to me: "You must go, and not wait a day longer than you have to. You are meeting people and this

could ruin them. Young people come to see you, trying to help you and openly showing their sympathy for you. They are defenseless—they won't get invitations from Western universities or be written about in the Western press. As long as you are here they are in serious danger. Any of them might be given the sack one day. Surely you realize your responsibility toward them and all of us. Even the older ones are in danger of losing their jobs or at best being retired early. You must go." (Etkind 1978, 244)

It is commonly remarked that Soviet people "used Communist morality for their own ends" (Field 1998, 610). But I invite you to notice how those ends were narrated, to notice a great overlap between the collectivist narratives in which people explain their late Soviet actions, the collectivist stance promoted by late Soviet media and educational texts, and the chief demands of the Third Party Platform itself: the collectivist ethics that were to bring Soviet society to communism. It was, I wager, collectivist turtles all the way down.

A Section Untitled

But this topology of collectivist turtles was encumbered, annoyingly, by the form of a certain beached whale.

It has often been argued that the late-Soviet state's ideological demands became "hypernormalized," that people tended to treat them pragmatically without engaging their substantive meaning (Yurchak 2006), and that "crimes of substitution" (Oushakine 2003) were often possible, so long as this ideological form was maintained. Parade participants could often get away with yelling mura (hogwash) instead of ura (hooray), just so long as they sounded enthusiastic. With parades, Sergei explained, "They needed to have a large column of bodies from the plant. And they gave bonuses, days-off—especially for carrying a banner. And the same with being sent down to a kolkhoz help harvest potatoes—like, they would have to send twenty people from the sector. Someone might go willingly. And everyone else has to be forced. Who do they make go? Alcoholics, trouble makers."[15] People of all walks of life told me that the late Soviet state's ideological demands were ubiquitous, but often a fact of form only, an everyday hassle to be resolved collectively so that everyone could get on with life. I heard this from former manual workers like Sergei, I heard it from scientists and engineers, I heard it from former members of the Communist Party.

In 2017, I talked with Fred Firsov, a historian who worked for three decades (1957–92) at the Institute of Marxism-Leninism, the party's premier ideological organ. Like the speakers of chapter 1, who recalled smuggling glass trinkets and flasks of sunflower oil home past their enterprise pass-gates, Firsov recalled the "good relations" and social tricks by which he skirted the archive's rules to write his articles about the history of the Communist Party properly, as he felt they ought to be written. He told me that he wrote in two notebooks: one for himself, which he smuggled out, and one that he showed for inspection to the archive employee responsible for cutting out the extracts that Firsov might not have been entitled to copy. Dealing with classified material, Firsov was required to keep his hand-copied extracts in his office at the Institute—in a locked safe. But he routinely took them home. There was a person who had to come through and inspect, "but people don't stop being humane. She would call me the night before and let me know she was coming. So I would bring my notebooks to work and put them in the safe."[16] The surprising laxity Firsov recalls might be explained by the fact that, while historians at other institutes were monitored by their institutes' KGB departments, the party historians of Marxism-Leninism were monitored by other party officials. But it also has much to do with late Soviet collectivist ethics; with the language of humanism and mutual aid, in which Firsov recalls having skirted the archive's censorship rules, and Sergei recalls having held Komsomol meetings in form only "to give the impression of busyness." The ubiquitous presence of ideological and classificatory rules was one theme running through the stories I heard about everyday late Soviet life. The collectivist schemes by which people surmounted these rules was another.

Most of my interlocutors had either themselves worked a clearance-level job in late-Soviet Leningrad or knew someone who did—even the position of translator at the Geology Institute required clearance because accurate maps were classified.[17] Classified enterprises were called "PO Boxes" because their real names were kept secret to throw off the foreign spy. But their own pass-gates were porous enough to permit the transmission of many useful things, like those we saw in chapter 1: flasks and knitting needles, ski rope-tow hooks, and ski bindings made on the Marker model. People told me fantastic stories about how they lined their country-house ground wells with rust-proof fuel nozzles pilfered from a classified military aviation plant; about how they tinted spectacles by exposing them to gamma-radiation: the radiation source was underground, below a layer of water, and glasses were lowered down on a string. I heard about this method of tinting spectacles from several people, who all recalled them being made at the Ioffe Physics Institute, in one of its classified sectors. Other sectors at the Institute were unclassified, but this border was also porous. A friend of mine, who had been a graduate student there, recalled being pressed into breaking up classified components of supposedly highly secret radio-technology, "which everyone knew was just called 'microwave' over in the free world." He recalled his resentment: he did not have clearance, and did not want it, and was afraid of being slapped with it, once he had seen the thing; moreover, its destruction was labor-intensive and tedious: there was a copper part that had to be sanded down by hand past the point of recognizability.

I often heard people muse about the pointlessness of classification, about how they did not know what exactly was classified, or why it should be. "Soviet people developed a certain sense of smell," Firsov told me. "For a historian of that time the most important was: what have recent party documents said about this question? If they say this, then it is this. If they say that, then it is that. If they criticize, that means that you can. If they are silent, it means that you should not discuss it." Classification rules affected both work and leisure. Western radio and music recordings, texts about history and philosophy, poetry and psychoanalysis, the *Joy of Sex* and *Kama Sutra* circulated through underground channels. So did karate manuals.[18] "Sure it irritated!" a mathematician told me, recounting his life in late Soviet Leningrad. "There were things some idiot did not want me to know." Those people who cared nothing about Western fashion or Russian esoterica, religion, and underground literature could also be frustrated by classification rules if they were, for example, interested in activities like rock climbing or mushroom gathering. Many wilderness areas that were limited to military or otherwise classified personnel could also be accessed through the proverbial hole in the fence. In 1987, Dobrova worked a brief stint as a security guard of a classified radio tower by Tosno, a small town nearby Leningrad, armed with one shot in her rifle. In case of attack, she was supposed to fire into the air and await reinforcements. She told me that she never saw any spies, but did occasionally have to explain to people how to find the hole in the fence to get back to the rail line. Local residents, having crossed into the classified zone to pick mushrooms and lost their way, were glad to have found her: "Hey! Hey you! Up there in the guard tower! How do I get out of here?" Even if I wanted to detain them—she told me in 2010—I would only have gotten into trouble for getting my superiors in trouble for having a gaping hole in the fence.

   The proverbial fence, I was told time and again, had a hole in it, and many people knew about this hole, and the fence was pointless to begin with, but yet failing to maintain the form of guarding the classified fence could cause very serious problems. It could cut a person off from access to higher education, career advancement, and material distribution, unless this person had high-powered personal connections to pull him or her through. Refusing or failing to join the Komsomol could keep one from entering college, while an inopportunely expressed youthful love of Salvador Dali could cause workplace problems for the next quarter century.[19] But for the most part, the stories I heard about how people had run afoul of the state's rules were characterized not by terror but by irritation. While Stalin-era oral histories are sewn through with genuine fear of unpredictable state violence, in the stories I heard the state's ideological regulations were an unjust and unnecessary hassle, a system whose pointless but incessant demands waste everyone's time and get in the way of good people's everyday lives.

Stalin's Lingering Vestiges

And this was the promise of perestroika: to sweep away this unjust bureaucratic rigamarole, this formalized language, and these pointless ideological requirements that had little relation to how people lived. "In the last years of L.I. Brezhnev's life, attainments widely came to be nonobjectively assessed," explained *Pravda* in 1986, "A disjuncture emerged between word and deed . . . The lack of consistent democratism, widespread glasnost, criticism, and self-criticism . . . [was] also echoed in the work of ideology and propaganda—where formalism took root, and where detachment from life became characteristic. In the party, and among the people, ripened a comprehension of the necessity of changing for the better, of energetic practical actions" (1986, 3). Perestroika promised to be a cleansing rebirth of socialism. It promised to tap into socialism's vast social resources (as well as its stockpiled material scraps) by activating "the personality, the human factor [*lichnosti, chelovecheskgo faktora*]" (Gorbachev 1987, 32). It promised to make socialism realize its full potential, to make it truly a "society for people, for the flourishing of their creative labor, their well-being, their physical and spiritual development; a society in which a person feels him/herself to be a legitimate *khoziain*, and is in fact such a *khoziain*" (Gorbachev 1987, 32).

To this end, there was one overbearing, pejoratively capitalized *khozi-ain* who had to be expunged from society's consciousness, the one whose ghost still lingered at the heart of an "administrative system," demanding mindless execution of centrally determined commands (Popov [1986] 1987). Promising to liberate Soviet people from the regulations that kept them from feeling like the legitimate *khoziaeva* of the socialist household, and positing his own perestroika reforms as the logical continuation of Khrushchev's Thaw, Gorbachev traced the indefinitely stagnant bureaucratic system to Stalin, through Brezhnev. He accused both of thwarting democracy: Stalin with fear, Brezhnev with cynicism. If Stalin's cult of personality created an "atmosphere of intolerance, hostility, suspicion" that kept Soviet society from democratically surmounting the harsh administer-command methods by which class enemies had been destroyed, Brezhnev's long rein generated social alienation and amorality, and "the growing discrepancy between the high principles of socialism and the daily reality of life [that, by 1985] has become intolerable" (Gorbachev 1987, 29). Perestroika publicists avidly picked up this new Party line. Accusing the indefinite administer-command system of fostering economic stagnation, "stale political verbosity, corruption and . . . the decline of moral values," they found the roots of this system in Stalin's personality cult, and its fruits in the Brezhnev regime's corrupt, truthless cynicism (Burlatsky 1988, 13). In the words of Fyodor Burlatsky, one of the authors of the *Moral Codex of the Builder of Communism*, Brezhnev's cabinet "possessed the unique skill of garbling any fruitful idea with a barely noticeable turn," and used such empty language to cover over the corrupt shadow economy, from which they profited and which they did nothing to stop: a truthless verbosity that was "in many ways a return to the command-administrative system of Stalin's epoch," whose fruits were economic stagnation and "endemic moral degradation" (Burlatsky 1988, 14).

But Khrushchev's era was no less responsible for this truthless formalism than Stalin's and Brezhnev's. This was a formalism born of the Third Party Platform's demand that people take personal responsibility for collectively solving their everyday problems. As the ostensibly voluntary actions of social self-management became problems to be collectively resolved—so that everyone could get on with life—they fostered that characteristically indirect linguistic style that perestroika authors denounced for formulaic verbosity: an indirect style that allowed people to perform the form of required public utterance, without tripping over potentially unspeakable themes. Among the most unspeakable topics was Stalin: his name and his place in Soviet history. Tiptoeing around this all-important persona of Soviet history—while still managing to say something about Soviet history—Brezhnev-era texts developed an extremely convoluted style of writing. This, for example, is how the 1980 volume of the *History of the USSR* explains the cult of personality with one long sentence, whose subject and verb are buried under numerous clauses and subclauses:

> Developing the decisions of the 20th Congress of the CPSU, with the intention of fundamentally explaining to communists and to all workers a phenomenon as complex as the cult of personality, of exposing the abhorrent slanderous campaign, started by the capitalist countries' bourgeoise press, which used some facts connected with the CPSU condemnation of the cult of personality of J. V. Stalin, on June 30, 1956, the CC CPSU accepted the resolution "About surmounting the cult of personality and its consequences," unveiling the essence of this phenomenon, and characterizing the conditions and causes that begat it. (Ponomarev 1980, 387–88)

The Brezhnev era is often said to have brought Stalin's partial rehabilitation. "The spirit of Stalin has a grip on the country," warns a 1969 CIA intelligence report, now declassified (*Neo-Stalinism* 1969, 20).[20] But this rehabilitation concerned nothing more than the recognition that Stalin had indeed been the Soviet Generalissimus in World War II: Stalin's photograph at the Yalta conference appeared in some history books, and the five-film epic World War II drama *Liberation* (1970–71) showed Stalin commanding Soviet forces. In other matters, Brezhnevite neo-Stalinism amounted to the further effacement of Stalin's image from history. Stalin's role in the history of the Soviet Union was no more discussed in official histories under Brezhnev than it had been under Khrushchev; history texts published between 1956 and 1964 mention that Stalin's suspiciousness led to the cult of personality and the repressions of the 1930s, those published after 1964 tend to avoid discussing both Stalin and the cult. By 1974, the Soviet National Anthem once again had lyrics—with the offending mention of Stalin replaced by two more lines about Lenin—and Aleksandr Solzhenitsyn's *Ivan Denisovich* was once again censored by order of the GlavLit, which ordered all library copies to be confiscated and destroyed. "If in the beginning of the 1960s, Stalinist repressions were called Stalinist repressions," write Pyotr Vail and Alexander Genis, "by the end of that decade they got the complex

title 'disruption of legality, noted in our memories of the year 1937'"
([1988] 1998, 165).

Vail and Genis's description of the language of Stalinist repressions
is a particularly apt illustration of what those repressions were not
said to have been: not, for example, the violent dispossession of people's land, labor, and property, and often also their lives, for the sake of
the socialist accumulation necessary to build the socialist household.
Neither a marker of the primitive dispossession underlying the socialist economy nor a marker of the institutions of forced labor, Stalinist
repressions instead became the mark of a certain subjective unfreedom,
of, as Khrushchev had put it, "conditions of insecurity, fear and even
desperation" (Khrushchev 1956, S15). Made indefinitely unspeakable,
softly excluded from public mention without being explicitly named,
Stalin became a universally known but unspeakable subject, a symbol of
the more general experience of suffering under an oppressive system of
corporate top-down control. Excised from public discourse by Khrushchev's famous 1956 speech, he became a persistent rumor. And then,
brought back into public discourse by Gorbachev's famous 1987 speech,
he became a symbol of all that which held Soviet society from accelerat-
ing into true socialism.

Contemporary anglophone commentators picked up such denounce-
ments of Stalinism into distinctly totalitarian terms, happily noting that

> "History" cast Mikhail Gorbachev as an instigator and initiator,
> emancipator and catalyst—the one who returned to his people the
> *meaning of language*. . . . Being able to express the truth for the first
> time in recent memory, the Soviet people are whelmed in revela-
> tions, many of them very unpleasant. Still, all this is undertaken
> with the spirit of exorcism and expiation, set against the backdrop
> of hope. Regardless of the backsliding into "command and admin-
> ister" forms of administration, the society as a whole seems to be
> lurching, sometimes kicking and screaming, into the strong light
> of reality, beginning to find its legs again after many, many years
> of being tossed about in the sickening swells of Stalinism. (Eisen
> 1990, ix–x)[21]

Thus framed, the Soviet Union's undoing, which caught Sovietologists
and CIA analysts utterly off-guard (Burawoy 1992; Aron 2006), appeared
to be the long-awaited culmination of history, an "unabashed victory
of economic and political liberalism . . . the universalization of Western
liberal democracy as the final form of human government" (Fukuyama

1989, 3–4). Gorbachev, his advisers, and the country's leading publicists seemed to finally admit what Western cold warriors had known all along: that the centralized control and administration of life is not only ineffective, but also immoral; that it stifles freedom and creativity, deters progress, and mutilates language into newspeak by attempting to control truth itself.

But these were two different totalitarianisms; they differed in their evil origins. On the liberal side of the Cold War, the totalitarian image found its evil root, ultimately, in the planned economy: in a state whose zealous drive to control material exchange leads it to stamp out all that ought to be private, from private property to private spheres. But the Soviet version of the Stalinist administer-command system was rooted in a different evil: in a law that refused to wither away, a force that frustrated people in their personal striving for important personally collectivist interests. These two totalitarianisms therefore had different solutions. If the root of totalitarianism is central planning, the way to destroy it would be to introduce free market institutions and electoral democracy. These institutions, however, were not part of Gorbachev's plan. Instead, perestroika promised to destroy the Stalinist administer-command system with more socialism, not less. It promised more socialism, more democracy, and more socialist social self-management.

Yet it is not hard to see why the Western cold warriors understood perestroika-era condemnations of Stalinism in totalitarian terms. The two concepts do look very similar. They are similarly unconcerned with material and institutional history. Instead, they both focus on individual feelings of subjective unfreedom. "The clearest sign that the Soviet Union can no longer be called totalitarian in the strict sense of the term," explains Hannah Arendt in her 1966 preface to *The Origins of Totalitarianism*, "is, of course, the amazingly swift and rich recovery of the arts during the last decade" (1973: xxxvi). In light of radical post-Stalin institutional reform—which disbanded the GULAG, decriminalized labor laws, and released millions of people—Arendt's focus on the Moscow art scene may seem surprising. But it need not be. It simply attests that particular institutions are not a necessary and sufficient condition of totalitarianism, that totalitarianism is concerned with mental unfreedom, rather than with particular institutions of labor, law, or incarceration. No particular institution can make a state "totalitarian" or safeguard it from becoming so. Totalitarianism is only established by the subjective experience of a person radically stripped of his privacy—or the liberal theorist's imagination of what it would feel like to be such a person.[22]

Perestroika's administer-command system was similarly vague: more mindset and morale than law, institutions, and forms of ownership. In the words of Len Karpinskii, commentator for the *Moscow Times*:

> Stalinism is not only Stalin and not just the cult of his personality. Stalinism is a huge knot of social interdependencies, a tightly interwoven agglomerate of economic, political, ideological and moral formations that had become ingrained in society over the previous years. . . . One of the grievous crimes of Stalinism was the inoculation of a slave mentality into people's lives. People's complete dependence on prescriptions from "above," the yoke of countless "prohibitions" at every step formed a stable social experience. . . . Today's troubles stem from the fact that by the mid-1980s the administer-command system was no longer a bare social "skeleton," a general schema standing above a given person and pressing upon him externally. Bureaucracy is not simply Moloch. It unceremoniously accommodated itself within us: inhabited our minds, took over our souls, ingrained itself into the sacred "I" of our personalities. (Karpinskii 1988, 649–50)

Reformers promised that by fully liberating personal striving from this Stalinist slave mentality, perestroika would allow for the full expression of socialist social self-management. But this image of Stalinism as a personally experienced, soul-crushing bureaucracy masked the foundational violence that begot the socialist household itself; it masked the violent enclosure act that created the socialist commons.

Returning Stalin back into official Soviet historiography, Gorbachev largely repeated Khrushchev's historiographic moves. Khrushchev claimed that the cult of personality was foreign to the nature of socialism, Gorbachev claimed that the administer-command system was nothing more than Stalinism's unresolved historical vestige. The party's endorsement of this historical narrative surely contributed to the historiographic riddle with which I opened this chapter—the widespread assumption that Khrushchev was the counter position to Stalin, almost an antidote. But also, and much more significantly, it contributed to the economic disaster of perestroika. Following Gorbachev's new party line, his economic advisers proposed cleansing socialism of this misplaced historical vestige by expanding relations of social self-management directly into formal economic material relations. They proposed liberating people from those irritating rules that got in everyone's way: that frustrated people's efforts to obtain materials, access, and information for their upstanding, collectivist, socially relevant personal ends. And this attempt to speed up the socialist household proved fatal. Theorized in a historiography that occluded the violent dispossession that had created the Soviet system's material base, the perestroika reforms inadvertently gave away that socialist commons to personal collectivist use. They dissolved the commons, and the Soviet Union collapsed.

CHAPTER 4

Chuvstvo Khoziaina

The Feeling of Being an Owner

Each of this book's chapters is framed by a riddle: by questions that came from my ethnographic fieldwork and whose answers I found in the history of Soviet socialist property law. Chapter 1 asked about the Soviet things of postsocialism. Chapter 2 asked whether nostalgic narratives about Soviet times made any historical sense. Chapter 3 asked why people so insistently assumed Khrushchev to be the historical answer to Stalinism. And now there is one riddle left that I need to tell you to complete the story of personal and socialist property. It is the riddle of Gorbachev's perestroika reforms, after which this property regime was no longer. The riddle is this: What were the economic reforms of perestroika (1985–91)? How were they theorized, what did their architects hope to achieve, and what methods did they find applicable? Considering how much has been written about perestroika and how often people talked about it still in the 2010s, it might be surprising that this is a riddle at all. But it is, and that is the riddle. Analyses of perestroika—oral and written, in Russian and English, academic and popular—have surprisingly little to say about Gorbachev's plan to speed up the socialist household economy. This silence is one of the few things about which contesting parties agree: people who herald perestroika for having destroyed the Soviet Union do not see it as a consistent economic reform project, and neither do people who denounce it for letting the country be taken apart by the screws.

In published accounts and in daily chatter, Gorbachev's perestroika is typically glossed as an economically irrational project, or as not an economic project at all. Texts concerned with the post-Soviet transition typically focus on the political, social, and ideological aspects of perestroika (Verdery 1996; Kotkin 2001; Yurchak 2006). Economic studies of the transition typically dismiss the economic policies of perestroika as a contradictory, indecisive, and piecemeal attempt to implement aspects of a market economy into the Soviet system (Sachs 1991; Boettke 1993; Aslund 2007; Travin 2010). This image of Gorbachev's piecemeal perestroika reforms lends support to the notion that the market reforms of the 1990s restructured an unaltered Soviet system. "Dismantling the Soviet-era system seemed to be a mission of great moral rightness," writes Jeffrey Sachs, recalling his work for Yegor Gaidar's reform team in 1991. "I certainly hoped, and rather expected, that Russia would feel a wave of elation at the new freedom" (Sachs 2012). Some studies skip over perestroika entirely, passing straight from the Brezhnev era to 1990 (Collier 2011; Grazhdankin and Kara-Murza 2015, 4). So do many everyday conversations. In the 2010s, I heard perestroika spoken about endlessly. But closer inspection showed that many of these narratives were set in the mid-to-late 1990s, well after the Soviet Union collapsed. And when I specifically asked people about the economic reforms of perestroika, I often heard about some features of the early post-Soviet reforms, like currency devaluation and privatization vouchers.

The post-1990 focus makes sense: it was then that the Soviet collapse became sensible as a project of actual market reform, locatable on one side of the divide between markets and command-style economies. But this focus does not help us understand what happened to the *sotsialisticheskoe khoziaistvo*. To understand why the Soviet Union fell apart as it did, when it did, we need to examine the mission of perestroika itself: the system that Gorbachev and his advisers intended to create with their reform project, and the ways they planned to do so. For this, it is imperative to notice two things. First, a market economy was never the goal of perestroika: these reforms tried to perfect the socialist household, not destroy it. Second, this was a holistic project, whose laws enacted what its theories had promised. The reformers who, by 1990, loudly blamed each other for perestroika's catastrophic outcomes were very much in consensus circa 1986–88. Gorbachev's speeches, his advisers' texts, publicist essays claiming to further perestroika—and, most important, the two main perestroika reform laws, the 1987 Law on State Enterprise (*Pravda* 1987) and the 1988 Law on Cooperatives (Frenkel 1989)—all worked around the same theory. Laid down at the 27th Party Congress in 1986, this theory is reasonable by the logic of its political imaginary. And in light of this book's previous chapters, this imaginary will not be surprising. It is, in short, that the socialist household could be perfected by giving people more space to act as the *khoziaeva* of their enterprises. As Leonid Abalkin, one of Gorbachev's premier economists, explained in a 1986 interview: "we need to activate the feeling of being a *khoziain* that is inherent in everyone" (Abalkin 1988, 34).

Another group of Soviet economists offered a different theory. The economy, they argued, was regulated not by commands but by negotiation between actors in different positions of administrative power: superiors wielding material resources, money, requirements, and incentives, and subordinates wielding labor for production assignments and ostensibly voluntary labor drives (Aven and Shironin 1987). Seen thus, the Soviet economy was based not on commands but on getting approvals, whereby a "system of vertical bargaining was supplemented by illegal, legalized or legal horizontal bargaining, implying various exchanges among organisations" (Naishul' 1993, 30). Many of the economists who worked with this "bargaining model" subsequently formed the core of Gaidar's post-Soviet economic reform team, and many of their theories have been seen as the forerunners of Russian neoliberalism (Rupprecht 2022). But their approach was wholly ignored by the perestroika reform project (Sutela and Mau 1998, 56–57). Instead, Gorbachev and his economic advisers built on and developed the party line that was laid down at the 27th Party Congress. This party line is incompatible with theories of bargaining, because it is written in terms of socialist householding: based on the assumption that those transactions that could be called bargaining were the ethical actions of a good *khoziain*.

The drive to activate the feeling of being a *khoziain* had been critical to prior reform projects too. But the perestroika reformers proposed something fundamentally new; they proposed activating such ownerly feelings by tying workers' material well-being directly to their enterprises' market success. "It would be naive," Leonid Abalkin explains, "to suppose that this [activating the feeling of being a *khoziain*] can be achieved with verbal appeals and commands. The relationship one has to property is formed by the particular conditions into which a worker is placed, by the real possibilities of him influencing the management and organization of the production, distribution and use of the products of labor. For this reason, we must strengthen socialist self-management" (Abalkin 1988, 34). Socialist self-management was to be strengthened with a combination of personal material interest and personal socialist ethics. Perestroika promised to stimulate the feeling of being a *khoziain* with new market mechanisms. It promised to crack the whip of fiscal responsibility over the socialist household, stimulating the resourceful and punishing the lazy by making individuals' incomes relate automatically to their work collective's successful use of socialist property.

There was a tragic flaw in this theory. But it is not—as is often assumed—in well-connected individuals' private greed (Barnes 2006, 43). It is rather in that question we left at the end of chapter 2, in the demarcating line of vested interest that threatened the ideological consistency on which the socialist household relied. Combining two major twentieth-century visions of self-governing systems—the ethical self-governance of the Third Party Platform and the economic self-governance of liberal markets—perestroika ran afoul not of actors' private greed but of their personal collectivist obligations.

A Self-Regulating System

At the heart of perestroika's economic reform theory is the idea that economic mechanisms could naturally make enterprise employees pick up the slack. Abalkin explains:

> The essence of the problem is to create a massive economic accountability [*khozraschetnyi*] press which, with the power of economic necessity would press [upon people] and compel them to do good, rather than bad. . . . The might of the economic-accountability press is determined by the fact that it realizes national [*obshego-sudarstvennye*] interests by way of an active pressing upon the economic interests of work-collectives, brigades, individual workers. It is irreplaceable as an effective method of linking [these] interests and of educating an ownerly attitude to work [*khoziaiskogo otnosheniia k delu*]. (Abalkin 1987, 86–88)

Such economic accountability pressing was to create a naturally self-regulating system, in which actors' management of socialist property would be evaluated immanently—with better management automatically generating greater profit—rather than administratively, according to predetermined workplans. In some ways, this automatism seems similar to the liberal common sense that markets naturally determine the most effective solutions. And perestroika reform texts themselves often draw this connection. The popular economist Nikolai Shmelev for example, explains that "our experience and world experience show [that] self-tuning, self-regulation, and self-development are the principal condition for the viability and effectiveness of complex social systems. Attempts to subordinate entirely the socioeconomic 'Brownian movement' with its inevitable but ultimately acceptable costs to a certain central control center were fruitless from the very beginning. With the passage of time, this has become increasingly apparent" (Shmelev [1987] 1988, 13; see also Shmelev and Popov 1989, 390). But the perestroika proposal also differed in one very significant way from self-regulating liberal markets: it lacked free market prices.

For twentieth-century liberal theorists like Ludwig von Mises and Friedrich Hayek, and for theorists of socially disembedded economies like Karl Polanyi, freely determined market prices are the mechanism that turns disparate social relations of exchange into a unified self-regulating system, by automatically connecting scarcity to cost (Polanyi 2001, 71). In such a system, prices mediate between all actors' desires and material scarcity. Per Hayek's famous example, if there is a shortage of tin anywhere in this economy, everyone reacts to it instantly, because the price of tin rises. "The mere fact that there is one price for any commodity—or rather that local prices are connected in a manner determined by the cost of transport, etc.—brings about the solution which (it is just conceptually possible) might have been arrived at by one single mind possessing all the information which is in fact dispersed among all the people involved in the process" (Hayek 1945, 526). The perestroika imaginary was based on a similar dream of automatic self-governance and all-knowing central planning.[1] But reform texts also insist that prices on this "socialist market" will remain unproblematically under central control. And while they lament the inaccuracy of state prices, they envision price reform as a program of more accurate pricing rather than of price of liberalization as such (see Abalkin 1987, 178–79; Pavlov 1988). In practice, such price reform was only applied selectively, and only after the main economic reform law, the 1987 Law On State Enterprise, was implemented. In other words, the 1987 law made enterprises responsible for their own gains and losses, while requiring them to trade at state-set prices that, as reformers themselves repeatedly acknowledged, did not correspond to actual production costs.

Perestroika reform theory was little concerned with prices because these reforms did not intend to create a self-regulating market. They intended to educate feelings of ownership and responsibility by legibly relating personal profit to the assiduous use of socialist property.[2] Claiming that "the most important aspect of perestroika is the reconstruction [lit. perestroika] of consciousness" (Abalkin 1988, 20), Gorbachev's economists lamented that administrative methods of management, based on top-down commands, have made workers lose the feeling of being a *khoziain*, leading them to grossly mismanage materials and labor time. Attempts to educate the feeling of being a *khoziain* have a long history in Soviet economic reform. Lenin, calling for workers' self-disciple in 1918, also claimed that "it is a question of every politically conscious worker feeling that he is not only the *khoziain* in his own factory but that he is also a representative of the country, of his feeling his responsibility" (Lenin 1965, 403).[3] Legal scholars writing in support of the draconian 1932 antitheft law insisted that "we must engrain in the consciousness of every collective farm member the feeling of being a *khoziain* and the feeling of responsibility for his collective *khoziaistvo*" (Man 1932, 9). Discussions at the 1961 22nd Party Congress claimed that eliminating Stalin's cult of personality and attracting the masses to the task of governing the state had "heightened within all soviet people the proud feeling of being a *khoziain* of the whole country, immeasurably raised the laborers' enthusiasm [*aktivnost'*] and initiative in the task of building communism" (CPSU 1962, 273). The perestroika reforms also have a more direct predecessor: their texts often replicate the language of the reforms proposed by Yuri Andropov, Gorbachev's predecessor and political mentor. Even the title of Abalkin's foundational 1987 book, *New Type of Economic Thinking*, comes from a phrase popularized by discussions of the 1983 Labor Collectives Law. Andropov had also attempted to bring the economy to heel during his short time in office (1982–84), and his 1983 reform law demanded that "each laborer must feel himself to be a *khoziain* in his enterprise, and a representative of the entire country" (Zakon SSSR 1983, 2). But Andropov's reforms intended to instill such feelings of responsibility by giving workers greater control over the distribution of material benefits within enterprises. Perestroika extended the logic to the material basis of the socialist household economy itself. Criticizing previous reform projects for "not touching upon the actual productive relations that frame economic [*khoziaistvennaia*] life . . . not [being] accompanied by any sort of a serious reformation of the relations of production," reformers proposed making "the work collective . . . genuinely interested in the best, the most effective use of the resources assigned to it" by connecting workers' personal material interests directly to their enterprises' success in trading on the "socialist market" (Abalkin 1987, 156, 86).

And this was truly novel.

"We must raise workers' interest in the better use and increase of our national wealth [*narodnogo bogatstva*]," Gorbachev declared at the 27th Party Congress. "How can we solve this problem? It would be naïve to imagine that the feeling of being an owner [*chuvstvo khoziaina*] can be educated by words alone. The relationship one has to property is formed first and foremost by the actual conditions in which a person finds himself, by the possibilities he has to influence the production, distribution and utilization of the results of his labor. The problem thus consists in a further entrenchment of socialist self-management within the economy" (Gorbachev 1986, 50). This ownerly attitude did not imply possession. The socialist self-management advocated by the perestroika reformers rested firmly on the foundation of socialist property. Even as they theorized that market mechanisms would automatically speed up the economy by making enterprises' success imminent to workers' fiscal losses and gains, they did not imagine that the institution of socialist property would itself need to be radically restructured.[4] The plan was only to stimulate the "multifaceted system of relations" that comprise socialist property and to make people manage such socialist property with greater assiduousness (Gorbachev 1986, 49–50). Abel Aganbegyan, one of Gorbachev's chief economic advisers, explains in a 1988 text:

> The main form of socialist property is national state property [*obshchenarodnaia gosudarstvennaia sobstvennost'*]. The earth, its mineral resources, state enterprises, and factories are all objects of such national property. The entire society possesses [*vladeet*] it collectively. A potential danger of such collective possession is that such property appears to belong to everyone and no one in particular. Individual or group feelings of ownership [*chuvstva khoziaina*] are dimmed. And people might develop the attitude that national goods as no one's: workers might use national resources uneconomically, since these resources are not their own; they may work worse in the collective household than they work for themselves; they may treat the equipment at state enterprises unsparingly, compared to how they treat their own automobiles. (Aganbegyan 1988a, 93–94)

To make people treat factory equipment as lovingly as they treat their own automobiles, reform theory proposed turning "the worker into a co-owner of public manufacturing" by making property relations "flexible" and "filled with actual content . . . : effectively joining the interests of society, of the work collective, and of each individual worker. Doing so means requiring people to realize the inevitability of feeling themselves to be authentic *khoziaeva*" (Abalkin 1987, 84). Enacting these proposals, the 1987 Law on State Enterprise decrees that "at a state enterprise, the labor collective, using national property [*obshenarodnuiu sobstvenost'*] as an owner [*khoziain*], creates and multiplies national wealth [*narodnoe bogatsvo*], provides for a combination of social, collective, and individual worker interests" (*Pravda* 1987, 1, article 1.2).

The ubiquitous late-Soviet mismanagement of material resources gave perestroika its urgency and its moral justification. Pointing to the hoarded stockpiles that lie around enterprise warehouses as deadweight, reform texts insist that a proper *khoziain* would put these misused materials to work, turning them into useful things for the Soviet people. "We should give enterprises and organizations the right to independently actualize products made in excess of the plan [*sverkhplanovuiu*]," says Gorbachev in 1986, "as well as unused stock, materials, equipment, and so on. Such things need to be legalized in interactions with the population as well. Is it sensible to destroy or throw into the dump that which could be useful for the household, for building housing, garages, little garden houses?" (Gorbachev [1986] 1987, 63). Certainly, such waste is not sensible. And to this end, the 1987 Law on State Enterprise entitled enterprises to sell—at state-set price—the material stockpiles that they had amassed (*Pravda* 1987, 1, article 4.4). These sales were theorized to not only encourage assiduousness, but also to provide the newly legalized small cooperative ventures with raw materials from which to produce consumer goods. Thus drawing on the Soviet economy's hidden internal reserves—on material stockpiles and on workers' untapped enthusiasm—the reforms would require neither "considerable capital" nor the abolishment of "the funded ('rationed') supply system." "All that is required is boldness, firmness, and consistency in liberation of internal economic forces . . . State enterprise reserves have any amount—billions of rubles' worth!—of surplus or obsolete equipment and raw materials and supplies hidden away for any contingency, if they were sold freely, it would be possible to satisfy offhand the initial basic needs of small-scale personal and cooperative enterprises" (Shmelev 1988, 14, 19–20; see also Aganbegyan 1988b, 28).

And critically, such sales of socialist property would not threaten the *sotsialisticheskoe khoziaistvo* itself, because they would only concern the household economy's excesses—its stockpiles, which would have been wasted; and its over-plan production, which would have never been made. The reformers' logic here will be familiar to theorists of house-holding. Polanyi, attributing to Aristotle this "most prophetic pointer ever made in the realm of the social sciences," notes that only produc-tion *for gain* creates a market economy. The mere market sale of surpluses need not threaten the household: "as long as the cash crop would also otherwise be raised on the farm for sustenance, as cattle or grain, the sale of the surpluses need not destroy the basis of householding . . . as long as markets and money were mere accessories to an otherwise self-sufficient household, the principle of production for use could oper-ate" (Polanyi 2001, 56). Following this same logic, perestroika reformers suggested that legalizing the sale of excesses would encourage employ-ees to more assiduously use the socialist property their enterprises had been allotted. Although the "transfer of assets to a privately controlled subsidiary looks like the plundering of state property," explains Simon Clarke, it was not illegal. "Although the 1987 Law on State Enterprise defined the enterprise as proprietor of its assets, this property did not have the capitalist form . . . provided that the enterprise maintained its deliveries, the state lost nothing if the enterprise assigned the user-rights to its assets to a [subsidiary private-cooperative venture] . . . From this perspective the profits of the co-operative or leased enterprise did not derive from plundering the state, but from the ability of its workers and managers to produce above the 'scientifically' determined norms" (Clarke et al. 1993, 208).

Gleaning

Seen through the logics of householding, perestroika reform theory does not seem unreasonable. What harm could come of letting people profit on that which would have been wasted? Or of holding them personally responsible for their enterprises' success? Intending to strengthen the institute of central planning by ensuring better fulfillment of its plans, these reforms would, after all, have only affected the "forms and meth-ods of disseminating the state plan's tasks to the [economy's] primary links—the enterprises and conglomerates" while the economy, and the "links constituting [it as a] totality," remained unproblematically under central control (Abalkin 1987, 169, also 132–33).

But the socialist household also differed significantly from Aristotle's ideal. Built on a commons of socialist property, that sacred and inviolable basis of the Soviet order, it was a large corporate structure, made up of a nestled multiplicity of smaller ones: all of them bound to each other by relations of distribution, and managed by people who had been allotted the right to use some of this sacred foundational property. In practice, because people often had trouble getting their hands on this property, it also relied on the customary use-rights that its many *khoziaeva* staked to the sacred commons.

Perestroika proposed giving managers more space to personally sort out their enterprises' mismanaged materials and labor time: to act as *khoziaeva*. "Imagine a present-day enterprise," Aganbegyan writes,

> it must make applications for rolled steel and other materials long before the plan of production for the following year has been determined. Not yet knowing the details of its final plans, these applications are naturally exaggerated. Much is acquired that is not needed. So difficult is the existing bureaucratic method of passing on unneeded resources to another enterprise, that it is easier to leave the unneeded materials in the storehouse. Thus shortages gradually accumulated and stocks grew in enterprises and organisations of materials that were withdrawn from circulation. (1988b, 136)

These stockpiles, however, were not simply warehoused. They were the roots and the fruits of good management. They had been skimmed from the plan of distribution by the socialist household's diligent *khoziaeva*, intentionally set aside as scrap to protect against shortage. "Everyone tried to raise the norms"—as we heard Ivan recall in Chapter 1, explaining how he obtained metal to make ice-screws—"because that's the way the Soviet system worked. How much will they give you next year? As much as this year, plus you could ask for a little more. And if you did not eat everything, next year they would give you less. So everyone tried to take a little more, and it all accumulated, accumulated." These stocks accumulated but did not lie dormant.[5] They were used by many different actors, for many different ends: to cover the enterprise's own unforeseen shortages, to help procurement officers from other enterprises, to cement and maintain personal relationships, and to make useful things, like kayaks and tombstones. The successful *khoziain* in this socialist household economy was a creator and user of such intentional leftovers, at once the household's owner and gleaner.

Foregrounding the management ethic that had shadowed and underpinned the *sotsialisticheskoe khoziaistvo*, perestroika made it central to the formal economy itself. This was the whole point: to make the economy imminently self-managing by making people act as *khoziaeva*. And the reforms were phenomenally successful in achieving this stated aim. Faced with the need to secure supplies for everything above their state-minimum work order and free to sell all their excesses at state-set price, enterprise managers acted as resourceful *khoziaeva*; they traded preferentially with partners who could help them obtain the materials they needed. Such preferential trading quickly broke apart the centrally planned economy's extant supply ties—making the right to acquire goods itself a highly valued, personally negotiated good—and disastrous effects were quickly felt (Filtzer 1991; Humphrey 1991; Burawoy and Krotov 1992). The worse things got, the more people relied on their nonmonetary personal social relationships, their customary use-rights to socialist property. This was also part of the plan. The reform laws themselves obligated enterprises to maintain their affiliates' well-being through explicitly nonmonetary distribution. "An enormous effort will have to made," urged the reform economist Stanislav Shatalin in 1986, "so that the prestige of a given enterprise becomes a real economic phenomenon that all its personnel are interested in working for, so that the loss of a job at the enterprise would have serious economic implications in a worker's life" (Shatalin [1986]1987, 18). The 1987 Law on State Enterprise implemented these theoretical demands in the requirement that enterprises offer their affiliates various forms of moral and social support, from medical treatment and children's organizations, to apartment buildings, vacation packages, and dacha gardening plots (*Pravda* 1987, article 13).

The prestige that Shatalin theorized as a real economic phenomenon was not an explicitly monetary one. It was customary: it fortified those social relationships that a market economy is typically said to cut off as it divorces "the economic motive from all concrete social relationships" (Polanyi 2001, 57). And so while foreign observers noted a "generalized supply crisis" gripping the Soviet economy (Filtzer 1991, 996), Soviet analyses often described the situation in moral terms. Around 1988–91, the term "group egoism" emerged both in mainstream newspapers like *Izvestia* and *Pravda* and in political discourse. Speakers used it to blame perestroika's disastrous outcomes on the selfishness of certain economic actors who acted to maximize profit, instead of ensuring the public good.[6] With accusations of mismanagement framed thus as a question of public morality, the answers to such accusations were also often posited as a question of morals: in the further perestroika of mindsets.[7] In 1988, for example, the Obkom secretary from Lipetsk noted that,

> The work collective of our Novolipetsk metal plant is in a persistently good mood, for much is done there to better the conditions of labor, life, culture, and health. But I recently visited the "Petrovskii" kolkhoz—they lack this, that, and the other, and the workers are in very different spirits. They are also "for" perestroika, but they chide it, doubt its perspectives. They say that as soon as the director went on holiday, his assistant quickly "organized" a three-bedroom apartment for a relative of his. And truly: what sort of perestroika is it, if its fate is in the hands of one good boss [*nachal'nik*], which are—alas!—not everywhere. It is imperative that the spiritual sphere, our morality, also—like the economic mechanism—become a self-correcting, self-regulating system that automatically guarantees protection from arbitrariness and despotism. (Manaenkov 1988, 3)

Other commentators reacted with greater alarm, pointing out that "a natural-exchange market has formed in the country. And the feeling of being a *khoziain* on this market is experienced by those who produce deficit goods. For example, for rolls of paper today one can buy anything, from French cosmetics to automobiles and audio equipment. But what about those enterprises that produce machine tools, electric locomotives, mining equipment?" (*Rabochaya Tribuna* 1990, 1).

Bolstering their ability to obtain supplies, economic actors combined into large monopolies of distribution: "suzerainties" (Humphrey 1991) of economic and territorial powers, which distributed the right to buy everything from industrial rolls of paper to furniture and food (Burawoy and Hendley 1992; Burawoy and Krotov 1992; Naishul 1992). These arrangements made actors' ability to get goods contingent on affiliation with such a suzerainty, and on what the latter had managed to obtain for redistribution.[8] And such affiliation—as a nonmarket, nonmonetary relationship—was itself subject to subsequent customary redistribution. Thus, for example, Oleg, the artisanal leather worker we met in chapter 1, recalled that around 1992–94, when "the Soviet Union had already collapsed, but the factory was still state-based," he obtained allocation rights through his personal relationship with the director of a five-star restaurant. He framed his recollection with the explanation that "a lot has changed since Soviet times . . . first of all, in the Soviet Union, I could not just come to the factory and buy leather," and he explained that he used his personal charm to fill that allocation quota with the products he needed.

> OLEG: When I got access to that factory, I took a bottle of champagne, a box of chocolates, and I went—not to the distribution department, but straight to the warehouse, to the girls who worked there . . . and they said: "Oh! Well, you go ahead and pick out what you need." And that's not something you could do there in those times. I'd come, choose, I could take my pick of a stack this high—I could pull out a sheet from the very bottom, so long as I had the strength to. And then I go to the payment department—and they say HOW? You were supposed to have gone to the distribution department, and then here, and then there, how could you have gone straight through? And I say, "what's the difference? You have the payment sheets? Settle me." And after a while they stopped paying attention—I'd just go straight to the warehouse with a bottle of champagne.
> XC: So, this was legally bought leather?
> OLEG: Yes, it was legal.
> XC: What price did you pay for it?
> OLEG: The state-set price.
> XC: Then what was the difference?
> OLEG: The difference is that I chose the leather I needed, instead of taking whatever they gave me.

Such "crimes of substitution" (Oushakine 2003) were the very instantiation of perestroika reform theory's stated aim: they were practices of being a good *khoziain,* practices by which people formally tasked with the management of socialist property created personally managed stockpiles.

The people I talked to in the 2010s often recalled perestroika as an era of social collapse and total commodity deficit, during which workers were paid in kind, in everything from thermoses and planes of glass to televisions and industrial quantities of aluminum foil. But they often narrated the logic of such non-monetary transactions as fundamentally Soviet. This was true for the enterprise-based distribution of welfare that, in chapter 1, Vera referred to as Svetlana's great material base: "a medical center, a pool, sauna, circular shower; lunch hour aerobics. A polyclinic, a dentist—for free—everything was free then, all during working hours." And it was true for the personally negotiated transactions by which people obtained materials to make sellable goods. Boris, the alpinist gear-designer whom we met in chapter 1, retired from his factory job in 1988 and by 1995 had registered a firm making personal belay devices for first respondents like firemen. A personal-rappelling device is comprised of a simple belay device and a fanny pack with a coiled cord. It allows one to escape from a dangerous situation by lowering oneself to safety. The cord used in such a device has to be light and strong and, most important, fire proof. Talking about how he got raw materials for his mid-1990s firm, Boris cited "Soviet specifics":

> BORIS: Actually, this material existed—it's just that the information was classified. It was unobtainable. There were organizations that had Kevlar, it was used for the space program—but it was classified.
>
> XC: And after 1991?
>
> BORIS: Then everything opened. The ropes need to be made from a fire-proof material—and it existed! It was Kevlar. It existed, but we didn't know anything about it. And the firemen didn't know about it. But it existed.
>
> XC: But how did you manage to get the material once you learned about it?
>
> BORIS: Well, that's just Soviet specifics. There were loads of it—you just had to know where to look. It existed. It existed— I just did not know about it. I was a machine-builder. Those materials that were used for the space program, they were unknown to machine-builders. But I also developed and tested gear for the Mountaineering Committee, so I had some connections.
>
> XC: But then, it was de-classified and what? Was it openly sold?
>
> BORIS: Oh, it stayed just where it was. Where would it go? Who needs it? If even I didn't know about it? Who would buy it? It's not a mass-consumer good after all. The material itself—it's just a thread—who would notice it?

Using his connections in the Mountaineering Committee to obtain Kevlar thread, Boris had it spun into ropes at the Kaliningrad Science-Research Institute of Industrial Fishing, which primarily made nets, but which had also spun small batches of climbing rope for the alpinism camps to which trip packages were distributed through mountaineering sections at various enterprises throughout the Soviet Union, until, he told me, "everything fell apart there . . . when this perestroika that came down upon our heads sent everything flying heads over tails."

Much excellent work has described the informal relationships through which people survived the Soviet collapse: the barter conglomerates that distributed goods and acquisition rights through nonmonetary transactions, the phatic labor that made these relationships possible, and the institutional practices into which they solidified (Burawoy 1997; Bridger and Pine 1997; Woodruff 1999; Burawoy and Verdery 1999; Seabright 2000; Pisano 2009; Collier 2011). But one interesting fact has received much less scholarly attention; the fact that perestroika reform theory framed such nonmonetary transactions as a social good: an explicitly noneconomic question of welfare. This is true even when such nonmonetary deals concerned international barter.

Vastly increasing the distributive power of bartering firms and motivating them to move resources abroad, international barter deals were hotly contested throughout the 1990s. But they were typically discussed in political and moral terms, rather than economic ones: as a question of rights rather than of taxation. The right to perform such operations was withheld by new regulations (Gorbachev 1990), obtained through legal loopholes (*Kommersant Vlast'* 1991a), granted to miners to quell strikes (*Kommersant Vlast'* 1991b), and exchanged between enterprises (Burawoy and Krotov 1993). But in all cases, these rights licensed untaxed exchanges; even the export of natural resources like oil and coal could avoid the 73 percent tax on profit from monetary sales abroad if enterprises performed such transactions with the extra production they made above their state-determined work plan, and if they performed them as barter (Rogers 2014). Contemporaneous economic discussions of taxation focused on profit (Pavlov 1990) and barter involved no money, consequently, it involved no profit. It did, however, involve immense redistribution, serving to underwrite other forms of commerce. "Some mines have an elaborate system of distribution among their employees," write Michael Burawoy and Pavel Krotov in their study of the Vorkuta coal mines: "at mine Number Six, for example, 5,600 rubles buys workers goods worth up to $10,000, i.e. at an exchange rate of one ruble for almost two dollars, including televisions, videos, mixers, fridges, shoes and even cars" (Burawoy and Krotov 1993, 59). But within the logic of socialist householding, the goods thus acquired and distributed to affiliates at fixed and generous exchange rates counted not as profit but as the provision of affiliates' well-being, the "concrete social relationships"

(Polanyi 2001, 57) that the 1987 Law on State Enterprise also explicitly required enterprises to maintain.

Perestroika reform discourse framed international barter deals as a social good, as transactions that could stabilize the ruble by filling the consumer market with imported commodities gotten in exchange for useless industrial scrap. Explaining the worsening commodity deficit by an "imbalance between money and commodity flows" that had been growing since the 1960s, economists proposed restoring the balance by mopping up excess money with extra commodities and an expanded "sphere of paid services . . . since it is impossible to provide for the money mass in circulation with commodities alone" (Krasvina 1990, 7).[9] They were therefore concerned with regulating the export of deficit products—like Soviet fridges, irons, and televisions—but not with the barter monopolies formed by the redistribution of imported goods (Krasvina 1990, 13; see also Konstantinov 1989; Shmelev [1990] 2007a; Golovatyi 1989; *Finansy SSSR* 1989, 9). "We did not even tax barter deals, wanting to encourage the inexperienced and none too wealthy 'sellers,'" writes Nikolai Ryzhkov, 1985–91 chairman of the Council of Ministers, in his 1992 autobiography *Perestroika: A History of Betrayals*.

> Barter could quickly and reliably stop up some national-economy [*khoziaistvennye*] holes—in the industrial sense as well as in the social. Who could have predicted then [in 1988] that czar-barter will eventually start forcing out all other forms of trade from our external market! But the first deals seemed quite reasonable. For example, in 1988, the Council of Ministers permitted the Novo-Lipetsky metalworks plant to sell its above-plan metal in exchange for a new ready-to-operate factory of household refrigerators, with the productive capacity of one million fridges a year. That, I still think, was a fine exchange! And later on I supported similar requests and offers, although I was constantly chided: barter ought to be forbidden, no good comes of it for the state budget. I protested: maybe no good for the budget, but a great deal of good for the state and the people. Those same Lipetsk fridges—don't we need them? . . . It's the same budget, just actualized in commodity form. (Ryzhkov 1992, 256)

The dream of speeding up the Soviet economy with the gleanings of its nestled households, the dream that a particular household's excesses could be used for the benefit of all—those fridges, don't we need them?—this is the dream of socialist social self-management. Party ideologues had insisted since the 1960s that the socialist household would become automatically self-governing once people learned to live by the ethical rules of comradely mutual aid, allowing society to outgrow the law. Perestroika actualized this striving in the material relations of production themselves. Liberating people to manage their enterprises' inputs and outputs, limits and plans, stockpiles and shortages, it promised to finally cleanse society of that irrational and violent administrative control that made it ineffective and stagnant.

Existing Stalinism

Following Gorbachev's 1987 call to "evaluate the past with a feeling of historical responsibility and on the basis of historical truth" (Gorbachev 1987, 14), the perestroika reforms mobilized a historiographically complicated maneuver of liberating the past: cleansing Leninist ideals from Stalinist methods to "remove the rust of bureaucratism from socialist ideals, to clean them of all everything inhuman . . . [to] liberate people's finest creative forces, to ensure the spiritual blossoming of personality [*lichnosti*]" (Gorbachev 1989, 66). This battle for de-Stalinization was nothing less than revolutionary. Shmelev wrote,

> An actual revolutionary situation has developed in the country. The "upper strata" cannot govern, and the "lower strata" do not want to live in the old way any longer. But revolution means revolution. We have already embarked on this path. The potential consequences of the decisions of the June [1987] Plenum of the CPSU Central Committee hold truly revolutionary significance for the fate of the nation. However, revolution from above is by no means easier than revolution from below.
>
> Its success, like the success of any revolution, depends primarily on the staunchness and resoluteness of revolutionary forces and their ability to break the resistance of outmoded social structures. (Shmelev [1988] 1989, 37–38)

But if the lower strata were to be led, with staunch resoluteness, by the Communist Party, who was in charge of the upper strata that was failing to govern? Where was Stalinism? "Existing Stalinism" (Shmelev [1987] 1988, 18) was neither a question of particular late-Soviet institutions, nor of the property relations that were established by the 1936 Stalin Constitution; it lingered in the mental unfreedom forced upon Soviet people by the vestigial administrative-command system.

The term "administrative system" (used interchangeably with "command system" and "administrative-command") was coined in 1986 by Gavriil Popov, editor of the journal *Questions of Economics*, in his review of Alexander Bek's novel about a fictional Stalin-era metal works' manager. The book, Popov writes in his review essay, tells the tragic story of a man who had given himself to the system completely, had sacrificed his personal relationships—with his family and friends, with his own health and his leisure—and was beholden only to his superiors' commands. The protagonist lets no one off the hook, and he lets no one glean: not even the women peeling potatoes in the factory's cafeteria, whom he suspects of "filching [the peelings] home to feed their piglets" (Popov [1986] 1987, 56). His saving grace is that he demands no less of himself than of others. The administrative system depended on such people, who sacrificed their whole lives to it, who were endlessly faithful to Stalin. Yet, even in Stalin's time, this system's rigidity inescapably led to what Ivan Pavlov called "collisions" of contrasting impulses, when "a person's internal motivation demands that he act one way, but he forces himself to do the opposite, as is demanded by the logic of administration and the habit of unconditionally fulfilling any order from above" (Popov [1986] 1987, 58). After Stalin's death this system lost its strictness but retained its rigidity; what had once been collisions, now became cynicism. A sort of doublethink emerged—a gap between actions and words—and many people found ways to use the system's rigidity for their personal avaricious profit by doing one thing while saying another.

Initially slated for publication in 1965, Bek's book was shelved because of the protests of a former minister's widow, who claimed that it slandered her deceased husband. In his defense, Bek insisted that the character was entirely fictional (Beliaev 2002). When it was finally published in 1986, Popov took this fictionalized image of Stalinism as a compelling description of that administrative system from which perestroika was now to liberate Soviet society. Deduced thus from a work of historical fiction—in a review essay titled "From an Economist's Point of View"—the administrative system is an economic theory of sentiment. Seen through its prism, late Soviet society had to be de-Stalinized through the wholesale liberation of mindsets. And so the perestroika reformers did not attempt to dismantle this administer-command system by radically restructuring systems of governance. They demanded instead that systems of governance be rid of those who cling to the old administer-command mindset, who are against perestroika.[10] "We must

learn to recognize, bring to light, neutralize the maneuvers of the enemies of perestroika," Gorbachev insisted: "those who hinder our affairs,
who put up road blocks, who try to drag us into the past" (Gorbachev
1987, 41). These people have "no place in perestroika," and they put perestroika in danger (Karpinsky 1988, 669). But it is not clear who exactly
they are because, as Popov put it in a 1988 interview, "today, at least in
principle, everyone is for" perestroika.

> This is the fundamental characteristic of the present moment;
> and, in my opinion, a rather dangerous one. How can we determine
> who is really for [perestroika], and who is against? By speeches and
> declarations? But where is the guarantee that the speeches are not
> dictated by a desire to please the authorities, that the declarations
> are not driven by the striving to attain a higher position? . . . The
> opponents of perestroika have not been defeated organizationally,
> the government apparatus has not been cleaned of them (Popov
> 1989 [1988], 315–16).

These unnamed "quasi-supporters of perestroika," who drag their
feet and try to hinder the reforms, even as they claim to support them
(Zaslavskaya [1988] 1989, 48), who cannot be clearly defined, person-
ify the "existing Stalinism" that lingers in late-Soviet society (Shmelev
[1987] 1988, 18). They, or rather it, is a "slave mentality" (Karpinskii
1988, 650): a stagnant way of thought that everyone must fight inside
his own head. A fight against such administrative methods, writes
Popov, "necessarily becomes an attempt to break not only the apparatus, but also the stereotypes of life that have formed within each of us"
(Popov [1988] 1989, 329). "Our consciousness," explains the economic
sociologist Tatyana Zaslavskaya, "is littered with a multitude of mistaken assumptions, imagined taboos, skepticism . . . but the fate of perestroika now greatly depends upon the level of society's consciousness"
(Zaslavskaya [1988] 1989, 46).[11]

The call to liberate mindsets from stagnant thought was far-reaching.
Popular periodicals noted a "veritable explosion of interest in people
with unusual abilities" (Romanenko and Izvekova 1989), and the Soviet
school of parapsychological energo-informational radiation enjoyed its
public triumph (Chudakova 2015, Velminski 2017). Millions of people
throughout the Soviet Union set jars of water before their TV screens
to be charged energetically by the extrasense healer Allan Chumak's
weekly broadcasts. Djuna, an extra-sense healer who was rumored to
have worked for Brezhnev, headlined *Pravda*'s 1990 "Festival of Truth,"
joined by the vice minister of health of the USSR; they discussed whether

medicine is an art or a science (Bogdanov 1990). Leading newspapers explained that Soviet parapsychology had been trapped in a double bind: on the one hand, incredulous public opinion "assumes such studies are 'pseudoscience,'" on the other hand, "conservatives in *Minzdrav* [the Ministry of Health] and the Academy of Medical Sciences 'gag' new scientific developments, like cybernetics and genetics had once been 'strangled'" (Konovalov 1986, 6). Specialists in bio-fields, torsion fields, and energo-informational radiation were joined by prophets, shamans, and priests, and all of them promised privileged access to the Secret that had laid just out of reach, obscured by state censorship, foreclosed by the scientific establishment, precluded by prudish morality and bankrupt habitual thought (Herzog 1993). The fast and large profits that some people now turned, with much fanfare, on the material excesses they gleaned through their personal ties gave visible proof to these specialists' claims: from a believer's point of view, the abundant gleanings of formerly socialist property looked like just rewards for those who had dared to open their minds to the true laws of God, society, and nature (Cherkaev 2020).

This explosion of supernatural discourses is often explained by a "spiritual vacuum caused by the downfall of Communism" (Menzel 2012, 14–15). But if we focus on perestroika's presences, instead of its vacuous absences, we will notice a curious overlap between the time's economic and extrasensorial theories. Both discourses hold as axiomatic that the Stalinist administer-command system stifled truth, that this truth exists abroad or had existed in pre-Stalinist Russia, and that individuals' personal mindsets, experiences, and feelings can directly affect the material world. To both, this stifled truth was quite serious: the truth of nature itself. Perestroika-era parapsychologists insisted that mindsets liberated from administrative stagnation could effect great material change; that, in the words of a 1989 article about a retired engineer turned parapsychologist, "in the light, in glasnost, everything will be seen and it will be easier to choose the true way of healing mankind and nature" (Shikin 1989, 49). Economists similarly claimed to return the economy to its natural laws whose scientific study the Stalinist administrative system had wrongly suppressed. Shmelev wrote in 1989:

> Why is it that the same people who never would have taken a crowbar to a nuclear reactor (it will blow!) did not hesitate for a second to come with that same crowbar at the economy, when, as was clear to any peasant with a church-school education, the

consequences will be much worse, much more frightening, than
an explosion of all of the country's explosives? . . . With your
hand on your heart, answer me: how many people in all of our
nation's present generations understand that the laws of nature
and the law of the economy are one and the same? And that people, despite all of their pride and presumption, can only come
to know these laws, obey them, use them, but under no consequences come at them with fists or, worse, with a machine gun?
Because truly: it will blow! And it blew. And thank God, at least
we are alive, even if maimed and damaged in our minds. (Shmelev
[1989] 2007b, 83–84)

In the revolutionary drive to overcome this totalitarian disregard for
natural law, even the factual collapse of the Soviet economy could
be justified. "The long rule of the totalitarian sociopolitical system
dragged our society into a profound crisis," explains the 500 Days
Plan for market transition, written in 1990 for Gorbachev and Boris
Yeltsin but vetoed by Nikolai Ryzhkov and not implemented (Shatalin
1990, 8).[12] Framed by an introduction titled "Person, Freedom, Market," the 500 Days Plan argues that full marketization is the only way
to escape a "return to 1937" and, constructing a rhetorical opposition
between the rich oppressive state and its impoverished people, sets "as
its goal to take everything possible from the state and give it to people"
(Shatalin 1990, 8). The 500 Days Plan celebrates the fact that perestroika
radically worsened the country's economic situation. "Paradoxical
though it may seem, the 1985–1990 period was objectively necessary
for society to realize the hopelessness of the extant social-economic
system, and to develop a program for transitioning to another model
of development" (Shatalin 1990, 25).

    And socialist property? Amid revolutionary calls to liberate mindsets
and economics from Stalinism, to return to the "universality of laws
that control the economy and the society in general" (Shatalin 1990,
28), amid finger-pointing accusations of whom to blame for the Soviet
Union's quick economic collapse, the sacred and inviolable basis of the
Soviet order had quietly withered away. The year before the Russian
Soviet Federative Socialist Republic officially quit the Soviet Union and
ceased to be socialist, a curiously laconic decree appeared in its Constitution. It states: "Persons threatening property are punished by law."[13]
Half a year prior, the June 16, 1990 edition of this same article 59 stated:
"A citizen of the RSFSR is obligated to protect and strengthen socialist

property. . . . Persons threatening socialist property are punished by law." But as the socialist household strove for greater self-management, the inviolable material basis that Stalin had personally ordained with such cruel violence had become curiously divorced from the image of Stalinism that perestroika reformers now accused of stagnating the economy by inoculating "a slave mentality into people's lives" (Karpinskii 1988, 650). Socialist property was never privatized. By the time privatization and price liberalization were implemented, there was no longer a socialist commons to speak of.[14]

"All the projects of perestroika, including the 500-Day Plan, were projects for introducing a fairy-tale market in a fantasy land," quipped Vitali Naishul (1992, 491). Naishul, one of the Soviet economists whose bargaining model was wholly ignored by Gorbachev's reformers, explained such magical thinking by the fact that decades of Soviet totalitarianism had suppressed truthful information about society, leaving people unable to comprehend their actual situation. From my vantage point thirty years later, the problem looks more like the short-circuiting of two totalitarian myths. The market reforms that Gorbachev's economic advisers heralded for their peaceful and efficient trading lacked that critical mechanism which, in the liberal myth of the one of the many, was to relate trading to peace and prosperity: they lacked free market prices. Reformers failed to notice this lack because their own assumptions of how individuals should relate to society had derived from another, different, parallel myth. This second myth had also grown from the debate of the one and the many. It had fortified in direct dispute with the claim that in a society built on collectivist principles "all people but the great dictators would be deprived of their essential human quality. They would become mere soulless pawns in the hands of a monster" (Mises [1957] 2007, 61). In this socialist myth, the individual's place in modern society was properly mediated not by market price but by a common collectivist striving.

Turning the good of one mythic image against the evil of its historical twin, perestroika accidentally gave away the socialist commons without noticing it. And this breakup was ethical. Mandated to glean for their own particular collectives' benefit, the socialist household's many *khoziaeva* split up the commons. They unfurled the delicate balance on which these customary use-rights relied. They did, in the end, make the state wither away. And the collapse of the Soviet Union may therefore be best explained neither by the slow death of an unnatural system, nor by the perestroika reformers' indecisiveness and half-hearted measures, but rather by the success of a holist reform project that had planned to liberate personal responsibility, common sense ethics and the laws of nature itself from the incessant oppression of Stalinism—a Stalinism, albeit, that had explicitly nothing to do with that sacred commons of socialist property that Stalin had, with such violence and cruelty, founded.

But the feeling of being a *khoziain* lived on. It entered popular lore as a question of ethics and history. It was this feeling that people recalled in the 2010s as they told me about Soviet times: the popular memory of those customary relations that made the Soviet plan function, despite its deficiencies, the customary right to a drop of the socialist glue.

Conclusion
Russian Socialism

I had promised that each of this book's chapters would be framed by a riddle and that, taken together, they would tell the story of the Soviet socialist household economy: its history, theory, and afterlife. But now there is one more riddle. A bonus. Another joke that I had played on myself, another critical ethnographic fact I had mistaken for a workaday truth. The riddle is this: What is this book about, really? I thought I was writing the history of an overlooked political morality. But now as I finish the text, it looks to me more like an ethnography of 2010s Russia, a story of the Putin era obsession with Soviet times.

In February 2022, Russia invaded Ukraine—and this undeclared war seemed to change everything. The apparently calm affluence of high Putinism cracked with the 2014 annexation of Crimea, caved with the 2020 Constitution and COVID, and now it seemed dead. Or maybe redoubled. In either case, a teutonic shift was at hand. I looked back at this book from my new vantage, and I saw that it was a beast of its time.

In the mid-2010s, I followed a popular historical narrative into the documentary archive, looking for Soviet collectivism. But why did people remember the past in this way? Not least because this story was everywhere. The Soviet past was a constant point of comparison. It blended into the present. Soldiers of World War II chronicles marched off projection screens and became flesh and blood reconstructions in a "visually unbroken flow of time" (Oushakine 2013, 271). Dead relatives were marched through city streets by their living heirs (Hanukai 2020). Privately curated collections, museums, walk-through panoramas, and historical reconstruction pageants compensated for "the decreasing prominence of the firsthand knowledge of socialist lifestyle" with the "increasing visibility and importance of socialist things" (Oushakine 2019, 39). In military parades and in textbooks, street festivals, children's organizations, and local museums of Soviet junk, the state looked around for a "usable past" (Brandenberger 2015, 192). And the usable past that it found now gave formal justification to its undeclared war on Ukraine: a "special military operation" that could not legally be called a war, popularized by the broadly collectivist slogan "We do not forsake our own." Officially, Russia had invaded Ukraine to cleanse it of Nazism. And most people around me in St. Petersburg did not find this outrageous. Some found it reasonable; others just did not care to talk about politics (Anonymous 2022).

This discourse of de-Nazification has the same roots as this book. Both stem from a particular image of the Soviet past that had been cultivated throughout the 2000s and 2010s: a narrative about glorious victory and voluntary, selfless struggle, of cheerful neighborliness in the face of material hardship. More than the "ethics of solidarity" commonly shared by postsocialist, post-Fordist nostalgia (Muehlebach 2017), this Soviet image was colored with a distinctly presentist ethnonationalist hue. Constitutional amendments adopted in 2020 named the Russian Federation the "successor of the USSR," and the Russian ethnos "nation forming." They also extended legal protection over the patriotic image of Soviet history with a Constitutional demand to "honor the memory of the defenders of the Fatherland and protect historical truth." Appropriate public utterance had already been carefully husbanded for quite some time. Over the course of the 2010s, people across different walks of life became increasingly dependent on a system of grants, tenders, and contracts; a competitive game from which you could be canceled for improper statements. In Russia, as elsewhere, people learned fast enough to avoid crossing indefinite lines.

But the patriotic image of the Soviet past was not a state thing. In many ways, it was itself antistatist. It developed the image of Soviet society from late Soviet film: an image of morally upstanding and generally happy people, self-effacing and friendly, ready to lend a hand, to overcome difficulties by all available means, and to work together in the face of hardship. World War II, as shown in these films, was a war won by people helping each other defend their country while regularly breaking the state's regulations and rules. Maverick commanders hopped out of their self-propelled artillery machines to lead them on foot across the battlefield, against all orders (Tregubovich 1969); underage boys jumped into parked planes and take off into the sky to do battle, against the rules (Bykov 1973); old men demanded to be allowed to join military regiments, against the regulations, and then refused to follow orders when assigned less dangerous secondary missions (Chkheidze 1964). Uniting these good Soviet people was a fight against Nazism—an ultimate evil. Often, narrative action took place in Ukraine.

This idealized Soviet past was made personal in the tactile details of things, in local museums, edutainment activities, and family archives. Around 2018, a friend of mine worked as a ghostwriter for a popular walk-through 3D panorama about the Great Patriotic War (funded generously by a state grant). The other crew members were artists and history buffs, genuinely concerned with realism in its minute historical details: the life-sized mannequins' lifelike expressions and poses, the real World War II-era machinery that visitors were invited to touch. Visitors appreciated such tactile realism too, and their guest-book comments related the panorama's historical details to their own personal family stories. And although the audio guide began by explaining that the story was fictional, many visitors refused to believe that it was not real. They left asking what happened to the hero after the war. Did he ever remarry?

The truth of this historical narrative was a personal one, and its factual details were endlessly debated. Between the truth of one's own relative's story and heated discussions of whether this or that scrap was part of this or that larger puzzle, a particular historical reality was created: one that made the Soviet people's heroic, willing and unified struggle against an abstract Nazism an indisputable fact.

In the spring of 2022, this mythic narrative of good people fighting an indefinite Nazism on the territory of Ukraine came alive in an actual savage war on the territory of the real Ukraine, which now lay in ruins: thousands of people dead, their homes destroyed, their ports, factories, hospitals burned to the ground. As the months passed, the Russian Federation's claims of de-Nazification grew to take on the evil of Western civilization itself: a civilization epitomized by the doctrine of the "Golden Billion," which, in the words of Security Council Secretary Nikolai Patrushev, "implies that only select few are entitled to prosperity in this world." Drawing on this image of saponaceous global elites,

Patrushev now accused "the Anglo-Saxon world" of hiding its selfish ambitions behind the rhetoric of human rights, freedom, and democracy (TASS 2022; Cherkaev 2022). Against this image of the morally rotting West, patriotic narratives countered an image of hardy and morally strong Russian Soviets. "We lived through the 1990s, we'll live through this too!" people now told me, laughing in the face of Western sanctions, sure of their resilience in the face of material hardship.

So in one sense, this book is firmly anchored to its particular decade. This is one way of answering the final riddle. But in another sense, it also tells of one episode in a much longer tale. Wrestling with the idea of liberal modernity, generations of Russian thinkers have counterposed the ethical practice of collective self-governance to the misery of capitalism and formalized systems of law. The *sotsialisticheskoe khoziaistvo* is one instance of this intellectual history. The Putin-era popular image of the "Russian World" is perhaps another: a hopscotching continuity with the past deliberately created by the state-led civil society itself.

One of these continuities hops back to the 1840s, when the Slavophile movement idealized the peasant commune in contradistinction to the heartlessly individualistic West. Alexander Herzen—Marx's contemporary and fellow exile—then flipped their assumption that peasants were inherently communal in character to argue that the peasants were communal due to their socioeconomic institutions. Herzen saw the peasant commune as radically collectivist and antistatist: qualities that he saw as opening the way to a specifically Russian socialism, built up of such self-managing social organizations (Ely 2022, 45). The peasant commune for Herzen, writes Martin Malia, "was socialist because it was the living negation of all authority not based on the voluntary association of autonomous individuals" (Malia 1961, 409). And yet the peasants were themselves "Baptized Property" (Herzen [1853] 1857). The peasant commune was a commune of serfs. Could the peasants' collective ownership be retained if they were themselves no longer owned? And could the promise of individual freedom and rights be realized in a society that does not crush poor people by iron laws of the market? Advocating for an end to serfdom that would come with a preservation of the peasant collective's material basis, Herzen wrote,

> Two extreme, lopsided ways of development have created two absurd situations: on the one hand, the independent Englishman, who is proud of his rights and whose freedom is based on courteous anthropophagy; on the other hand, the poor Russian peasant,

facelessly lost in the commune, rightlessly given in serfdom and made into victuals for the nobles.

How may these two ways of development be reconciled, the contradiction between them resolved? How may the Englishman's independence be preserved without cannibalism and the personality of the peasant developed without loss of its communal basis? (Herzen [1853] 1857, 17–18)

How might the liberal promise of civic equality be reconciled with a society in which power is not displaced from socially embedded relations to a "fantastic form of a relation between things" (Marx [1867] 1976, 165)? Riffing on the Declaration of the Rights of Man and Citizen, the Soviet socialist household economy gave one answer to this question: it declared socialist property to be the sacred and inviolable basis of a new system of personal rights. But it was also a beast of its own historical era, a political imaginary borne and fortified in a mythic standoff with fledgling neoliberalism. In this angry dialogue about which version of modernity crushes freedom and dignity, which provides for the flourishing of individual personalities and rights, the *sotsialisticheskoe khoziaistvo* was born. And in this same standoff it perished, when the two mythic images of just modern worlds crossed and short-circuited in an economic reform theory that took its sacred socialist commons for granted.

But now in the radiant afterglow of this mythic clash, there is still one more question with which I would like to leave you. It is very simple: Can we form a society without eating each other? In other words, must someone always be crushed by the law, the collective, the market? And who should it be? For what sins and misdeeds, by what stroke of bad luck, by what sacrificial logics? This question contains "the entire painful task of our era, the essence of socialism" for us today still, as it had for Herzen ([1853] 1857). Whatever answer we settle on, we should keep sight of the question of property—and with it enclosure and dispossession. Property regimes are no more stable than personal social relations, but they always leave someone fenced out of the field.

Notes

Introduction

Viktor Tsoi "The Idler" track 5 on 45, AnTrop Records, 1982, magnitizdat.

1. See also Plehwe (2009, 10–15) for a discussion of the emergence and consolidation of the term "neoliberalism." For a discussion of how to delimit and study the intellectual history of neoliberalism as a "thought collective," see Plehwe (2018). See Pietz (1988), Moyn (2004) for a discussion of totalitarianism in postwar critical theory.

2. For background on how this conversation about rationality brought together early neoliberals, anthropologists, and critical theorists, see Chris Hann (1992), Julia Elyachar (2020), Callison (2019). For a brief study of the intellectual history behind Mises' thoughts on barbarism and civilization, see Whyte (2020). For background to Karl Polanyi's socialist-democratic intervention in the socialist calculation debate, see Bockman et al. (2016).

3. See Humphrey (2021) for a discussion of the contesting definitions of the term "corruption" in Russia, as misuse of power and as taking above one's rank.

4. There was likewise no entry for "capitalism." As Steven Marks notes, the term entered mainstream American political discourse slowly and in opposition to Soviet communism: "at nearly every moment since the word came into use it was defined by way of comparison with the dreaded Soviet Frankenstein economy" (2012, 163).

5. Pashukanis's "commodity exchange theory of law" posits that commodity exchange lies at the basis of law as such, that criminal law derives from private (civil) law—an idea that may be fruitfully compared to the Chicago school's law-and-economics understanding of crime, whereby even murder may be seen as that which attempts to circumvent the rules of the market (Harcourt 2011, 136). For background on Pashukanis, see Fuller (1949), Beirne and Sharlet (1990), Milovanovic (2002).

6. This point was especially clear in 2022 when Russia's war on Ukraine was conducted under the slogan *svoikh ne brosaem* (we do not forsake our own), but the exclusionary nature of *svoi* traces a much longer history. For a discussion of how the term "svoi" was used among Soviet underground entrepreneurs moonlighting at Soviet enterprises to produce black-market goods (*tsekhoviki*), see Zhevakina (2020).

7. The institution of personal property had existed previously in Russian property law, but the unity of socialist property had not. In 1861, peasants were emancipated from serfdom but remained legally insolvent: real estate, equipment, seed, livestock, and draft animals were all owned collectively by

the peasant commune (Kotsonis 1999, 20–24). Wrestling with the question of how to modernize such a society without private property, a generation of Russian theorists and activists turned to the idea of socialism built on the peasant commune. See Ely (2022) for a general overview; Mullin (2020) for a discussion of such *narodnik* populist socialism in relation to Russian marxism; Malia (1965, 310–23, 395–406) for a discussion Alexander Herzen's influential mid-nineteenth-century socialist theories specifically. Emerging also from this intellectual tradition, Alexander Chayanov's early twentieth-century theories opened a possibility of a thriving peasant household economy within Soviet socialism. Employing a sort of nonmonetary marginalism, Chayanov argued that the peasant family strives to balance the drudgery of labor with its consumer needs (Bruisch 2010; Worobec 2020). But while Chayanov's theories became influential for Western peasant studies, they proved incompatible with the socialist household economy, whose basic unit was not the family household but the individual citizen, endowed with personal rights to the commons of socialist property. In 1937, Chayanov was executed. His wife, Olga Chayanova, was sentenced to ten years imprisonment and rearrested after her release. In 1969, the American Economics Association voted to send her $300, "in view of the fact that publication of Chayanov's book on peasant economy was issued in the AEA 'Translation Series' without a royalties payment" (Coleman and Taitslin 2008, 103).

8. For background on A.Ya. Vyshinsky, see Sharlet and Beirne (1990), Vaksberg (1991).

9. For background on Soviet acquisition managers (known as *snabzhentsy* or *tolkachi*), see Berliner (1957, 207–30), Humphrey (1983, 223–24), Khlevniuk (2018). For an autobiographical memoir, see Anisimov (2003). For a theoretical discussion of "fixers" across different economic contexts, see Jeffrey et al. (2011).

10. This anticollectivist critique that became central to fledgling neoliberalism had particular urgency on the brink of World War II. "The absolutism that we see in Russia, Germany, and Italy is not transitory, but the essential principle of a full-blown collectivist order," warned Lippmann in 1937. "For in so far as men embrace the belief that the coercive power of the state shall plan, shape, and direct their economy, they commit themselves to the suppression of the contrariness arising from the diversity of human interests and purposes. They cannot escape it. If a society is to be planned, its population must conform to the plan; if it is to have an official purpose, there must be no private purposes that conflict with it" (Lippmann [1937] 2004, 51).

11. For background on these debates, see Halfin and Hellbeck (1996), Krylova (2000), Chatterjee and Petrone (2008). This conversation has predominantly focused on the Stalinist period, but for a discussion of its applicability to the late Soviet period, see Platt and Nathans (2011).

12. For legal analysis, see Berman (1963, 97–151).

1. The "Soviet" Things of Postsocialism

1. The practice of gleaning industrial materials to create useful things deserves its own discussion, beyond the scope of this book. For an artist's

collection of such early post-Soviet things, see Arkhipov (2006); for an ethnographic study of how such DIY practices continue in a postsocialist working-class Russian town, see Jeremy Morris (2013, 2016). For similar practices in other state socialist contexts, see Kreis (2018); in a large French aeronautic plant, see Anteby (2008); in eighteenth-century English shipyards, see (Linebaugh 1991, 379). For a theory of the ethics of gleaning time from work to make such useful things, see De Certeau (1984, 24–28).

2. DIY Soviet objects are typically termed "self-made" in Anglophone studies, as a literal translation of the Russian terms "samopal," "samodel'nyi" (Golubev and Smolyak 2013; Cherkaev 2018; Vasilyeva 2019; Golubev 2020). Although admittedly, this translation is flawed in that it suggests a thing that has made itself, like a "self-made man."

3. For a similar analysis of popular historiographies of the Soviet in a different working-class setting, see Morris (2014).

4. In a 1982 article on "The 'Shadow Economy,'" Grossman analyzes second economy actions that are done for the good of the enterprises themselves, arguing that this shadow economy helps assuage the deficiencies of the planned economy, thereby supporting continued centralization. But interestingly, for the Soviet economic sociologist Tatyana Zaslavskaya, from whom Grossman borrows the term, the "shadow economy" is a negative phenomenon: something that lowers the effectiveness of centralized planning and that creates "clandestine redistribution of profit between social groups, often to the detriment of state interests" (Zaslavskaya 1980, 30).

5. The suggested use of industrial materials in DIY gear construction is an explicitly late-Soviet phenomenon. Guides published after the 1960s often suggest using duralumin to make everything from camping stoves to tent poles (A. Berman 1968) and suggest industrial materials like phenoplast and polyurethane as an environmentally friendly way to insulate tents in the winter, in "our century of polymers," instead of chopping fir branches (Maerkovich and Gur'ian 1971). These titles are part of a wider DIY literature: as Alexey Golubev and Olga Smolyak note, "the Brezhnev period saw a dramatic rise in the circulation of magazines and the number of brochures and books which offered all sorts of advice on how to make things with one's own hands using simple technologies and available materials" (2014, 518). Some such texts cite the store *Iunyi Tekhnik* as a place where recommended materials can be bought (Strogonov 1974, 90–93), but most are silent on the question of where readers can obtain the recommended industrial materials. "There are many types of pitons: regular (round), cork-screw, spiral," explains Nikolai Volkov in his 1974 book *Sports trekking in the mountains*. "Old types of pitons are made of steel, most self-made pitons are made of titanium or duralumin" (1974, 49). The question of how one might obtain titanium or duralumin to make one's own pitons, however, is beyond the scope of the book. By contrast, early Soviet DIY gear construction guides are often explicitly concerned with which materials can be bought (Semenovskii 1929); and those published in the 1930s–1940s emphasize readers' capacity to independently produce tourist gear "out of the most ordinary materials," including silk, satin, percale, down feather, and rubber glue (Zatulovskii 1939, 2). While such materials were neither cheap nor easy to find,

they were also not industrial materials but consumer goods. By 1987, DIY texts narrated the unplanned transactions of industrial stockpiles as entirely licit and socially upstanding actions that directly followed the party's perestroika reform program and received full institutional support. Citing Gorbachev's call to "create conditions for technological creativity," the 1987 book *Alpine Touring Gear* opens with the "obvious question where to get the materials necessary to make one's own gear—the fabrics, metal, nylon strapping? Many clubs and touristic sections obtain industrial scrap from sewing factories—nylon fabric, synthetic filler—and buy spent parachute nylon, top cords and harness systems from warehouses of written-off aviation gear" (Direktor 1987, 6–7).

6. For a history of the Stalin-era origins of Soviet mountaineering camps, see Maurer (2006). Boris's sharp condemnation of independent mountaineering is specifically addressed at large-scale ascents rather than at local camping and rock-climbing. The latter was quite popular among late-Soviet Leningrad climbers, and found official support in the form of published trail guides. See, for example, Maerkovich and Gur'ian (1971).

7. For a study of such relations in the context of an early postsocialist enterprise, see Alasheev (1995).

8. On alcohol thus facilitating exchange see Ssorin-Chaikov (2000), Rogers (2005).

9. For a discussion of popular nostalgia for the 1970s as that for the socially embedded gifting economy begotten by Soviet commodity deficit and distribution, see Aleksandr Kustarev (2007).

2. Gleaning for the Common Good

1. Grammatically, there are more potential "we's" in Nadezhda Kuzmenichna's statement than can be conveyed by a clean translation to English. In Russian, the subject and object pronouns may be presupposed by the verb, so phrases like "there was none of this *tuneiadstvo* as they made them work" may just as well be translated as "we made them," "they made us," or "we made us."

2. Implemented in 1922, the first Soviet Civil Codex regulated property relations of the New Economic Policy. See Rosenberg (1994) for background on the political-economic context circa 1914–26; Gsovski (1938) and Newton (2015) for a history of Soviet civil law; Berman (1946) for a focus on family law. For a discussion of individual and collective taxation policies in late-Imperial and early-Soviet Russia, see Kotsonis (2004); on how Bolshevik nationalization policies partially answered the problem of fragmented late-imperial property rights, see Pravilova (2014, 270–89).

3. For background on P. I. Stuchka, see Sharlet, Maggs, and Beirne (1990).

4. See Raff and Taitslin (2014) for an overview of how property rights were conceptualized in Russian law from the early nineteenth century through the 1994 Civil Code, with a focus on the socialist period.

5. The word *obshchestvennoe* may be translated as societal, common, or municipal. Contemporary cognates include *obshchestvo* (society), *obshchenie*

(communication, hanging out), *obobshchenie* (generalization). One cognate deserves special mention: Steven Grant argues that the *obshchina* (peasant commune) emerged in the nineteenth century among Slavophile intellectuals. The peasants themselves knew their village organization as *mir* (Grant 1976, 651). For a contemporary sociological breakdown of the term *obshchee* (common), see Chernysheva and Sezneva (2020).

6. For contemporaneous discussion of these debates, see Amfiteatrov (1937), Bratus' (1937). For a brief legal history, see Małecki (2017); for late perestroika-era civilists' commentary on this legal history, see Martem'ianov ([1991] 2010).

7. Shortly thereafter, in 1937, Ginzburg was arrested along with many other civilists working with the dual legislation approach of Soviet property law. He was sentenced to ten years' imprisonment. For a brief biography, see Lushnikov and Lushnikova (2010, 499–517).

8. On inheritance, see Cowley (2014).

9. By the early 1930s, as Katerina Clark writes, the myth of the "great family" with Stalin as the father, other party bosses as smaller fathers, Soviet heroes (aviators, border guards, etc.) as brothers under these fathers replaced the 1920s socialist realist narrative of "the little man" (Clark 1981). This great family could also overlap with actual families, fictive or real. See Alexey Tikhomirov's study of the letters sent to Voroshilov and Khrushchev by people claiming to be their blood relatives and asking for material boons (Tikhomirov 2017).

10. The choice of the instrument is likely significant here, as the button accordion was itself widely popularized in the early years of the socialist household economy as an instrument for the masses. See Imkhanitskii (2006, 195–208).

11. For a history of the emergence of *sobstvennost'* as the private property of nobles, enclosed from other customary use by the decrees of Catherine the Great, see Pravilova (2014, 24–34).

12. For a discussion of this hierarchical structure in its laws and in practice, see Ioffe (1982). For such nestled sovereignty as a defining feature of the "Russian legal tradition" more generally, Borisova and Burbank (2018).

13. The Harvard Interview Project was a US Air Force-funded study that conducted oral history interviews with Soviet emigres and refugees between 1949 and 1953. The resource is fascinating, but hardly unproblematic especially as the interviews were recorded in English translation. For a brief history and guide to the archive, see Brandenberger (2020); for its centrality to American studies of the Soviet Union, see Edele (2007); for an oral historian's critical analysis, see Prendergast (2017). The transcripts are digitized and published at https://library.harvard.edu/collections/hpsss/index.html.

14. Harvard Project on the Soviet Social System, Schedule A, Vol. 33, Case 338, nrs.harvard.edu/urn-3:FHCL:962324?n=4; Vol. 19, Case 358, http://nrs.harvard.edu/urn-3:FHCL:955638?n=13; Vol. 27, Case 523, nrs.harvard.edu/urn-3:FHCL:959080?n=8.

15. This political morality of collectivist use-right existed against the background of the harsh punishment of economic crimes, like bribery, embezzlement,

and misappropriation. Theft of socialist property was prosecuted all through-out the history of the *sotsialisticheskoe khoziaistvo*'s existence and on all levels: from the minor gleaning of coal and grain for personal use (Reut 2014) to grand schemes in the millions of rubles. But while jobs dealing directly with the distri-bution of large amounts of socialist property required employees to take mate-rial liability which made them especially vulnerable to prosecution (Kondrat'eva 2005), the political morality of collectivist use-right remained effective even in such cases: speaking in their defense, those accused of high-level theft could claim to be "helping out friends or acquaintances" (Heinzen 2016, 102) or per-forming actions that necessitated by their job description (Duhamel 2004, 206; Cadiot 2018).

16. The process of enclosure extended to wage laboring trades as well. "By enclosure we include the complete separation of the worker from the means of production—this was most obvious in the case of land (the commons)—it also obtained in the many trades and crafts of London, indeed it was prerequisite to mechanization. The shoemaker kept some of the leather he worked with ('clicking'). The tailor kept cloth remnants he called 'cabbage.' The weavers kept their 'fents' and 'thrums' after the cloth was cut from the loom. Servants expected 'vails' and would strike if they were not forthcoming. Sailors treasured their 'adventures.' Wet coopers felt entitled to 'waxers.' The ship-builders and sawyers took their 'chips.' The dockers (or longshoremen) were called 'lump-ers,' and worked with sailors, watermen, lightermen, coopers, warehousemen, porters, and when the containers of the cargo broke or the cargo spilled they took as custom their 'spillings,' 'sweepings,' or 'scrapings.' The cook licked his own fingers" (Linebaugh 2014, 32). For a detailed study of how these custom-ary rights were contested and fought over in eighteenth-century London, see Linebaugh 1991.

17. Cited is Stalin's July 24, 1932 letter to Molotov and Kaganovich, which Stalin sent as the August 7 decree was being drafted weeks before it was imple-mented. Stalin used this same explanation—that socialist property must be made sacred, like private property had been—in subsequent speeches, and his words were echoed by contemporaneous Soviet civilist literature. See Venedik-tov (1949, 58–59). For a discussion of the history of the August 7 decree, see Peter Solomon's *Soviet Criminal Justice under Stalin* (1996, 109).

18. Granted to nobles alone, private property rights thereby intensified the unfreedom of serfs, who were tied to their land (Pipes 1998, 435); on debates about whether serfs could be property, see Pravilova (2018, 49). Following emancipation, peasants' assumed "immaturity" was used to justify their lim-ited rights to individually own and alienate property, to post it in a bank as collateral, and to pay individual income tax to the state (Kotsonis 1999, 2004). This changed significantly with the 1906 land reforms, stirring conflicts about welfare, fairness, and collectivist custom that were factually cut short of World War I (Gaudin 1998; Pallot 1999).

19. For example, while the Russian property law of 1649 "protected the property rights of forest beekeepers (as well as the rights of those who used other use-rights [*ugod'ia*]) from incursions by the forest-owners," reflecting a system in which different ownership rights intersected in the same territory,

"in the laws of 1760s, the emphasis shifted: they stressed the limited rights not of land-owners but of those persons who held beekeeping, hunting or fishing acreage [*ugod'ia*] on others' land. The law explained that forest beekeepers have rights only to their trade [*promysel*], but not to the trees themselves or to the land" (Loskutova and Fedotova 2019, 81–82). For Marx's analysis of primitive accumulation as the "usurpation of feudal and clan property and its transformation into modern private property under circumstances of ruthless terrorism," see (Marx [1867] 1976, 874–95, quote at 895). For an early study of enclosure as a process whereby "the law of movables, which was always Roman law, has suspended and annulled the feudal law of the land" see Henry Sumner Maine's *Ancient Law* (1906, 237–94, quote at 274).

20. On collectivization as an attack on peasant custom, and on the customary relations by which peasants resisted it, see Viola (1996). The 1932 law met resistance from a wide spectrum of Soviet society, who balked at its excessive harshness. Judges dismissed cases, gave sentences lower than the ten-year minimum, and tried cases of theft by a previous, milder, antitheft law (Solomon 1996, 115–16). Khlevniuk quotes People's Commissar for Justice Nikolai Krylenko: "Sometimes, one encounters not only a lack of understanding but also a direct unwillingness to strictly apply the law. One People's Court judge told me, 'I do not have the heart to sign a person away for ten years for the theft of four stalks.' We see here a deep prejudice, learned at the mother's breast, and with traditions of the old forms of bourgeoise juridical notions that such-and-such cannot be done, that judgment must rely not on the political direction of the party and government, but on ideas of 'higher-order justice'" (Khlevniuk 1992, 23). The renewed emphasis from Stalin and party ensured that the law was enforced. In 1933 over 100,000 people were found guilty. This number fell rapidly in the following years—from over 37,000 in 1934 to 241 persons in 1939 (Solomon 1996, 126n40), but the specter of the law was subsequently raised to crack down on theft during World War II (e.g., Schechter 2019, 87). In 1947, another harsh antitheft law was issued, replacing prior legislation (Gorlizki 1999).

21. In his study of how a village economy was impacted by a developmental nongovernmental organization, Paul Kockelman (2016) compares value systems that foreground the substitution of things (as they are lost or wear out) and people (if they fail to meet their commitments) with value systems that foreground abstract universal values (exchange value but also other abstract measurements, like inches and yards). In the former, things are measured in context to see whether they fit well enough, and what is extra may be lopped off as remainder. In the latter, everything is measured against abstract universal standards, allowing one to take only the exact amount that is called for. In the latter economy, therefore, abstract exchange-value can circulate losslessly through particular use-values, casting off disposable use-value skins with every iteration while keeping its own valuable self safe and sound. In use-value economies, such extras may be regarded as blessings, as in the early Byzantine monastic *oikonomia* described by Daniel Caner (2008). But in liberal metaphors of gainful circulation, wherein "money acts as a foundation of social life by being a mechanism for the exchange of things that might otherwise perish and

be wasted," they have often been used to justify enclosure and dispossession (Neocleous 2011, 511). However, metaphors of replacement and use can justify dispossession as well. In her study of legal and illegal fuel economies at one roadside Kenyan town, Amiel Bize (2020) shows that whether one sees an economy of use-value replacement or of exchange-value circulation depends on one's point of view: people who distribute fuel legally describe licit and illicit fuel economies in metaphors of circulating liquid flows, people who distribute fuel illegally describe both of these same fuel economies as the movement of fixed quantity-sets that must be replaced as they are used up, but whose remainders may be gleaned with impunity.

22. Released in celebration of the fifteenth anniversary of the Revolution, *Counterplan* is probably best known for Dmitri Shostakovich's theme song and soundtrack (Riley 2004).

23. In 1932 the RSFSR Supreme Court explicitly warned the lower courts to be careful in prosecuting mismanagement (*bezkhoziaistvennost'*). While actions of mismanagement could manifest from explicitly anti-Soviet wrecking—in which case they ought to be prosecuted to the fullest extent of the law—they could also be the result of an honest mistake or an experimental new management method, and "special care should be taken in all cases when new techniques and methods of leading a *khoziaistvo* are being explored, as this is inevitably tied to a certain risk and the possibility of losses. The courts must remember that the fight against *bezkhoziaistvennost'* turns into its opposite in every case of unjustified criminal prosecution for *bezkhoziaistvennost'* as a result of the use of new techniques and methods in the *khoziaistvo*, since this creates uncertainty and destroys the initiative of officials of the *khoziaistvennyi* apparatus" (Uskov 1932, 292).

24. Put differently: in the managers' own recollections, their relations of irregular redistribution were not exchange but reciprocity, not acts of self-interested tit for tat barter, but material transactions performed as "momentary episode[s] in a continuous social relation" (Sahlins 1972, 185–86), striving for socially upstanding ends like solidarity, fraternity, and mutual aid. If, as Parry (1986) argues, the notion of reciprocity aspires to the ideal of the "pure gift" in societies dominated by self-interested market exchange, in the socialist household economy, it aspired to an ideal of "pure mutual aid"; it focused on the management of property, rather than on the possession thereof, on the gifting of *usus*.

3. Songs of Stalin and Khrushchev

1. In his 1991 memoir, Felix Chuev recalls that in one of their 1971 conversations, an aged Molotov had recalled Stalin having uttered the statement sometime during World War II. Another text pegs the phrase with greater specificity. The memoirs of Chief Marshal of Soviet Aviation Alexander Golovanov attribute Stalin's words to 1943, uttered in Teheran. This text was drafted in the 1970s and published in 2007. See Chuev (1991), Golovanov (2007).

2. In a characteristic passage, Starikov writes: "Soviet history through the eyes of a contemporary liberal is a collection of stamps, myths, and stupidities that tend to be repeated by [these] half-defenders of human rights and the proponents of "human values." . . . [T]his nonsense liberals seriously write into history textbooks, from where it enters our young peoples' heads. The problem is that nearly ALL contemporary Russian textbooks are written with foreign grants. With the corresponding content. And our liberals don't cease telling us: 'in the West they told the truth about history long ago. And Russia should follow this example'" (Starikov 2011). For background on such neo-Stalinist literature, see Chapkovski (2017). For background on how this historical narrative fits into post-Soviet Russian conspiratorial thought, see Borenstein (2019), on how it fits in with neo-Soviet imperialism, especially as it concerns Russia's 2014 annexation of Crimea, see Bluth (2017).

3. Citation amended to keep with accepted usage: in the annotated 1956 English translation I cite here, *lichnost'* is translated as "individual" rather than "personality."

4. See Dmitrii Kozlov (2017) for the debates of mid-century historians and pedagogues about these historiographic revisions; Cherkaev (2015, 116–21) for a comparison of key passages from different editions of Soviet textbooks, reflecting critical changes in the official historiographic line from Khrushchev to Gorbachev; Martin (2019) for a study of dissident histories that ran afoul of the party line.

5. For a collection of archival documents concerning Beria's reforms, see Naumov and Sigachev's *Lavrentii Beria* (1999). See Knight (1996) for a study of Beria's political career; Elie (2013) for a study of the different penal reforms implemented after Stalin's death; Service (1981) for an analysis of how Beria's execution and elimination from Soviet history itself also went missing from the studies of American Sovietologists. Academic texts continuing to associate de-Stalinization with Khrushchev are too numerous to list. One striking example, the title of Miriam Dobson's *Khrushchev's Cold Summer* (2009) alludes to a 1987 film about people released on Beria's March 1953 amnesty—*Cold Summer of 1953* (Proshkin 1987)—but for some reason attributes that cold summer to Khrushchev. The book does not name Khrushchev directly responsible for the March amnesty, but discusses it in the passive voice, as something "decreed on 27 March 1953 by the Supreme Soviet and announced on Pravda's front page the following day" (Dobson 2009, 37).

6. Vail and Genis's book *1960s: The World of a Soviet Person* ([1988] 1998) is notable for basing its analysis of the Thaw on a discussion of the Third Party Platform, but it is an outlier. Most academic and publicist histories of the Thaw do not foreground these reforms. As Denis Kozlov and Eleonory Gilburd write, "the Third Party Program is . . . regarded sceptically, as the ultimate embodiment of Khrushchev's hopeless utopianism, and more broadly, the utopianism of the 'Soviet project'" (2013, 35). For analysis of the Third Party Platform in its contemporaneous Anglophone legal journals, see Berman (1965, 1972), Berman and Spindler (1963), Kline (1963). For historical analysis, see Titov (2009), Nemtsev (2016), and Fokin (2017).

7. Prosecutor General Vyshinsky set the tone for these discussions with his condemnation of the "enemies of communism, slanderers who tell lies about communism as an order that supposedly suppresses individual personalities and does not recognize any categories other than society, economy [*khoziaistvo*], production" (Vyshinsky 1937, 3).

8. As new deposits were discovered in the Volga-Ural region and in Siberia throughout the late 1950s, Soviet oil production rose steadily, from just under 3 million barrels per day in 1960, to 12.1 million in 1980. World market price for crude oil also rose steadily during these decades—from $27 in 1960, to $127 in 1980—and the export-oriented side of the Soviet economy cashed in on this windfall. "By 1976, oil exports were responsible for around half of the Soviet Union's hard currency earnings and energy exports for almost 80 percent" (Painter 2017, 286). The practice of putting all eggs in one basket would become disastrous as prices crashed in the later 1980s (down to 13$/barrel in 1986), but while surplus oil profits lasted, they gave a good material foundation to the Third Party Platform's ethical plans.

9. For a history of Soviet cybernetics, see Graham (1987), Gerovitch (2008). For a discussion of how mathematical modeling combined with the Soviet state's formal rejection of Western neoclassical economics, see Boldyrev and Düppe (2020).

10. Over 4,600 people were found guilty of anti-Soviet agitation between 1956 and 1960, nearly half of them in the two years before Khrushchev's speech (Kozlov Fitzpatrick and Mironenko 2011, 45).

11. For a legal analysis of such quasi-juridical organizations' place in late-Soviet law, see Berman (1972), Berman and Spindler (1963). For a history of some of the political debates around the adoption of such quasi-juridical institutions, see Gorlizki (1998; 2003), Fitzpatrick (2006). These institutions drew on early Soviet predecessors (Solomon 1981). They also revived aspects of pre-Soviet practices, such as the late imperial lay peasant *volost'* courts, which were "made up of elected peasant judges, who were often illiterate, [and which] applied customary peasant law more often than the sections of the criminal law" (Solomon 1981, 12); the peasant communes' power to exile potential criminals "in order to protect society from the possibility of further crime being committed"; and the customary "courts" held by the Siberian exiles' own criminal communes (Wood 1990, 397). For an overview of the customary laws regulating late-Imperial peasant communes, see Lewin (1985).

12. Ioffe was a leading late Soviet civilist. In 1981, he emigrated to the United States and continued to write about Soviet civil law for an anglophone audience. For a brief biographical sketch, see Harold Berman's (1985) and John Hazard's (1984) reviews of Ioffe's *Soviet Law in Theory and Practice* (1983).

13. Similarly, Yurchak notes that "it was not uncommon for people to participate in certain procedures without paying close attention to their literal meanings, such as voting in favor of resolutions without knowing what they said. This was not always the case, but it was certainly a dominant paradigm. Among small groups, the required Komsomol meetings were often reported without actually being held. Anna (born in 1961) remembers regular

Komsomol meetings in her student group (twenty to twenty-five people) in college in the early 1980s, where the komsorg (the meeting's convener) would often suggest: 'Maybe we should just write down that we had a discussion and voted in favor of the resolution, without actually having the discussion? I understand that everyone has things to attend to at home'" (2006, 16).

14. See Albert Baiburin (2017, 144–50) for a brief history of this rule that prohibited certain categories of people from settling within 100 kilometers of major cities. In 1927 when it first appeared in the books, it applied to people found guilty of counterrevolutionary activity. Subsequently, the excluded categories came to include many others, including dissidents, violent criminals, and social parasites like *tuneiadsty.* For the 1960s campaign to exile social parasites, see Fitzpatrick (2006), for a story of the practice's destructive effects, see Höjdestrand (2009, 115–16).

15. This, too, was a constant theme of late Soviet satire. In Eldar Ryazanov's 1979 classic *Garage,* the head of an institute publicly questions a zoology professor's moral character; she received complaints from "an influential organization" that customers buying bagged potatoes found his business card in every bag:

> DIRECTOR: "Who sent you to pack those potatoes?!"
> PROFESSOR: "But they sent all my co-workers. I found it impermissible not to accompany them. And I worked conscientiously! If I, with my 500-ruble salary spend my time packing potatoes, then I am responsible for every one. Where there any complaints about quality?"
> DIRECTOR: "Well, no, I don't think so." (Ryazanov 1979)

16. In 1992, after the Soviet Union collapsed and the Institute of Marxism-Leninism closed, Firsov stayed on as an archivist. He told me: "as an employee of the archive, director of the section of publications, I got access to those very documents, and to others that I had never seen before, and that the archivists had never seen. And when I saw them I understood that if I did not copy them, I would be a complete idiot, because such a chance you get once in a lifetime." By that point, Firsov was collaborating with an Italian research team and had a photocopier in his office. A historian of the Comintern, he is perhaps best known for having exported a large collection of copied documents, some of which were still classified, which are all now housed at Stanford's Hoover Institution. He writes about his experiences in his autobiography *34 Years in the Institute of Marxism-Leninism* (2013).

17. Semyon Faibisovich (1999) recounts that, while he was an architecture student, he was allowed into the director's office at the Institute of the General Plan of Moscow to read the accurate maps smuggled into the office for him. This was done at his advisor's request around 1972 to help him find a place for his thesis project.

18. Law enforcement officials themselves followed formalized rules, which could also, sometimes, be normatively circumvented. Alfat Makashev recalled organizing a karate tournament in 1972: "Since contacts with foreigners were not particularly welcome, and since I was an officer of the Soviet Army at

the time, and had had a few interactions with Finnish karate masters, I was detained by the KGB several times. Who knows what I am talking to the Finns about! Espionage, reconnaissance—they were thinking about things like that. So we were wary of foreigners participating in the karate championships. Then a Laotian came from Moscow, a man whose last name was Mang So. To keep the authorities from taking issue, we decided to baptize him Mangsoev, and call him a Yakut" (interviewed in the 2010 TV documentary *Karate. Leningradskaia makivara*).

19. I met only several members of the "last Soviet generation" (Yurchak 2006) who had not been Komsomol members. One person, the son of a famous writer, was subsequently accepted to study at a Leningrad institute. Another, the daughter of highly ranked scientists, was also accepted to a different institute. A third person, daughter of a low ranked engineer, had her application papers refused outright. The admitting officer refused to consider them, suggesting that she reapply after she got a job at a factory and joined the Komsomol there. There are many differences between these cases. For one thing, the former two declined to join the Communist Youth around 1970, while the third declined around 1980, at the height of Brezhnev's conservative swing and the start of the Afghan War. For another thing, the protagonists' parents' employment and social positions allowed for quite different possibilities. And this is the story about Salvador Dali. Evgeniy Vladimirov (2012) recalls being asked to share his "educated opinion" at a Komsomol dispute against abstract art in 1961, when he was a student at a Leningrad technical college. Something compelled him to say that criticizing something no one in the room has seen was wrong, and things escalated from there: when he was asked to name his favorite artist, he defiantly claimed Salvador Dali. Subsequently, his Komsomol cohort asked him to "admit his mistakes," but he claimed ignorance: "the impressionists were once misunderstood, and now they're canonical." This happened a few more times, until his persistent refusal got him kicked out of the Komsomol. From that point onward, Salvador Dali stalked his Soviet working life. Drafted into the army, he was twice passed up for promotion, in 1962 and 1964. In 1970, as head engineer at a Science Research Institute, he was passed up for a research trip to the GDR. In 1982, as an engineer at a different Science Research Institute, he was pressured to collaborate with the KGB (he refused). And finally in 1985, employed at yet another Leningrad science research institute, he was kept from joining a group of scientists studying ferromanganese nodules at their source, somewhere in the Pacific ocean. In all of these cases, the censoring official asked him to remember what he was going on about, regarding that Salvador Dali. For background about the relation between the Komsomol and the KGB, see Elkner (2009).

20. With Khrushchev ousted in 1964, fears rose that the 1966 23rd Party Congress could overturn prior party decisions, leading to a "partial or indirect rehabilitation of Stalin." Leading Soviet intellectuals sent Brezhnev open letters urging against such a decision. But "against all expectations, the question of Stalin's rehabilitation was eventually kept off the Congress' agenda," writes Barbara Martin in her study of the party's shifting position on Stalin's

historical role, "it is likely that the combination of liberal protests, added to the lack of a consensus on this question within the Soviet leadership, led to this compromise. It consisted of tacitly ending de-Stalinization, but without any official sanction of this new course—in other words, no reversal of any prior resolutions and no official rehabilitation of Stalin. From then on, the accomplishments of the Stalin era would be celebrated, but whenever possible they would be attributed to the people and the Party instead of Stalin, and his mistakes and crimes would be kept silent" (Martin 2018, 177). The solution to this historiographic void, she argues, was a new public cult of World War II: "While Stalin the General Secretary of the Communist Party was responsible for the death of millions of innocent Soviet citizens, Stalin the wartime military leader could be acclaimed for his role in the victory. This convenient dissociation allowed the Brezhnev leadership to resort of this usable past without fully denouncing the resolutions of the 20th and 22nd Party Congresses" (Martin 2018, 182).

21. Similarly, see Sokol (2016) on the discourse of "returning to reality" in Poland's postsocialist reforms.

22. Les Adler and Thomas Paterson write, "this nightmare of 'Red Fascism' terrified a generation of Americans and left its mark on the events of the cold war and its warriors." They quote George Kennan: "When I try to picture totalitarianism to myself as a general phenomenon, what comes into my mind most prominently is neither the Soviet picture nor the Nazi picture as I have known them in the flesh, but rather the fictional and symbolic images created by such people as Orwell or Kafka or Koestler or the early Soviet satirists. The purest expression of the phenomenon, in other words, seems to me to have been rendered not in its physical reality but in its power as a dream, or a nightmare" (Adler and Paterson 1970, 1063).

4. Chuvstvo Khoziaina

1. In the 1960s economic reform thought that was perestroika's forebear, cybernetics were to allow central planning to "derive optimal prices for all resources and thus guide all economic activities in an indirect way . . . There would be no markets in his scheme, just the use of shadow prices derived by computers to simulate markets. Computers were even claimed to have advantages over markets. They would process information faster and avoid the fluctuations typical of markets searching for equilibrium" (Sutela 1991, 59–60). For a discussion of this image of the social planner who has "complete information about costs and preferences" in neoclassical economic theories, see Bockman (2011, 8).

2. In the intellectual history of Soviet economic thought, reformers' theories trace back to the 1960s: the Liberman-Kosygin reforms of 1965 also proposed using enterprises' fiscal profitability as a measure of efficiency and an incentive to workers. See Feygin (2017) for a detailed history of these earlier economic theories. See Mau ([1994] 1995), Sutela and Mau (1998) for their role in perestroika economic reform theory.

3. Citation amended with reference to the Russian original: "master" retranslated as "*khoziain*."

4. The possibility of thinking about economic processes apart from property relations emerged in the wake of the 1960s economic reforms as a split between theories of the "political economy" and the "*khoziaistvennyi* mechanism." Vladimir Mau explains: "Since the inviolability of socialist property was a seemingly predetermined prerequisite of further theoretical conjecture, realistically thinking economists soon found their political (or ideological) niche: taking the thesis about the inviolability of the fundamental foundations of the socialist system as a given, and leaving these questions as pay-off to the ideologized polit-economical orthodoxy (with all its above listed 'laws'), these economists formulated their conclusions needing to 'perfect the *khoziaistvennyi* mechanism' and started considering the latter as an independent object of study, which could be analyzed and reformed, leaving aside questions of property" (1995, 11).

5. Borrowing a phrase from Gustav Peebles: "one person's hoard may be constituted by another person's savings" (2020, 7).

6. The seemingly counterintuitive idea of group egoism became notably common circa 1988–91, as politicians and publicist commentators groped for an explanation of what went wrong with perestroika. A characteristic example from the report of the January 10, 1989 Central Committee meeting: "Still, the economy has not yet started working in the new way. People have not yet fully felt the results of perestroika . . . Consistently following the reform course, the party considers it indispensable to erect reliable barriers to the attempts to use economic instruments in narrow-group, egotistical interests, to the detriment of the population" (CPSU Central Committee 1989, 21–22). For a discussion of group egoism in the perestroika-era press, see Filtzer (1991, 1002), Cherkaev (2015, 167–77). For a curious quantitative illustration, see Google Book Ngram Viewer: the entire history of the Soviet Union maps neatly between spiking usage of the terms "group interests" [*gruppovye interesy*], spiked circa 1918, and "group egoism" [*gruppovoi egoism*], spiked circa 1990.

7. Asked in a 1987 interview with the newspaper *Argumenty i Fakty* whether the combination of markets and central planning would not create "terrible chaos," Shatalin replied that "this can neither be proven nor refuted. Honestly, we don't know for sure what will come out of this yet. But the main reason for introducing commodity-money relations is to better ensure the people's welfare. And in this case, I consider this policy is *deeply moral*, it liberates the economy, liberates the people's powers, their initiative" (1989, 213; emphasis added). "Ignorance and bureaucracy" were the main hindrance to perestroika, he added, remaining hopeful that they would soon be overcome with a critical mass of "knowledge and culture" (Shatalin 1989, 215).

8. Splitting up the socialist household economy into a "marketless market" (Filtzer 1991), these arrangements lasted, in various forms, throughout the 1990s, until the Russian Federation effectively instituted a series of anticorruption reforms to "bring all state inputs and outputs into a single, auditable, and transparent budget and treasury system," partially in response to

the International Monetary Fund and World Bank critiques about corruption and the lack of transparency (Rogers 2006, 935).

9. Balancing the population's expenses and money income had been a driving concern for economic planners since the 1930s. In their theories, writes Serguei Oushakine, "the 'commodity mass' was mirrored by a similarly faceless 'mass of money' accumulated by consumers . . . The process of commodity circulation was conceived as a form of barter, with money playing the role of a fixed-value commodity" (2014, 200, 221). For a history of the debates and fiscal reform policies around the Soviet ruble, see Ironside (2021). For a curious history of how, in the early 1960s, rural stores across the Soviet Union refused to accept rubles altogether and transformed pricelists from rubles to eggs, see Oberländer (2020).

10. "The rhetoric about the resistance to perestroika was an important element of politics from 1986 onward," note Michael Ellman and Vladimir Kontorovich in their interview-based study, "yet our authors provide no evidence of resistance to reforms" (1998, 22). See also Vladislav Zubok, who writes that reform-minded Soviet intellectuals "never recognized that the reforms of 1987–1988 were the main cause of the desperate economic situation later on. Instead, they (and Gorbachev along with them) blamed the problems on the resistance of the Soviet bureaucracy, the old enemy. The binary of innovators versus bureaucrats led Soviet analysts astray—the deeper the economic problems and consumer dissatisfaction became, the more they concluded that the entire old party—state system should be dismantled. In ideological terms, it was now a struggle against "totalitarianism" to the end, until the full destruction of all forms of Soviet life" (Zubok 2019, 60–61).

11. For background on these theories of "activating the human factor," see Alymov (2018). Reformers, he writes, "often had 'pro-peasant' sympathies, but in their thinking the image of the peasant was associated with a whole complex of 'market' ideas which had been repressed by the Soviet regime along with the 'real' peasantry. One of the most important components of this complex was the idea that Homo *oeconomicus* was 'natural' and even biologically predetermined. The return of society to normality was envisaged through the overcoming of the command-administrative system, which impeded people's natural economic activity" (2018, 162).

12. This reform program is known in Russian as the "Shatalin plan" (or simply the 500 Days Plan); in English it is better known as the "Yavlinksy plan" (Yavlinsky et al. [1990] 1991).

13. Constitution of the RSFSR, December 15, 1990, http://www.rusconsti tution.ru/library/constitution/articles/1286/. A formal desacralization took place some decade prior, barely noticed: the Stalinist language of the sacred and inviolable socialist commons did not make it into Brezhnev's 1977 Constitution.

14. See Clarke (1992) for economic analysis; for legal analysis, Schneider (1989, 1992), Stephan (1991). Zubok writes that "the majority of those who supported Yeltsin did not realize that they were participating in the rapid dismantling of the Soviet Union. They acted on the belief that the old

totalitarian statehood had to be destroyed at any cost. After that, they imagined, new democratic institutions and transition to a market economy would quickly fix the endemic problems of the post-Soviet polity and economy. The Western economist Michael Ellman was astonished in 1990 to see tens of thousands of people from the institutes of Academy of Science and the military—industrial complex marching in support of market liberalism. All of a sudden, this was a new utopia of capitalist prosperity and emancipation, which replaced social-ism with a human face. Ellman called those people 'the turkey that celebrated Thanksgiving.' The vast majority of these people would lose their status, jobs and livelihoods within a couple of years" (Zubok 2019, 61–62).

References

Abalkin, L.I. 1987. *Novyi tip ekonomicheskogo myshleniia*. Moscow: Ekonomika.

Abalkin, L.I. 1988. *Perestroika: Puti i problemy. Interv'iu direktora instituta ekonomiki AN SSSR Akademika L.I. Abalkina s sovetskimi i inostrannymi zhurnalistami (Sentiabr' 1986–Mai 1988)*. Moscow: Ekonomika.

Adler, Les K., and Thomas G. Paterson. 1970. "Red Fascism: The Merger of Nazi Germany Soviet Russia in the American Image of Totalitarianism, 1930's–1950's." *American Historical Review* 75 (4): 1046–64. https://doi.org/10.2307/1852269.

Adzhubei, Rada Nikitichna. 2009. "'Nauka i zhizn' vchera, segodnia, zavtra. K 75-letiiu vozobnovleniia vykhoda zhurnala 'Nauka i Zhizn'.'" http://www.nkj.ru/interview/16363/.

Aganbegyan, Abel Gezevich. 1988a. *Sovetskaia ekonomika: vzgliad v budushchee*. Moscow: Sovetskaia Ekonomika.

Aganbegyan, Abel. 1988b. *The Economic Challenge of Perestroika*. Bloomington: Indiana University Press.

Alasheev, Sergei Iur'evich. 1995. "Neformal'nye otnosheniia v protsesse proizvodstva: 'Vzgliad iznutri.'" *Sotsiologicheskie Issledovaniia*, no. 2: 12–19.

Aleksandrov, Grigorii, dir. 1936. *Tsirk*. Mosfilm.

Alexopoulos, Golfo. 2003. *Stalin's Outcasts: Aliens, Citizens, and the Soviet State, 1926–1936*. Ithaca: Cornell University Press.

Allen, D. W., and Y. Barzel. 2009. "The Evolution of Criminal Law and Police during the Pre-Modern Era." *Journal of Law, Economics, and Organization* 27 (3): 540–67. https://doi.org/10.1093/jleo/ewp030.

Allisson, François. 2015. *Value and Prices in Russian Economic Thought: A Journey Inside the Russian Synthesis, 1890–1920*. New York: Routledge.

Althusser, Louis. (1970) 2001. "Ideology and the Ideological State Apparatuses." In *Lenin and Philosophy and Other Essays*. 85–132. New York: Monthly Review Press.

Alymov, Sergei. 2018. "Activating the 'Human Factor': Do the Roots of Neoliberal Subjectivity Lie in the 'Stagnation'?" *Forum for Anthropology and Culture*, no. 14: 137–68. https://doi.org/10.31250/1815-8927-2018-14-14-137-168.

Amfiteatrov, G. N. 1937. "O sostoianii teoreticheskoi raboty po sovetskomu grazhdanskomu pravu." In *Problemy sotsialisticheskogo prava*, edited by N.V. Krylenko, vol. 1, 34–48. Moscow: Iuridicheskoe izdatel'stvo NKIu Soiuza SSR.

Anisimov, Valentin Anatol'evich. 2003. "Ispoved' snabzhentsa." *Zvezda*, no. 11: 196–204.

Anonymous. 2022. "This Troubled Silence—in Russia We Don't Talk about War or Politics." *Mother Jones*, March 23, sec. Politics. https://www.moth erjones.com/politics/2022/03/this-troubled-silence-in-russia-we-dont-talk-about-war-or-politics/.

Anteby, Michel. 2008. *Moral Gray Zones: Side-Production, Identity, and Regulation in an Aeronautic Plant*. Princeton: Princeton University Press.

Arendt, Hannah. 1973. *The Origins of Totalitarianism*. New York: Harcourt Brace Jovanovich.

Arkhipov, Vladimir. 2006. *Home-Made: Contemporary Russian Folk Artifacts*. London: Fuel Publishing.

Aron, Leon Rabinovich. 2006. "The 'Mystery' of the Soviet Collapse." *Journal of Democracy* 17 (2): 21–35. https://doi.org/10.1353/jod.2006.0022.

Arvatov, Boris. (1925) 1997. "Everyday Life and the Culture of the Thing (Toward the Formulation of the Question)." *October* 81: 119–28.

Aslund, Anders. 2007. *Russia's Capitalist Revolution: Why Market Reform Succeeded and Democracy Failed*. Washington, DC: Peterson Institute.

Aven, P. O., and V. M. Shironin. 1987. "Reforma khoziaistvennogo mekhanizma: Real'nost' namechaemykh preobrazovanii." *Izvestiia sibirskogo otdeleniia Akademii Nauk SSSR, seriia "Ekonomika i prikladnaia sotsiologiia,"* 13(3): 32–41.

Baiburin, Albert. 2017. *Sovetskii pasport: Istoriia, struktura, praktiki*. St. Petersburg: EUSPB.

Barnes, Andrew. 2006. *Owning Russia: The Struggle over Factories, Farms and Power*. Ithaca: Cornel University Press.

Barnett, Vincent, and Joachim Zweynert. 2008. *Economics in Russia: Studies in Intellectual History*. Hampshire, England: Ashgate.

Baron, Nick. 2001. "Conflict and Complicity: The Expansion of the Karelian Gulag, 1923–1933." *Cahiers du Monde Russe* 42 (2–4): 615–48. https://doi.org/10.4000/monderusse.8471.

Bear, Laura, Karen Ho, Anna Tsing, and Sylvia Yanagisako. 2015. "Gens: A Feminist Manifesto for the Study of Capitalism." *Fieldsights,* Cultural Anthropology Website Theorizing the Contemporary, March 30. https://culanth.org/fieldsights/652-gens-a-feminist-manifesto-for-the-study-of-capitalism.

Beirne, Piers, and Robert Sharlet. 1990. "Toward a General Theory of Law and Marxism: E. B. Pashukanis." In *Revolution in Law: Contributions to the Development of Soviet Legal Theory, 1917–1938*, edited by Piers Beirne, 17–44. Armonk, NY: M.E. Sharpe.

Beliaev, A. 2002. "Na staroi ploshchadi." *Voprosy literatury*, no. 3: 243–70.

Beliaev, Dmitrii Pavlovich. 2014. *Razrukha v golovakh. Informatsionnaia voina protiv Rossii*. SPb: Piter.

Benjamin, Walter. (1936) 1968. "The Storyteller." In *Illuminations*, ed. H. Arendt, trans. H. Zohn, 26–55. New York: Schocken Books.

Berliner, Joseph. 1957. *Factory and Manager in the U.S.S.R.* Cambridge MA: Cambridge: Harvard University Press.

Berman, A. 1968. *Puteshestvie na lyzhakh*. Moscow: Fizkul'tura i sport.

Berman, Harold J. 1946. "Soviet Family Law in the Light of Russian History and Marxist Theory." *Yale Law Journal* 56 (1): 26–57. https://doi.org/10.2307/793249.

Berman, Harold J. 1948. "The Challenge of Soviet Law." *Harvard Law Review* 62 (2): 220–65. https://doi.org/10.2307/1336434.

Berman, Harold J. 1963. *Justice in the U.S.S.R: An Interpretation of Soviet Law*. Cambridge MA: Harvard University Press.

Berman, Harold J. 1965. "USSR: Legality vs. Terror: The Post-Stalin Law Reforms." In *Politics in Europe: 5 Cases in European Government*, edited by Gwendolen M. Carter and Alan F. Westin, 179–205. New York: Harcourt, Brace & World.

Berman, Harold J. 1972. "The Educational Role of the Soviet Court." *International and Comparative Law Quarterly* 21 (1): 81–94. https://doi.org/10.1093/iclqaj/21.1.81.

Berman, Harold J. 1985. *Review of Soviet Law in Theory and Practice*, edited by Peter B. Maggs and Olympiad S. Ioffe. *Russian Review* 44 (1): 72–74. https://doi.org/10.2307/129262.

Berman, Harold J., and James W. Spindler. 1963. "Soviet Comrades' Courts." *Washington Law Review* 38 (842): 842–910.

Bize, Amiel. 2020. "The Right to the Remainder: Gleaning in the Fuel Economies of East Africa's Northern Corridor." *Cultural Anthropology* 35 (3): 462–86. https://doi.org/10.14506/ca35.3.05.

Bluth, Natasha. 2017. "Fringe Benefits: How a Russian Ultranationalist Think Tank Is Laying the 'Intellectual' Foundations for a Far-Right Movement." *World Policy Journal* 34 (4): 87–92. https://doi.org/10.1215/07402775-4373262.

Boas, Franz. 1895. "The Potlatch." In *The Social Organization and the Secret Societies of the Kwakiutl Indians. Based on Personal Observations and on Notes Made by George Hunt*, 341–57. Report of the United States National Museum for the year ending June 30, 1895, 309–738. https://repository.si.edu/handle/10088/29967.

Bockman, Johanna. 2011. *Markets in the Name of Socialism: The Left-Wing Origins of Neoliberalism*. Stanford: Stanford University Press.

Bockman, Johanna, Ariane Fischer, and David Woodruff. 2016. "'Socialist Accounting' by Karl Polanyi: With Preface 'Socialism and the Embedded Economy.'" *Theory and Society* 45 (5): 385–427. https://doi.org/10.1007/s11186-016-9276-9.

Boettke, Peter. J. 1993. *Why Perestroika Failed: The Politics and Economics of Socialist Transformation*. New York: Routledge.

Bogdanov, A. 1990 "Zhivu vo imia cheloveka." *Pravda*, May 8.

Boldyrev, Ivan, and Olessia Kirtchik. 2017. "The Cultures of Mathematical Economics in the Postwar Soviet Union: More Than a Method, Less Than a Discipline." *Studies in History and Philosophy of Science Part A* 63 (Supplement C): 1–10. https://doi.org/10.1016/j.shpsa.2017.03.011.

Boldyrev, Ivan, and Till Düppe. 2020. "Programming the USSR: Leonid V. Kantorovich in Context." *British Journal for the History of Science* 53 (2): 255–78. https://doi.org/10.1017/S0007087420000059.

Borenstein, Eliot. 2019. *Plots against Russia: Conspiracy and Fantasy after Socialism*. Ithaca: Cornell University Press.

Borisova, Tatiana, and Jane Burbank. 2018. "Russia's Legal Trajectories." *Kritika: Explorations in Russian and Eurasian History* 19 (3): 469–508. https://doi.org/10.1353/kri.2018.0027.

Boyer, Dominic. 2016. "Introduction: Crisis of Liberalism." *Fieldsights*, October 27. https://culanth.org/fieldsights/introduction-crisis-of-liberalism.

Brandenberger, David. 2015. "Promotion of a Usable Past: Official Efforts to Rewrite Russo-Soviet History, 2000-2014." In *Remembrance, History, and Justice: Coming to Terms with Traumatic Pasts in Democratic Societies*, edited by Vladimir Tismaneanu and Bogdan C. Iacob, 191–212. Central European University Press. https://www.jstor.org/stable/10.7829/j.ctt19z399m.10.

Brandenberger, David. 2020. *A Guide to Working with the Harvard Project on the Soviet Social System Online.* Harvard College Library. https://library.harvard.edu/collections/hpsss/HPSSSguide2020.pdf.

Bratus', S.N. "O sostoianii teoreticheskoi raboty po sovetskomu grazhdanskomu pravu." *Sovetskoe Gosudarstvo*, no. 1–2: 48–64.

Bridger, Sue, and Frances Pine, eds. 1997. *Surviving Post-Socialism: Local Strategies and Regional Responses in Eastern Europe and the Former Soviet Union.* London: Routledge.

Brown, Wendy. 2015. *Undoing the Demos: Neoliberalism's Stealth Revolution.* Cambridge MA: Zone Books.

Bruisch, Katja. 2010. "Historicizing Chaianov: Intellectual and Scientific Roots of the Theory of Peasant Economy." *Jahrbuch Für Geschichte Des Ländlichen Raumes* 7: 96–113. https://doi.org/10.25365/RHY-2010-7.

Buck-Morss, Susan. 2002. *Dreamworld and Catastrophe: The Passing of Mass Utopia in East and West.* Cambridge: MIT Press.

Bukharin, Nikolai. (1919) 1927. *Economic Theory of the Leisure Class.* New York: International Publishers.

Burawoy, Michael. 1992. "Review: The End of Sovietology and the Renaissance of Modernization Theory." *Contemporary Sociology* 21 (6): 774–85. https://doi.org/10.2307/2075622.

Burawoy, Michael. 1997. "The Soviet Dissent into Capitalism." *American Journal of Sociology* 102 (5): 1430–44. https://doi.org/10.1086/231090.

Burawoy, Michael, and Kathryn Hendley. 1992. "Between Perestroika and Privatisation: Divided Strategies and Political Crisis in a Soviet Enterprise." *Soviet Studies* 44 (3): 371–402. https://doi.org/10.1080/09668139208412022.

Burawoy, Michael, and Pavel Krotov. 1992. "The Soviet Transition from Socialism to Capitalism: Worker Control and Economic Bargaining in the Wood Industry." *American Sociological Review* 57 (1): 16–38. https://doi.org/10.2307/2096142.

Burawoy, Michael, and Pavel Krotov. 1993. "The Economic Basis of Russia's Political Crisis." *New Left Review*, no. 198 (April): 49–70.

Burawoy, Michael, and Katherine Verdery, eds. 1999. *Uncertain Transition: Ethnographies of Change in the Post-Socialist World.* Lanham, MD: Rowman & Littlefield.

Burlatsky, Fedor. 1988. "Brezhnev i krushenie ottepeli." *Literaturnaia Gazeta*, no 37, September 14.

Bykov, Leonid, dir. 1973. *V voi idut odni "stariki."* Dovzhenko Film Studios.

Cadiot, Juliette. 2018. "L'affaire Hain." *Cahiers du Monde Russe. Russie—Empire Russe—Union Soviétique et États Indépendants* 59 (2–3): 255–88. https://doi.org/10.4000/monderusse.10415.

Callison, William Andrew. 2019. "Political Deficits: The Dawn of Neoliberal Rationality and the Eclipse of Critical Theory." PhD diss., UC Berkeley.

Campeanu, Pavel. 1988. "The Genesis of the Stalinist Social Order." Translated by Michel Vale. *International Journal of Sociology* 18 (1/2): 1, 3–159, 161–65.

Caner, Daniel. 2008. "Wealth, Stewardship, and Charitable 'Blessings' in Early Byzantine Monasticism." In *Wealth and Poverty in Early Church and Society*, edited by Susan R. Holman, 221–42. Holy Cross Studies in Patristic Theology and History. Grand Rapids, MI: Baker Academic.

Chapkovski, Philipp. 2017. "'We Should Be Proud Not Sorry': Neo-Stalinist Literature in Contemporary Russia." In *War and Memory in Russia, Ukraine and Belarus*, 189–207. Cham: Palgrave Macmillan.

Chatterjee, Choi, and Karen Petrone. 2008. "Models of Selfhood and Subjectivity: The Soviet Case in Historical Perspective." *Slavic Review* 67 (4): 967–86. https://doi.org/10.2307/27653033.

Cherkaev, Xenia. 2014. "On Warped Mourning and Omissions in Post-Soviet Historiography." *Ab Imperio*, no. 4: 365–85. https://doi.org/10.1353/imp.2014.0121.

Cherkaev, Xenia. 2015. "Language, Historiography and Economy in Late- and Post-Soviet Leningrad: 'The Entire Soviet People Became the Authentic Creator of the Fundamental Law of Their Government.'" PhD diss., Columbia University.

Cherkaev, Xenia. 2017. "How Grades Had Been Gotten for Penguins and Money." *Anthropology and Humanism* 42 (1): 127–34. https://doi.org/10.1111/anhu.12167.

Cherkaev, Xenia. 2018. "Self-Made Boats and Social Self-Management. The Late-Soviet Ethics of Mutual Aid." *Cahiers du Monde Russe* 59 (2–3): 289–310. https://doi.org/10.4000/monderusse.10422.

Cherkaev, Xenia. 2018b. "Dostoinstvo lichnosti kak lichnaia sobstvennost': Metamorfoza rossiiskikh zakonov o porochashchikh svedeniiakh." *Novoe literaturnoe obozrenie* 3 (151): 65–80.

Cherkaev, Xenia. 2020. "St. Xenia and the Gleaners of Leningrad." *American Historical Review* 125 (3): 906–14. https://doi.org/10.1093/ahr/rhaa241.

Cherkaev, Xenia. 2022. "The Golden Billion: Russia, COVID, Murderous Global Elites." *Anthropology and Humanism* 47 (2). https://doi.org/10.1111/anhu.12386.

Cherkaev, Xenia, and Elena Tipikina. 2018. "Interspecies Affection and Military Aims: Was There a Totalitarian Dog?" *Environmental Humanities* 10 (1): 20–39. https://doi.org/10.1215/22011919-4385453.

Chernysheva, Liubov, and Olga Sezneva. 2020. "Commoning beyond 'Commons': The Case of the Russian 'Obshcheye.'" *Sociological Review* 68 (2): 322–40. https://doi.org/10.1177/0038026120905474.

Cherviakov, Yevgeni, dir. 1936. *Zakliuchennye*. Mosfilm.

Chkheidze, Rezo, dir. 1964. *Otets soldata*. Gruziiafil'm.

Chudakova, Tatiana. 2015. "The Pulse in the Machine: Automating Tibetan Diagnostic Palpation in Postsocialist Russia." *Comparative Studies in Society and History* 57 (02): 407–34. https://doi.org/10.1017/S0010417515000080.

Chuev, Felix. 1991. *Sto sorok besed s Molotovym*. Moscow: TERRA.

Clark, Katerina. 1981. "The Stalinist Myth of the 'Great Family.'" In *The Soviet Novel: History as Ritual*, 114–35. Chicago: University of Chicago Press.

Clarke, Simon. 1992. "Privatization and the Development of Capitalism in Russia." *New Left Review*, no. 196 (December): 3–27.

Clarke, Simon, Peter Fairbrother, Michael Burawoy, and Pavel Krotov. 1993. *What about the Workers? Workers and the Transition to Capitalism in Russia*. London: Verso.

Cohen, Stephen F., and Katarina Vanden Heuvel. 1989. *Voices of Glasnost: Interviews with Gorbachev's Reformers*. New York: W.W. Norton.

Coleman, William, and Anna Taitslin. 2008. "The Enigma of A.V. Chayanov." In *Economics in Russia: Studies in Intellectual History*, edited by Vincent Barnett and Joachim Zweynert, 91–105. Burlington, VT: Ashgate.

Collier, Stephen J. 2011. *Post-Soviet Social: Neoliberalism, Social Modernity, Biopolitics*. Princeton: Princeton University Press.

Cowley, Marcie K. 2014. "The Right of Inheritance and the Stalin Revolution." *Kritika: Explorations in Russian and Eurasian History* 15 (1): 103–23. https://doi.org/10.1353/kri.2014.0014.

CPSU. 1961. *Programme of the Communist Party of the Soviet Union: Adopted by the 22nd Congress of the C.P.S.U October 31, 1961*. Moscow: Foreign Languages Publishing House.

CPSU. 1962. *22 S"ezd Kommunisticheskoi Partii Sovetskogo Soiuza 17–31 Oktiabria 1961: Stenograficheskii otchet. Vol. 2: Stenogrammy 11–20 zasedanii*. Moscow: Gosudarstvennoe izdatel'stvo politicheskoi literatury.

CPSU Central Committee. 1989. *Materialy Plenuma Tsentral'nogo Komiteta KPSS, 10 Jan 1989*. Moscow: Politizdat.

Davis, John. 1988. *Conflict and Control: Law and Order in Nineteenth-Century Italy*. London: Macmillan Education.

Dawisha, Karen. 2014. *Putin's Kleptocracy: Who Owns Russia?* New York: Simon & Schuster.

Dem'ianov, D.V. 1937. *Pesnia o Rodine*. Noginsk: Noginskii zavod gramplastinok. https://russian-records.com/details.php?image_id=8705.

De Certeau, Michel. 1984. *The Practice of Everyday Life*. Berkeley: University of California Press.

Deutscher, Isaac. 1953. "The Beria Affair." *International Journal* 8: 227–39. https://doi.org/10.1177/002070205300800401.

Diamond, Larry. 2016. "Russia and the Threat to Liberal Democracy." *The Atlantic*, December 9, 2016. https://www.theatlantic.com/international/archive/2016/12/russia-liberal-democracy/510011/.

Direktor, L. B. 1987. *Snariazhenie dlia gornogo turizma*. Moscow: Profizdat.

Ditton, Jason. 1977. "Perks, Pilferage, and the Fiddle: The Historical Structure of Invisible Wages." *Theory and Society* 4 (1): 39–71. https://doi.org/10.1007/BF00209744.

Dobson, Miriam. 2009. *Khrushchev's Cold Summer: Gulag Returnees, Crime, and the Fate of Reform after Stalin*. Ithaca: Cornell University Press.

Duhamel, Luc. 2004. "The Last Campaign against Corruption in Soviet Moscow." *Europe-Asia Studies* 56 (2): 187–212.

Edele, Mark. 2007. "Soviet Society, Social Structure, and Everyday Life: Major Frameworks Reconsidered." *Kritika: Explorations in Russian and Eurasian History* 8 (2): 349–73. https://doi.org/10.1353/kri.2007.0025.

Eisen, Joathan. 1990. *The Glasnost Reader*. New York: Penguin, NAL Books.

Elie, Marc. 2013. "Khrushchev's Gulag: The Soviet Penitentiary System after Stalin's Death, 1953–1964." In *The Thaw: Soviet Society and Culture during the 1950s and 1960s*, edited by Denis Kozlov and Eleonory Gilburd, 109–42. Toronto: Toronto University Press.

Elkner, Julie. 2009. "The Changing Face of Repression under Khrushchev." In *Soviet State and Society under Nikita Khrushchev*, edited by Melanie Ilic and Jeremy Smith, 142–61. Abingdon: Routledge.

Ellman, Michael, and Vladimir Kontorovich, eds. 1998. *The Destruction of the Soviet Economic System: An Insiders' History*. Armonk, NY: M.E. Sharpe.

Ely, Christopher. 2022. *Russian Populism: A History*. London: Bloomsbury Academic.

Elyachar, Julia. 2005. *Markets of Dispossession: NGO's, Economic Development, and the State in Cairo*. Durham: Duke University Press.

Elyachar, Julia. 2020. "Neoliberalism, Rationality, and the Savage Slot." In *Mutant Neoliberalism: Market Rule and Political Rupture*, edited by William Callison and Zachary Manfredi, 177–95. New York: Fordham University Press.

Ermler, Fridrikh, and Sergei Yutkevich, dirs. 1932. *Vstrechnyi*. Lenfilm.

Etkind, Alexander. 2014. "Mourning, Unwarped?" *Ab Imperio*, no. 4: 386–88. https://doi.org/10.1353/imp.2014.0126.

Etkind, Efim. 1978. *Notes of a Non-Conspirator*. Translated by Peter France. Oxford: Oxford University Press.

Evans-Pritchard, E. E. 1940. *The Nuer: A Description of the Modes of Livelihood and Political Institutions of a Nilotic People*. Oxford: Clarendon Press.

Faibisovich, Semyon. 1999. "Sekretnye materialy; obshchestvo slepykh." *Neprikosnovennyi Zapas* 4 (6). https://magazines.gorky.media/nz/1999/4/sekretnye-materialy-obshhestvo-slepyh.html

Feygin, Yakov. 2017. "Reforming the Cold War State: Economic Thought, Internationalization, and the Politics of Soviet Reform, 1955–1985." PhD diss, University of Pennsylvania. https://repository.upenn.edu/edissertations/2277.

Field, Deborah A. 1998. "Irreconcilable Differences: Divorce and Conceptions of Private Life in the Khrushchev Era." *Russian Review* 57 (4): 599–613. https://doi.org/10.1111/0036-0341.00047.

Field, Deborah A. 2007. *Private Life and Communist Morality in Khrushchev's Russia*. New York: Peter Lang.

Filtzer, Donald A. 1991. "The Contradictions of the Marketless Market: Self-Financing in the Soviet Industrial Enterprise, 1986–90." *Soviet Studies* 43 (6): 989–1009. https://doi.org/10.1080/09668139108411979.

Finansy SSSR. 1989. "S"ezd Narodnykh Deputatov i finansy," *Finansy SSSR*, no. 7: 3–10.

Firsov, Fred. 2013. *34 goda v Institute Maksizma-Leninizma. Vospominaniia istorika*. Moscow: AIRO-XXI.

Fitzpatrick, Sheila. 1993. "Ascribing Class: The Construction of Social Identity in Soviet Russia." *Journal of Modern History* 65 (4): 745–70. https://doi.org/10.1086/244724.

Fitzpatrick, Sheila. 2006. "Social Parasites. How Tramps, Idle Youth, and Busy Entrepreneurs Impeded the Soviet March to Communism." *Cahiers du Monde Russe* 47 (1–2): 377–408. https://doi.org/10.4000/monderusse.9607.

Fitzpatrick, Sheila. 2007. "Revisionism in Soviet History." *History and Theory* 46 (4): 77–91. https://doi.org/10.1111/j.1468-2303.2007.00429.x.

Fokin, Alexander. 2017. "Kommunizm ne za gorami." *Obrazy budushchego u vlasti i naseleniia SSSR na rubezhe 1950–1960.* Moscow: Politicheskaia Entsiklopediia.

Foucault, Michel. 2008. *The Birth of Biopolitics: Lectures at the College de France, 1978–1979.* Translated by Graham Burchell. New York: Palgrave Macmillan.

Frenkel, William G. 1989. "Union of Soviet Socialist Republics: Law on Cooperatives." *International Legal Materials* 28 (3): 719–53. https://doi.org/10.1017/S0020782900021902.

Fukuyama, Francis. 1989. "The End of History?" *National Interest*, no. 16: 3–18.

Fuller, Lon L. 1949. "Pashukanis and Vyshinsky: A Study in the Development of Marxian Legal Theory." *Michigan Law Review* 47 (8): 1157–66. https://doi.org/10.2307/1284239.

Gal, Susan. 2002. "A Semiotics of the Public/Private Distinction." *Differences* 13 (1): 77–95. https://doi.org/10.1215/10407391-13-1-77.

Gal, Susan. 2005. "Language Ideologies Compared: Metaphors of Public/Private." *Journal of Linguistic Anthropology* 15 (1): 23–37.

Gaudin, Corinne. 1998. "'No Place to Lay My Head': Marginalization and the Right to Land during the Stolypin Reforms." *Slavic Review* 57 (4): 747–73. https://doi.org/10.2307/2501045.

Gefter, Mikhail. 1989. "Destalinizatsiia." In *50/50. Opyt slovaria novogo myshleniia,* edited by Iurii Afanas'ev and Mark Ferro, 394–400. Moscow: Progress.

Gerovitch, Slava. 2008. "InterNyet: Why the Soviet Union Did Not Build a Nationwide Computer Network." *History and Technology* 24 (4): 335–50. https://doi.org/10.1080/07341510802044736.

Ginzburg, L. Ya. 1933. "Voprosy sovetskogo khoziaistvennogo prava na dannom etape." In *Voprosy sovetskogo khoziaistvennogo prava,* edited by L. Ginzburg and I. Suvorov, 1:3–15. Moscow: Sovetskoe zakonodatel'stvo.

Gleason, Abbott. 1995. *Totalitarianism: The Inner History of the Cold War.* New York: Oxford University Press.

Goldman, Wendy Z. 2022. "Blood on the Red Banner: Primitive Accumulation in the World's First Socialist State." *International Review of Social History*, 67(2), 211–29. https://doi.org/10.1017/S0020859022000104.

Golovanov, A. E. 2007. *Dal'niaia bombardirovochnaia . . . Vospominania glavnogo Marshala Aviatsii 1941–1945.* Moscow: Tsentropoligraph.

Golovatyi, A.I. 1989. "Perestroika vo vneshne-ekonomicheskoi sfere." *Finansy SSSR*, no. 4: 65–70.

Golubev, Alexey. 2020. *The Things of Life: Materiality in Late Soviet Russia.* Ithaca: Cornell University Press.

Golubev, Alexey, and Olga Smolyak. 2013. "Making Selves through Making Things." *Cahiers du Monde Russe* 54 (3–4): 517–41. https://doi.org/10.4000/monderusse.7964.

Gorbachev, M.S. (1986) 1987. *Politicheskii doklad Tsentral'nogo Komiteta KPSS XXVII S"ezda Kommunisticheskoi Partii Sovetskogo Soiuza.* Moscow: Izdatel'stvo politicheskoi literatury.

Gorbachev, M.S. 1987. *Oktiabr' i perestroika.* Moscow: Politizdat.

Gorbachev, M.S. 1989. "Revoliutsionnoi perestroike—ideologiiu obnovleniia. Rech' na plenume TsK KPSS 18 fevralia 1988 goda." In *Izbrannye rechi i stat'i: Period s ianvaria po oktiabr' 1988.* Vol. 65. Moscow: Izdatel'stvo politicheskoi literatury.

Gorbachev, M.S. 1990. *Ukaz Prezidenta SSSR ot 02.11.1990 N UP-975 ob osobom poriadke ispol'zovaniia valiutnykh resursov v 1991 godu.*

Gorlizki, Yoram. 1998. "Delegalization in Russia: Soviet Comrades' Courts in Retrospect." *American Journal of Comparative Law* 46 (3): 403–25. https://doi.org/10.2307/840839.

Gorlizki, Yoram. 1999. "Rules, Incentives and Soviet Campaign Justice after World War II." *Europe-Asia Studies* 51 (7): 1245–65. https://doi.org/10.1080/09668139998525.

Gorlizki, Yoram. 2003. "Policing Post-Stalin Society: The Militsiia and Public Order under Khrushchev." *Cahiers du Monde Russe* 44 (2–3): 465–80. https://doi.org/10.4000/monderusse.8619.

Gorlizki, Yoram. 2016. "Theft under Stalin: A Property Rights Analysis." *Economic History Review* 69 (1): 288–313. https://doi.org/10.1111/ehr.12121.

Graham, Loren R. 1987. "Cybernetics and Computers." In *Science, Philosophy, and Human Behavior in the Soviet Union*, 266–93. New York: Columbia University Press.

Grant, Steven A. 1976. "Obshchina and Mir." *Slavic Review* 35 (4): 636–51. https://doi.org/10.2307/2495655.

Grazhdankin, A. I., and S. G. Kara-Murza. 2015. *Belaia kniga Rossii. Stroitel'stvo, perestroika i reformy: 1950–2013.* Moscow: Nauchnyi Expert.

Grossman, Gregory. 1963. "Notes for a Theory of the Command Economy." *Soviet Studies* 15 (2): 101–23. https://doi.org/10.1080/09668136308410352.

Grossman, Gregory. 1977. "The 'Second Economy' of the USSR." *Problems of Communism* 26 (5): 25–40.

Grossman, Gregory. 1982. "The 'Shadow Economy' in the Socialist Sector of the USSR." In *The CMEA Five-Year Plans (1981–1985) in a New Perspective*, 99–115. Brussels: NATO.

Gsovski, Vladimir. 1938. "The Soviet Concept of Law." *Fordham Law Review* 7 (1): 1–44.

Gupta, Akhil. 1995. "Blurred Boundaries: The Discourse of Corruption, the Culture of Politics, and the Imagined State." *American Ethnologist* 22 (2): 375–402. https://doi.org/10.1525/ae.1995.22.2.02a00090.

Halfin, Igal, and Jochen Hellbeck. 1996. "Rethinking the Stalinist Subject: Stephen Kotkin's 'Magnetic Mountain' and the State of Soviet Historical Studies." *Jahrbücher Für Geschichte Osteuropas* 44 (2): 456–63.

Haller, Dieter, and Cris Shore. 2005. "Introduction—Sharp Practice: Anthropology and the Study of Corruption." In *Corruption: Anthropological Perspectives*, 1–12. Ann Arbor, MI: Pluto Press.

Hann, Christopher. 1992. "Radical Functionalism: The Life and Work of Karl Polanyi." *Dialectical Anthropology* 17 (2): 141:66. https://doi.org/10.1007/BF00258088.

Hanukai, Maksim. 2020. "Resurrection by Surrogation: Spectral Performance in Putin's Russia." *Slavic Review* 79 (4): 800–824. https://doi.org/10.1017/slr.2021.6.

Harcourt, Bernard E. 2011. *The Illusion of Free Markets: Punishment and the Myth of Natural Order*. Cambridge, MA: Harvard University Press.

Harris, James R. 1997. "The Growth of the Gulag: Forced Labor in the Urals Region, 1929–31." *Russian Review* 56 (2): 265–80. https://doi.org/10.2307/131659.

Hasty, Jennifer. 2005. "The Pleasures of Corruption: Desire and Discipline in Ghanaian Political Culture." *Cultural Anthropology* 20 (2): 271–301. https://doi.org/10.1525/can.2005.20.2.271.

Hayek, F. A. 1945. "The Use of Knowledge in Society." *American Economic Review* 35 (4): 519–30.

Hayek, F. A. (1979) 1998. *Law, Legislation and Liberty*. Vol. 3: *The Political Order of a Free People*. London: Routledge.

Hayek, F. A. (1933) 2007a. "Nazi-Socialism." In *The Road to Serfdom: Text and Documents*. Vol 2. Edited by Bruce Caldwell, 245–48. Chicago: University of Chicago Press.

Hayek, F. A. (1944) 2007b. *Road to Serfdom: Texts and Documents*. Vol 2. Edited by Bruce Caldwell. Vol. 2. Collected Works of F.A. Hayek. Chicago: University of Chicago Press.

Hazard, John N. 1984. "*Soviet Law in Theory and Practice*. By Olympiad S. Ioffe and Peter B. Maggs. London/Rome/New York: Oceana Publications, Inc., 1983, Pp. vii, 327. US $35 (Cloth)." *International Journal of Legal Information* 12 (1–2): 34–36. https://doi.org/10.1017/S0731126500016619.

Heidegger, Martin. (1927) 1962. *Being and Time*. New York: HarperCollins.

Heinzen, James. 2016. *The Art of the Bribe: Corruption Under Stalin, 1943–1953*. New Haven: Yale University Press.

Herzen, Alexander. (1853) 1857. *Kreshchenaia sobstvennost'*. London: Vol'naia russkaia knigopechatnia.

Herzog, Werner, dir. 1993. *Bells from the Deep: Faith and Superstition in Russia*. Werner Herzog Filmproduktion.

Hickel, Jason. 2015. *Democracy as Death: The Moral Order of Anti-Liberal Politics in South Africa*. Oakland: University of California Press.

Hickel, Jason, and Arsalan Khan. 2012. "The Culture of Capitalism and the Crisis of Critique." *Anthropological Quarterly* 85 (1): 203–27. https://doi.org/10.1353/anq.2012.0003.

Höjdestrand, Tova. 2009. *Needed by Nobody: Homelessness and Humanness in Post-Socialist Russia*. Ithaca: Cornell University Press.

Humphrey, Caroline. 1983. *Karl Marx Collective: Economy, Society, and Religion in a Siberian Collective Farm*. Cambridge: Cambridge University Press.

Humphrey, Caroline. 1991. "'Icebergs,' Barter, and the Mafia in Provincial Russia." *Anthropology Today* 7 (2): 8–13. https://doi.org/10.2307/30 33166.

Humphrey, Caroline. 2021. "Corruption." In *Words and Worlds: A Lexicon for Dark Times*, edited by Veena Das and Didier Fassin, 185–204. Durham: Duke University Press.

Huntington, Samuel. (1968) 2006. *Political Order in Changing Societies*. New Haven: Yale University Press.

Imkhanitskii, M. 2006. *Istoriia baiannogo i akkordeonnogo iskusstva*. Moscow: Rossiiskaia akademiia muzyki imeni Gnesinykh.

Ioffe, O. S. 1962. "Novaia kodifikatsiia sovetskogo grazhdanskogo zakonodatel'stva i okhrana chesti i dostoinstva grazhdan." *Sovetskoe Gosudarstvo i Pravo* 32 (7): 59–71.

Ioffe, Olympiad S. 1982. "Law and Economy in the USSR." *Harvard Law Review* 95 (7): 1591–1625. https://doi.org/10.2307/1340720.

Ioffe, Olympiad S., and Peter B. Maggs. 1983. *Soviet Law in Theory and Practice*. New York: Oceana.

Ironside, Kristy. 2021. *A Full-Value Ruble: The Promise of Prosperity in the Postwar Soviet Union*. Cambridge MA: Harvard University Press.

Jeffrey, Craig, Christine Philliou, Douglas Rogers, and Andrew Shryock. 2011. "Fixers in Motion. A Conversation." *Comparative Studies in Society and History* 53 (03): 692–707. https://doi.org/10.1017/S0010417511000302.

Jones, Polly, ed. 2006. *The Dilemmas of De-Stalinization Negotiating Cultural and Social Change in the Khrushchev Era*. London: Routledge.

Kalb, Don. 2009. "Conversations with a Polish Populist: Tracing Hidden Histories of Globalization, Class, and Dispossession in Postsocialism (and Beyond)." *American Ethnologist* 36 (2): 207–23. https://doi.org/10.1111/j.1548-1425.2009.01131.x.

"Karate. Leningradskaia makivara." 2010. *Kul'turnyi sloi*. 5 Kanal. St. Petersburg. https://www.5-tv.ru/programs/broadcast/502597.

Karpinskii, Len. 1988. "Pochemu stalinizm ne skhodit so stseny?" in *Inogo ne dano: Sud'by perestroiki. Vgliadyvaias' v proshloe vozvrashchenie k budushchemu*, edited by Yu. Afanas'ev, 648–70. Moscow: Progress.

Kharkhordin, Oleg. 1999. *The Collective and the Individual in Russia: A Study of Practices*. Berkeley: University of California Press.

Khlevniuk, O. V. 1992. *1937-i: Stalin, NKVD i sovetskoe obshchestvo*. Moscow: "Respublika" publishers.

Khlevniuk, O. V. 2010. *Khoziain. Stalin i utverzhdenie stalinskoi diktatury*. Moscow: ROSSPEN; Boris Yeltsin Fund.

Khlevniuk, Oleg V. 2018. "'Tolkachi,' Parallel'nye stimuly v stalinskoi ekonomicheskoi sisteme 1930-e–1950-e gody." *Cahiers du Monde Russe. Russie—Empire Russe—Union Soviétique et États Indépendants* 59 (2–3): 233–54. https://doi.org/10.4000/monderusse.10406.

Khlevniuk, O. V., R. U. Devis, L. P. Kosheleva, E. A. Ris, and L. A. Rogovaia, eds. 2001. *Stalin i Kaganovich. Perepiska. 1931–1936*. Moscow: ROSSPEN.

Khrushchev, Nikita S. 1956. *The Crimes of the Stalin Era, Special Report to the 20th Congress of the Communist Party of the Soviet Union*. New York: New Leader.

Khrushchev, Nikita S. 1959. "Doklad tov. N.S. Khrushcheva 'Kontrol'nye tsifry razvitiia narodnogo khoziaistva SSSR na 1959-1965 gody" In *Vneocherednoi 21 S"ezd Kommunisticheskoi Partii Sovetskogo Soiuza—stenograficheskii otchet.* Moscow: Gosudarstvennoe izdatel'stvo politicheskoi literatury.

Kiaer, Christina. 2005. *Imagine No Possessions: The Socialist Objects of Russian Constructivism.* Cambridge: MIT Press.

Klein, Joachim. 1995. "Belomorkanal: Literatur und Propaganda in der Stalinzeit." *Zeitschrift Für Slavische Philologie* 55 (1): 53–98.

Kline, G. L. 1963. "'Socialist Legality' and Communist Ethics." *American Journal of Jurisprudence* 8 (1): 21–34. https://doi.org/10.1093/ajj/8.1.21.

Knight, Amy W. 1996. *Beria: Stalin's First Lieutenant.* Princeton: Princeton University Press.

Kockelman, Paul. 2007. "From Status to Contract Revisited: Value, Temporality, Circulation and Subjectivity." *Anthropological Theory* 7: 151–76. https://doi.org/10.1177/1463499607077296.

Kockelman, Paul. 2016. *The Chicken and the Quetzal: Incommensurate Ontologies and Portable Values in Guatemala's Cloud Forest.* Durham: Duke University Press.

Kommersant Vlast'. 1991a. "Normal'nye geroi vsegda idut v obkhod." March 1991. https://www.kommersant.ru/doc/265504

Kommersant Vlast'. 1991b. "Shakhterskie zabastovki: Uglia ne budet, problemy ostanutsia." March 1991. http://kommersant.ru/doc/265512.

Kondrat'eva, Tamara Sergeevna. 2005. "Material'no otvetstvennye litsa pri rezhime sotsialisticheskoi sobstvennosti." *Neprikosnovennyi Zapas*, no. 4. https://magazines.gorky.media/nz/2005/4/materialno-otvetstvennye-licza-pri-rezhime-soczialisticheskoj-sobstvennosti.html.

Konovalov, B. 1986. "Extrasens glazami fiziki." *Izvestia*, July 3, 1986.

Konstantinov, Iu. A. 1989. "Valiutnaia politika i finansy v usloviakh perestroiki." *Finansy SSSR*, no. 6: 61–67.

Kornai, Janos. 1980. *Economics of Shortage.* Amsterdam: North Holland Publishing Company.

Kotkin, Stephen. 1995. *Magnetic Mountain: Stalinism as Civilization.* Berkeley: University of California Press.

Kotkin, Stephen. 2001. *Armageddon Averted: The Soviet Collapse, 1970–2000.* New York: Oxford University Press.

Kotsonis, Yanni. 1999. *Making Peasants Backward: Managing Populations in Russian Agricultural Cooperatives, 1861–1914.* New York: St. Martin's Press.

Kotsonis, Yanni. 2004. "'No Place to Go': Taxation and State Transformation in Late Imperial and Early Soviet Russia." *Journal of Modern History* 76 (3): 531–77. https://doi.org/10.1086/425440.

Koziol, Geoffrey. 2011. "Leadership: Why We Have Mirrors for Princes but None for Presidents." In *Why the Middle Ages Matter: Medieval Light on Modern Injustice*, edited by Celia Chazelle, Simon Doubleday, Felice Lifshitz, and Amy G. Remensnyder, 183–98. London: Routledge.

Kozlov, Denis, and Eleonory Gilburd. 2013. "The Thaw as an Event in Russian History." In *The Thaw: Soviet Society and Culture during the 1950s and 1960s*, 18–81. Toronto: University of Toronto Press.

Kozlov, Dmitrii. 2017. "'Pod vidom preodoleniia kul'ta lichnosti': Nerealizovan-naia reforma prepodavania istorii v shkole (1956–1957)." *Ab Imperio*, no. 2: 93–122. https://doi.org/10.1353/imp.2017.0032.

Kozlov, Vladimir, Sheila Fitzpatrick, and Sergei Mironenko, eds. 2011. *Sedition: Everyday Resistance in the Soviet Union under Khrushchev and Brezhnev*. New Haven: Yale University Press.

Krasvina, L. N. 1990. "Ot infliatsii k tverdomu rubliu." *Finansy SSSR*, no. 2: 3–14.

Kreis, Reinhild. 2018. "A 'Call to Tools': DIY between State Building and Consumption Practices in the GDR." *International Journal for History, Culture And Modernity* 6 (1): 49–75. https://doi.org/10.18352/hcm.539.

Krylova, Anna. 2000. "The Tenacious Liberal Subject in Soviet Studies." *Kritika: Explorations in Russian and Eurasian History* 1 (1): 119–46. https://doi.org/10.1353/kri.2008.0092.

Kustarev, Alksandr. 2007. "Zolotye 1970-e—nostalgiia i reabilitatsiiia." *Neprikosnovennyi zapas* 2: 6–12.

Ledeneva, Alena. 1998. *Russia's Economy of Favours: Blat, Networking, and Informal Exchange*. New York: Cambridge University Press.

Lenin, V. I. 1965. "Speech at the Second All-Russia Congress of Commissars for Labour." In *Lenin Collected Works*, vol. 27, 399–403. Moscow: Progress Publishers.

Lenin, V. I. 2014. *State and Revolution*. Edited by Todd Chretien. Chicago: Haymarket Books.

Lewin, Moshe. 1985. "Customary Law and Russian Rural Society in the Post-Reform Era." *Russian Review* 44 (1): 1–19. https://doi.org/10.2307/129255.

Linebaugh, Peter. 1991. *The London Hanged: Crime and Civil Society in the Eighteenth Century*. London: Penguin Books.

Linebaugh, Peter. 2014. *Stop, Thief!: The Commons, Enclosures, and Resistance*. Oakland, CA: PM Press.

Lippmann, Walter. (1937) 2004. *The Good Society*. New York: Routledge.

Loskutova, M. V., and A. A. Fedotova. 2019. "Pravitel'stvennaia politika v otnoshenii bortnogo pchelovodstva v Rossiiskoi imperii 18–19 vekov." *Izvestiia Russkogo Geograficheskogo Obshchestva* 151 (2): 78–95. https://doi.org/10.31857/S0869-6071151278-95.

Lukoyanov, P. I. 1986. *Samodel'noe turisticheskoe snariazhenie*. Moscow: Fizkul'tura i sport.

Lushnikov, A. M., and M. V. Lushnikova. 2010. *Rossiiskaia shkola trudovogo prava i prava sotsial'nogo obespecheniia: Portrety na fone vremeni*. Iaroslavl': Iaroslavskii gosudarstvennyi universitet imeni P. G. Demidova.

Maerkovich, V. V. and Yu. A. Gur'ian. 1971. *Na skaly!* Leningrad: Lenizdat.

Magerovskii, D., ed. 1927. *Osnovy sovetskogo prava*. Moscow: Gosudarsvtennoe izdatel'stvo.

Maine, Henry Sumner. 1906. *Ancient Law: Its Connections with the Early History of Society and Its Relation to Modern Ideas*. New York: Henry Holt.

Małecki, Witold. 2017. "The Scholar Discussion on the Concept of Economic Law in Soviet Union in the Years, 1956–1958." *Krakowskie Studia z Historii Państwa i Prawa* 9: 111–27. https://doi.org/10.4467/2084413 1KS.16.037.6975.

Malenkov, G. M. 1941. "O zadachakh partiinykh organizatsii v oblasti pro-myshlennosti i transporta." *Izvestia*, February 16, 1–2.

Malia, Martin. 1965. *Alexander Herzen and the Birth of Russian Socialism*. New York: Grosset & Dunlap.

Malinowski, Bronislaw. (1922) 1984. *Argonauts of the Western Pacific*. Long Grove, IL: Waveland Press.

Man, A. 1932. "Za okhranu sotsialisticheskogo urozhaia." *Sovetskaia Iustitsiia*, no. 27: 8–9.

Manaenkov, Iurii. 1988. "Utverzhdat' neobratimost' perestroiki." *Sovetskaia Kul'tura*, May 9.

Marks, Steven G. 2012. "The Word 'Capitalism': The Soviet Union's Gift to America." *Society* 49 (2): 155–63. https://doi.org/10.1007/s12115-011-9520-x.

Martem'ianov, V.S. 2010. "Iuridicheskaia tragediia." *Vserossiiskii nauchnyi zhurnal "Voprosy pravovedeniia,"* no. 3: 371–91.

Martin, Barbara. 2019. "A Selective Silence: Leonid Brezhnev's Compromise over the Memory of Stalin's Crimes." In *Truth, Silence and Violence in Emerging States: Histories of the Unspoken*, edited by Aidan Russell, 169–87. London: Routledge.

Martin, Barbara. 2019. *Dissident Histories in the Soviet Union: From De-Stalinization to Perestroika*. London: Bloomsbury Academic.

Marx, Karl. (1867) 1976. *Capital: A Critique of Political Economy*. Vol. 1. New York: Penguin Books.

Masco, Joseph. 2017. "The Crisis in Crisis." *Current Anthropology* 58 (S15): S65–76. https://doi.org/10.1086/688695.

Mau, V.A. (1994) 1995. *Ekonomika i vlast': Politicheskaia istoriia ekonomicheskoi reformy v Rossii 1985–1994*. Moscow: Delo LTD.

Maurer, Eva. 2006. "Alpinism as Mass Sport and Elite Recreation: Soviet Moun-taineering Camps under Stalin." In *Tourizm: The Russian and East European Tourist under Capitalism and Socialism*, edited by Anne E. Gorsuch and Diane Koenker, 141–62. Ithaca: Cornell University Press.

Mauss, Marcel. (1925) 1990. *The Gift*. Translated by W. D. Halls. New York: W.W. Norton.

Menzel, Birgit. 2012. "Introduction." In *The New Age of Russia: Occult and Esoteric Dimensions*, edited by Michael Hagemeister and Bernice Glatzer Rosenthal, 11–28. Munchen: Verlag Otto Sagner.

Milovanovic, Dragan. 2002. "Introduction to the Transaction Edition." In *General Theory of Law and Marxism*, edited by Evgeny Bronislavovich Pashu-kanis, vii–xxvi. New Brunswick, NJ: Transaction Publishers.

Mirowski, Philip. 1989. *More Heat Than Light. Economics as Social Physics, Physics as Nature's Economics*. Cambridge: Cambridge University Press.

Mises, Ludwig von. (1920) 1935. "Economic Calculation in the Socialist Com-monwealth." In *Collectivist Economic Planning*, edited by F. A. Hayek, 87–130. London: Routledge & Kegan Paul.

Mises, Ludwig von. (1922) 1951. *Socialism: An Economic and Sociological Analysis*. New Haven: Yale University Press.

Mises, Ludwig von. 2007. *Theory and History: An Interpretation of Social and Economic Evolution*. Auburn: Ludwig von Mises Institute.

Mitchell, Timothy. 1998. "Fixing the Economy." *Cultural Studies* 12 (1): 82–101. https://doi.org/10.1080/095023898335627.

Molotov, V.M. 1933. "Iz doklada t. Molotova na ob"edinennom plenume TsK I TsKK VKP(b) 8 ianvaria 1933: Zadachi pervogo goda vtoroi piatiletki." *Sovetskaia Iustitsiia*, no. 2–3: 16–17.

Morison, James. 1881. *The Pulpit Commentary*. Edited by H.D.M. Spence and Joseph S. Exell. Vol. 4: *Ruth*. London: C. Kegan Paul.

Morozov, M. A., ed. 1963. *Spravochnik agitatora*. Moscow: Gosudarstvennoe izdatel'stvo politicheskoi lieratury.

Morris, Jeremy. 2013. "Beyond Coping? Alternatives to Consumption within a Social Network of Russian Workers." *Ethnography* 14 (1): 85–103. https://doi.org/10.1177/1466138112448021.

Morris, Jeremy. 2014. "The Warm Home of Cacti and Other Soviet Memories: Russian Workers Reflect on the Socialist Period." *Central Europe* 12 (1): 16–31. https://doi.org/10.1179/1479096314Z.00000000020.

Morris, Jeremy. 2016. *Everyday Post-Socialism: Working-Class Communities in the Russian Margins*. London: Palgrave Macmillan.

Morris, Jeremy, and Abel Polese, eds. 2014. *The Informal Post-Socialist Economy*. London: Palgrave Macmillan.

Moyn, Samuel. 2004. "Of Savagery and Civil Society: Pierre Clastres and the Transformation of French Political Thought." *Modern Intellectual History* 1 (1): 55–80. https://doi.org/10.1017/S1479244303000076.

Muehlebach, Andrea. 2017. "The Body of Solidarity: Heritage, Memory, and Materiality in Post-Industrial Italy." *Comparative Studies in Society and History* 59 (01): 96–126. https://doi.org/10.1017/S0010417516000542.

Muir, Sarah. 2018. "Corruption and (Il)Liberal Politics Roundtable." *American Anthropological Association Meetings*. San Jose, CA, November 14–18.

Muir, Sarah, and Akhil Gupta. 2018. "Rethinking the Anthropology of Corruption: An Introduction to Supplement 18." *Current Anthropology* 59 (S18): S4–15. https://doi.org/10.1086/696161.

Mullin, Richard. 2020. "The Russian Narodniks and Their Relationship to Russian Marxism." In *Left Radicalism and Populism in Europe*, edited by Giorgos Charalambous and Gregoris Ioannou, 33–50. New York: Routledge.

Murnau, F. W., dir. 1931. *Tabu: A Story of the South Seas*. Paramount Pictures.

Naishul, Vitali. 1992. "Institutional Development in the USSR." *Cato Journal* 11: 489–96.

Naishul', Vitalii. 1993. "Liberalism, Customary Rights, and Economic Reform." *Communist Economies and Economic Transformation* 5 (1): 29–44. https://doi.org/10.1080/14631379308427743.

Naumov, V., and Yu. Sigachev. 1999. *Lavretii Beriia. 1953. Stenogramma iiul'skogo plenuma TsK KPSS i drugie dokumenty*. Moscow: Mezhdunarodnyi fond "Demokratiia."

Nemtsev, Mikhail. 2016. "K istorii sovetskoi akademicheskoi distsipliny 'Osnovy nauchnogo kommunizma.'" *Idei i idealy* 27 (1): 23–38.

Neocleous, Mark. 2011. "War on Waste: Law, Original Accumulation and the Violence of Capital." *Science & Society* 75 (4): 506–28. https://doi.org/10.1521/siso.2011.75.4.506.

Neo-Stalinism: Writing History and Making Policy. 1969. CIA Directorate of Intelligence. https://www.cia.gov/readingroom/docs/CIA-RDP03-02194R000200690001-7.pdf.

Newton, Scott. 2015. *Law and the Making of the Soviet World: The Red Demiurge.* Milton Park: Routledge.

Oberländer, Alexandra. 2020. "Hatching Money: The Political Economy of Eggs in the 1960s." *Cahiers du Monde Russe* 61 (1–2): 231–56.

Osokina, Elena. 2006. "Torgsin: Zoloto dlja industrializacii." *Cahiers du Monde Russe*, 47 (4): 715–48. https://doi.org/10.4000/monderusse.8849.

Osokina, Elena. 2018. *Nebesnaia golubizna angel'skikh odezhd. Sud'ba proizvedenii drevnerusskoi zhivopisi, 1920–1930.* Moscow: Novoe Literaturnoe Obozrenie.

Oushakine, Serguei Alex. 2003. "Crimes of Substitution: Detection in Late Soviet Society." *Public Culture* 15: 426–51.

Oushakine, Serguei. 2013. "Remembering in Public: On the Affective Management of History." *Ab Imperio*, no. 1: 269–302. https://doi.org/10.1353/imp.2013.0000.

Oushakine, Serguei. 2014. "'Against the Cult of Things': On Soviet Productivism, Storage Economy, and Commodities with No Destination." *Russian Review* 73 (2): 198–236. https://doi.org/10.1111/russ.10727.

Oushakine, Serguei. 2019. "Second-Hand Nostalgia: On Charms and Spells of the Soviet Trukhliashechka." In *Post-Soviet Nostalgia: Confronting the Empire's Legacies*, edited by Otto Boele, Boris Noordenbos, and Ksenia Robbe, 38–69. New York: Routledge.

Painter, David S. 2017. "From Linkage to Economic Warfare: Energy, Soviet-American Relations, and the End of the Cold War." In *Cold War Energy: A Transnational History of Soviet Oil and Gas*, edited by Jeronim Perović, 283–318. Cham: Springer International.

Palomera, Jaime, and Theodora Vetta. 2016. "Moral Economy: Rethinking a Radical Concept." *Anthropological Theory* 16 (4): 413–32. https://doi.org/10.1177/1463499616678097.

Pallot, Judith. 1999. *Land Reform in Russia 1906–1917: Peasant Responses to Stolypin's Project of Rural Transformation.* New York: Oxford University Press.

Pankratova, A. M., ed. 1957. *Istoriia SSSR: Uchebnik dlia 10 klassa srednei shkoly.* Vol. 3. Moscow: Izdatel'stvo Ministerstva Prosveshcheniia RSFSR.

Pavlov, A. 1937. "Protiv vreditel'skikh izvrashechenii v teorii sovetskogo grazhdanskogo prava." In *Problemy sotsialistichekogo prava*, edited by N. V. Krylenko, vol. 1, 49–62. Moscow: Iuridicheskoe Izdatel'stvo NKIu Soiuza SSR.

Pavlov, V. 1988. "Radikal'naia reforma tsenoobrazovaniia." In *Ritm Perestroiki. Novaia sistema upravleniia ekonomikoi, god 1987*, 34–39. Moscow: Ekonomika.

Pavlov V. S. 1990. "O proekte zakona SSSR 'O nalogakh s gosudarstvennykh, arendnykh, kooperativnykh, obshchestvennykh i innykh predpriiatii, ob"edinenii i organizatsii.' Doklad Ministra Finansov SSSR na tret'ei sessii Verkhovnogo Soveta SSSR. Vystuplenie i otvety na voprosy narodnykh deputatov SSSR." *Finansy SSSR*, no. 6: 3–21.

Parry, Jonathan. 1986. "The Gift, the Indian Gift and the 'Indian Gift.'" *JRAI* 21 (3): 453–73. https://doi.org/10.2307/2803096.

Pashukanis, Evgeny Bronislavovich. (1924) 2002. *General Theory of Law and Marxism*. New Brunswick, NJ: Transaction Publishers.

Pearson, Heath. 2000. "Homo Economicus Goes Native, 1859–1945: The Rise and Fall of Primitive Economics." *History of Political Economy* 32 (4): 933–89.

Peebles, Gustav. 2018. "Eradicating Poverty: Good for Humanity, Bad for the Planet?" *American Anthropologist* website, February 19. https://www.ameri cananthropologist.org/deprovincializing-development-series/eradicat ing-poverty-good-for-humanity-bad-for-the-planet.

Peebles, Gustav. 2020. "Hoarding and Saving." In *Oxford Research Encyclopedia of Anthropology*, edited by Gustav Peebles, 1–21. Oxford University Press. https://doi.org/10.1093/acrefore/9780190854584.013.80.

Pietz, William. 1988. "The 'Post-Colonialism' of Cold-War Discourse." *Social Text* no. 19/20, 55–75. https://doi.org/10.2307/466178.

Pipes, Richard. 1998. "Private Property Comes to Russia: The Reign of Catherine II." *Harvard Ukrainian Studies* 22: 431–42.

Pisano, Jessica. 2009. "Property: What Is It Good For?" *Social Research* 76 (1): 175–202.

Platt, Kevin, and Benjamin Nathans. 2011. "Newest Mythologies: Socialist in Form, Indeterminate in Content: The Ins and Outs of Late Soviet Culture." *Ab Imperio*, no. 2 (April): 301–24.

Plehwe, Dieter. 2009. "Introduction." In *The Road from Mont Pèlerin: The Making of the Neoliberal Thought Collective*, edited by Philip Mirowski and Dieter Plehwe, 1–42. Cambridge, MA: Harvard University Press.

Plehwe, Dieter. 2018. "Neoliberal Thought Collectives: Integrating Social Science and Intellectual History." In *The SAGE Handbook of Neoliberalism*. edited by Damien Cahill, Melinda Cooper, Martijn Konings, and David Primrose, 85–97. London: Sage.

Polanyi, Karl. (1944) 2001. *Great Transformation*. Boston: Beacon Press.

Ponomarev, B. N. 1980. "Sovetskii Soiuz na puti k razvitomu sotsializmu 1945–1960." In *Istoriia SSSR s drevneishikh vremen do nashikh dnei*. Vol. 11. Moscow: Nauka.

Popov, Gavriil Kharitonovich. (1986) 1987. "S tochki zreniia ekonomista." *Nauka i Zhizn'*, no. 4: 54–65.

Popov, Gavriil Kharitonovich. (1988) 1989. "Kto protiv." In *Puti Perestoiki: Mnenie Ekonomista*, 315–30. Moscow: Ekonomika.

Povinelli, Elizabeth A. 2017. "What Do White People Want?: Interest, Desire, and Affect in Late Liberalism." *E-Flux*, January. https://conversations.e-flux.com/t/elizabeth-a-povinelli-what-do-white-people-want-interest-de sire-and-affect-in-late-liberalism/5845.

Powell, Raymond P. 1977. "Plan Execution and the Workability of Soviet Planning." *Journal of Comparative Economics* 1: 51–76.

Pravda. 1986. "K 80-letiiu so dnia rozhdeniia L.I. Brezhneva." December 19.

Pravda. 1987. "Zakon Soiuza Sovetskikh Sotsialisticheskikh Respublik o gosudarstvennom predpriaitii (ob"edenenii)." July 1.

Pravilova, Ekaterina. 2014. *A Public Empire Property and the Quest for the Common Good in Imperial Russia*. Princeton: Princeton University Press.

Prendergast, Sam. 2017. "Revisiting the Harvard Project on the Soviet Social System." *Oral History Review* 44 (1): 19–38. https://doi.org/10.1093/ohr/ohw136.

Proshkin, Aleksandr, dir. 1987. *Kholodnoe leto piat'desiat tret'ego*. Mosfilm.

Rabochaya Tribuna. 1990. "Ot vorot povorot," March 18. No. 162 (March): 1.

Raff, Murray, and Anna Taitslin. 2014. "Property Rights under Socialist Civil Law." In *East European Faces of Law and Society: Values and Practices*, edited by William Simons, 251–306. Leiden: Brill.

Rakhmilovich, V. A. 1977. "O poniatii khozrascheta i ego pravovoi kharakteristike." In *Problemy sovershenstvovaniia sovetskogo zakonodatel'stva*, vol. 9, 19–31. Moscow: Ministerstvo iustitsii SSSR; Vsesoiuznyi nauchno-issledovatel'stkii institut sovetskogo zakonodatel'stva.

Rakopoulos, Theodoros, and Knut Rio. 2018. "Introduction to an Anthropology of Wealth." *History and Anthropology* 29 (3): 275–91. https://doi.org/10.1080/02757206.2018.1460600.

Rapoport, V., dir. 1964. Fitil': "Karty ne vrut." Gorky Film Studio.

Reid, Susan, and David Crowley. 2002. ed. *Socialist Spaces: Sites of Everyday Life in the Eastern Bloc*. Oxford: Berg.

Reinhoudt, Jurgen, and Serge Audier. 2018. *The Walter Lippmann Colloquium: The Birth of Neo-Liberalism*. Cham: Palgrave Macmillan.

Reisner, M. A. 1918. *Chto takoe sovetskaia vlast'?* Moscow: Izdatel'stvo narodnogo komissariata zemledeliia.

Reut, E. V. 2014. "Sotsial'noe iavlenie 'nesuny' na zavode #820 v pervye poslevoennye gody (1946–1953)." *Vestnik baltiiskogo federal'nogo universiteta imeni I. Kanta*, no. 12: 77–83.

Riley, John. 2004. "From the Factory to the Flat: Thirty Years of the Song of the Counterplan." In *Soviet Music and Society under Lenin and Stalin: The Baton and Sickle*, edited by Neil Edmunds, 67–80. London: Routledge.

Robbins, Joel. 2013. "Beyond the Suffering Subject: Toward an Anthropology of the Good." *Journal of the Royal Anthropological Institute* 19 (3): 447–62. https://doi.org/10.1111/1467-9655.12044.

Rogan, Tim. 2017. *The Moral Economists: R. H. Tawney, Karl Polanyi, E. P. Thompson, and the Critique of Capitalism*. Princeton: Princeton University Press.

Rogers, Douglas. 2005. "Moonshine, Money, and the Politics of Liquidity in Rural Russia." *American Ethnologist* 32 (1): 63–81. https://doi.org/10.1525/ae.2005.32.1.63.

Rogers, Douglas. 2006. "How to Be a Khoziain in a Transforming State: State Formation and the Ethics of Governance in Post-Soviet Russia." *Comparative Studies in Society and History* 48 (4): 915–45. https://doi.org/10.1017/S001041750600034X.

Rogers, Douglas. 2014. "Petrobarter: Oil, Inequality, and the Political Imagination in and after the Cold War." *Current Anthropology* 55 (2): 131–53. https://doi.org/10.1086/675498.

Roitman, Janet. 2013. *Anti-Crisis*. Durham: Duke University Press.

Romanenko, V., and O. Izvekova. 1989. "Institut cheloveka. Charlatanstvo ili panatsea?" *Argumenty i Fakty*, September 2.

Rosenberg, William G. 1994. "The Problem of Market Relations and the State in Revolutionary Russia." *Comparative Studies in Society and History* 36 (2): 356–96. https://doi.org/10.1017/S0010417500019083.

Rubinshtein, Boris Moiseevich. 1933. "K voprosu o khozraschete." In *Voprosy khoziaistvennogo prava*, edited by L. Ginzburg and I. Suvorov, 46–71. Moscow: Sovetskoe zakonodatel'stvo.

Rubinshtein, Boris Moiseevich. 1936. *Sovetskoe khoziaistvennoe i grazhdanskoe pravo: Uchebnik dlia iuridicheskikh shkol i posobie dlia vuzov.* Moscow: Gosudarstvennoe izdatel'stvo "Sovetskoe zakonodatel'stvo."

Rupprecht, Tobias. 2022. "The Road from Snake Hill. The Genesis of Russian Neoliberalism." In *Market Civilizations: Neoliberals East and South*, edited by Quinn Slobodian and Dieter Plehwe, 109–38. Brooklyn, NY: Zone Books.

Ryazanov, Eldar, dir. 1979. *Garage.* Mosfilm.

Ryzhkov, Nikolai. 1992. *Perestroika: Istoriia predatel'stv.* Moscow: Novosti.

Sachs, Jeffrey. 1991. "Helping Russia: Goodwill Is Not Enough." *Economist*, December 21.

Sachs, Jeffrey. 2012. "What I Did in Russia." Jeffsachs.org, March 12, 2012. http://jeffsachs.org/2012/03/what-i-did-in-russia/.

Sahlins, Marshall. 1972. *Stone Age Economics.* Chicago: Aldine Atherton.

Sampson, Steven. 2005. "Integrity Warriors: Global Morality and the Anti-Corruption Movement in the Balkans." In *Understanding Corruption: Anthropological Perspectives*, edited by Dieter Haller and Cris Shore, 103–30. Ann Arbor, MI: Pluto Press.

Sampson, Steven. 2010. "The Anti-Corruption Industry: From Movement to Institution." *Global Crime* 11 (2): 261–78. https://doi.org/10.1080/17440571003669258.

Sanchez-Sibony, Oscar. 2014. "Capitalism's Fellow Traveler: The Soviet Union, Bretton Woods, and the Cold War, 1944–1958." *Comparative Studies in Society and History* 56 (2): 290–319. https://doi.org/10.1017/S001041751400005X.

Schattenberg, Susan. 2006. "'Democracy' or 'Despotism' How the Secret Speech Was Translated into Everyday Life." In *The Dilemmas of De-Stalinization: Negotiating Cultural and Social Change in the Khrushchev Era*, 64–79. New York: Routledge.

Schechter, Brandon. 2017. "Khoziaistvo and Khoziaeva: The Properties and Proprietors of the Red Army, 1941–45." *Kritika: Explorations in Russian and Eurasian History* 18 (3): 487–510. https://doi.org/10.1353/kri.2017.0033.

Schechter, Brandon. 2019. *The Stuff of Soldiers: A History of the Red Army in World War II through Objects.* Ithaca: Cornell University Press.

Schneider, Richard C. 1989. "Developments in Soviet Property Law." *Fordham International Law Journal* 13 (4): 446–80.

Schneider, Richard C. 1992. "Property and Small-Scale Privatization in Russia." *St. Mary's Law Journal* 24: 507–38.

Seabright, Paul, ed. 2000. *The Vanishing Rouble: Barter Networks and Non-Monetary Transactions in Post-Soviet Societies.* Cambridge: Cambridge University Press.

Semenovskii, V. 1929. *Snariazhenie turista.* Moscow: Gosudarstvennoe Isdatel'stvo.

Service, R. J. 1981. "The Road to the Twentieth Party Congress: An Analysis of the Events Surrounding the Central Committee Plenum of July 1953." *Soviet Studies* 33 (2): 232–45. https://doi.org/10.1080/09668138108411353.

Sharlet, Robert, and Piers Beirne. 1990. "In Search of Vyshinsky: The Paradox of Law and Terror." In *Revolution in Law: Contributions to the Development of Soviet Legal Theory, 1917–1938,* edited by Piers Beirne, 136–56. Armonk, NY: M.E. Sharpe.

Sharlet, Robert, Peter B. Maggs, and Piers Beirne. 1990. "P.I. Stuchka and Soviet Law." In *Revolution in Law: Contributions to the Development of Soviet Legal Theory, 1917–1938,* edited by Piers Beirne, 45–60. NY: M.E. Sharpe.

Shatalin, S. S. 1987. "The Effective Utilization of Resources: Interests and Stimuli." *Problems of Economics* 30 (4): 6–21.

Shatalin, S. 1989. "Plan ili rynok?" In *Obratnogo khoda net,* edited by Gavriil Kharitonovich Popov, 211–15. Moscow: Izdatel'stvo Politicheskoi Literatury.

Shatalin, S., ed. 1990. *Perekhod k rynku (500 dnei).* Moscow: Arkhangel'skoe.

Shestakov, A.V. 1955. *Istoriia SSSR. Kratkii kurs. Uchebnik dlia 4–go klassa.* Moscow: Gosudarstvennoe Uchebno-Pedagogicheskoe Izdatel'stvo Ministerstva Prosvesheniia RSFSR.

Shikin, V. 1989. "Stalker iz Chertanova." *Priroda i Chelovek,* no. 7 (July): 46–49.

Shishkin, Alexander Fedorovich, ed. 1961. *Marksistskaia etika: Khrestomatiia.* Moscow: Izdatel'stvo Instituta Mezhdunarodsnykh Otnoshenii.

Shmelev, Nikolai. (1987) 1988. "Advances and Debts." *Problems of Economics* 30 (10): 7–43.

Shmelev, Nikolai. (1988) 1989. "New Anxieties." *Problems of Economics* 31 (9): 6–38.

Shmelev, Nikolai. (1990) 2007a. "Pravitel'stvo dolzhno poiti na ustupki." In *Avansy i dolgi ili vozvrashchenie k zdravomu smyslu. Stat'i i ocherki,* 158–80. Moscow: Letnii Sad.

Shmelev, Nikolai. (1989) 2007b. "Libo sila, libo rubl'." In *Avancy i dolgi ili vozvrashchenie k zrdavomy smyslu. Stat'i i ocherki,* 82–121. Moscow: Letnii Sad.

Shmelev N. P, and V. V. Popov. 1989. *Na perelome: Ekonomicheskaia perestroika v SSSR.* Moscow: Izdael'stvo Agentstva pechati "Novosti."

Siegelbaum, L., ed. 2006. "Introduction." In *Borders of Socialism: Private Spheres of Soviet Russia,* 1–21. New York: Palgrave Macmillan US.

Simmel, Georg. (1907) 1971. "Exchange." In *On Individuality and Social Forms,* 43–69. Chicago: University of Chicago Press.

Skidelsky, Robert. 2014. "The Moral Economy of Debt." *Guardian,* October 21, sec. Business. https://www.theguardian.com/business/2014/oct/21/morality-debt-disputes.

Slobodian, Quinn. 2014. "The World Economy and the Color Line: Wilhelm Röpke, Apartheid and the White Atlantic." *German Historical Institute Bulletin Supplement,* no. 10: 61–87.

Smart, Alan. 1993. "Gifts, Bribes, and Guanxi: A Reconsideration of Bourdieu's Social Capital." *Cultural Anthropology* 8 (3): 388–408. https://doi.org/10.1525/can.1993.8.3.02a00060.

Smith, Daniel Jordan. 2018. "Corruption and 'Culture' in Anthropology and in Nigeria." *Current Anthropology* 59 (S18): S83–S91. https://doi.org/10.1086/695714.

Sokol, Grzegorz. 2016. "Working through What Is: Depression and Agency in Poland's 'New Reality.'" PhD diss., The New School for Social Research.

Sokolov, Mikhail. 2017. "Putin kak Brezhnev." Radio Svoboda, October 6. https://www.svoboda.org/a/28777556.html

Solomon, Peter H. 1981. "Criminalization and Decriminalization in Soviet Criminal Policy, 1917–1941." *Law & Society Review* 16 (1): 9–44. https://doi.org/10.2307/3053548.

Solomon, Peter H. 1996. *Soviet Criminal Justice under Stalin.* Cambridge: Cambridge University Press.

Ssorin-Chaikov, Nikolai. 2000. "Bear Skins and Macaroni: The Social Life of Things at the Margins of a Siberian State Collective." In *Vanishing Rouble: Barter Networks and Non-Monetary Transactions in Post-Soviet Societies*, edited by Paul Seabright, 345–61. Cambridge: Cambridge University Press.

Stalin, J. V. 1926. "O khoziaistvennom polozhenii Sovetskogo soiuza i politike Partii: Doklad aktivu leningradskoi organizatsii o rabote Plenuma TsK VKP(b) 13 aprelia 1926." *Leningradskaia Pravda*, April 18.

Stalin, J. V. 1934. "Marxism Versus Liberalism. An Interview with H.G. Wells. 23 July 1934." Marxists Internet Archive. https://www.marxists.org/reference/archive/stalin/works/1934/07/23.htm.

Starikov, Nikolai. 2011. "Istoriia rossii—liberal'nyi variant." April 10. https://nstarikov.ru/istoriya-rossii-liberalnyj-variant-11901.

Starikov, Nikolai. 2013. *Stalin. Vspominaem vmeste.* SPb: Piter.

Steedman, Ian, ed. 1995. *Socialism and Marginalism in Economics: 1870–1930.* London: Routledge.

Stephan, Paul B. 1991. "Perestroyka and Property: The Law of Ownership in the Post-Socialist Soviet Union." *American Journal of Comparative Law* 39 (1): 35–65. https://doi.org/10.2307/840670.

Strogonov, Valentin. 1974. "Odnomestnaia razbornaia baidarka 'Taimen.'" *Katera i iakhty*, no. 51: 90–93.

Stuchka, Pyotr Ivanovich. 1931. *Kurs sovetskogo grazhdanskogo prava.* Vol. 3: *Osobennaia chast'.* Moscow: Gosudarstvennoe sotsial'no-ekonomicheskoe izdatel'stvo.

Sutela, Pekka. 1991. *Economic Thought and Economic Reform in the Soviet Union.* Cambridge Soviet Paperbacks. Cambridge: Cambridge University Press.

Sutela, Pekka, and Vladimir Mau. 1998. "Economics under Socialism: The Russian Case." In *Economic Thought in Communist and Post-Communist Europe*, edited by Hand-Jurgen Wagener, 33–79. London: Routledge.

TASS. 2022. "Top Russian Official Blasts Anglo-Saxon Doctrine of 'Select Few Entitled to Prosperity.'" TASS Russian News Agency, May 24. https://tass.com/politics/1455011.

Taylor, Charles. 1985. "The Person." In *The Category of the Person: Anthropology, Philosophy, History*, edited by Michael Carrithers and Steven Collins, 257–81. New York: Cambridge University Press.

Thompson, E. P. (1991) 1993. *Customs in Common.* London: Penguin.

Tikhomirov, Alexey. 2017. "The State as a Family: Speaking Kinship, Being Soviet and Reinventing Tradition in the USSR." *Journal of Modern European History* 15 (3): 395–417. https://doi.org/10.17104/1611-8944-2017-3-395.

Titov, Alexander. 2009. "The 1961 Party Programme and the Fate of Khrushchev's Reforms." In *Soviet State and Society under Nikita Khrushchev*, edited by Melanie Ilic and Jeremy Smith, 8–26. London: Routledge.

Travin, Dmitrii. 2010. *Ocherki noveishei istorii Rossii. Kniga pervaia: 1985–1999*. SPb: Norma.

Tregubovich, Viktor, dir. 1969. *Na voine, kak na voine*. Lenfilm.

Tret'iakov, Sergei. (1929) 2006. "The Biography of the Object." *October* 118: 57–62.

Tsoi, Viktor. 1982. "The Idler." Track 5 on *45*. AnTrop Records, magnitizdat.

Uskov, V., ed. 1932. *Sbornik raz"iasnenii Verkhovnogo Suda RSFSR*. Moscow: Gosudarstvennoe Izdatel'stvo "Sovetskoe Zakonodatel'stvo."

Vail, Pyotr, and Alexander Genis. (1988) 1998. *1960-e. Mir sovetskogo cheloveka*. Moscow: Novoe Literaturnoe Obozrenie.

Vaksberg, Arkadi. 1991. *Stalin's Prosecutor: The Life of Andrei Vyshinsky*. Translated by Jan Butler. New York: Grove Weidenfeld.

Vasilyeva, Zinaida. 2019. "From Skills to Selves: Recycling 'Soviet DIY' in Post-Soviet Russia." PhD diss., University of Neuchâtel.

Velminski, Wladimir. 2017. *Homo Sovieticus: Brain Waves, Mind Control, and Telepathic Destiny*. Cambridge: MIT Press.

Venediktov, Anatolii Vasil'evich. 1949. "Voprosy sotsialisticheskoi sobstvennosti v trudakh Iosifa Vissarionovicha Stalina." *Sovetskoe gosudarstvo i pravo*, no. 12 (December): 53–78.

Verdery, Katherine. 1996. *What Was Socialism and What Comes Next?* Princeton: Princeton University Press.

Viola, Lynne. 1996. *Peasant Rebels Under Stalin: Collectivization and the Culture of Peasant Resistance*. New York: Oxford University Press.

Vladimirov, Evgenii. 2012. "Vo vsem vinovat . . . Salvador Dali!" Maxpark May 1. http://maxpark.com/user/3138259138/content/1327872.

Volkov, Nikolai Nikolaevich. 1974. *Sportivnye pokhody v gorakh*. Moscow: Fizkul'tura Sport.

Vološinov, V. N. (1929) 1986. *Marxism and the Philosophy of Language*. Cambridge: Harvard University Press.

Vyshinsky, A. Ya. 1931. "Khozraschet i organy iustitsii: Doklad prokurora RSFSR tov. Vyshinskogo na zasedanii kollegii NKIu s aktivom moskovskikh sudebnykh rabotnikov 28 maia 1931." *Sovetsakia Iustittsiia*, no. 16: 1–8.

Vyshinsky, A. Ya. 1935. *Rech' tovarischa Stalina 4 maia i zadachi sovetskoi iustitsii*. Moscow: Gosudarstvennoe Izdatel'stvo "Sovetskoe Zakonodatel'stvo".

Vyshinsky, A. Ya. 1937. "Protiv antimarksistskoi teorii prava." *Pravda*, April 9, 2–3.

Vyshinsky, A. Ya., ed. 1938. *Sovetskoe gosudarstvennoe pravo: Uchebnik dlia iuridicheskikh institutov*. Moscow: Iuridicheskoe izdatel'stvo NKIu SSSR

Wedel, Janine R. 2012. "Rethinking Corruption in an Age of Ambiguity." *Annual Review of Law and Social Science* 8 (1): 453–98. https://doi.org/10.1146/annurev.lawsocsci.093008.131558.

Whyte, Jessica. 2019. *The Morals of the Market: Human Rights and the Rise of Neoliberalism*. London: Verso.

Whyte, Jessica. 2020. "Calculation and Conflict." *South Atlantic Quarterly* 119 (1): 31–51. https://doi.org/10.1215/00382876-8007641.

Wimberg, Ellen. 1992. "Socialism, Democratism and Criticism: The Soviet Press and the National Discussion of the 1936 Draft Constitution." *Soviet Studies* 44 (2): 313–32. https://doi.org/10.1080/09668139208412014.

Wood, Alan. 1990. "Administrative Exile and the Criminals' Commune in Siberia." In *Land Commune and Peasant Community in Russia: Communal Forms in Imperial and Early Soviet Society,* edited by Roger Bartlett, 395–414. London: Palgrave Macmillan.

Woodruff, David. 1999. *Money Unmade: Barter and the Fate of Russian Capitalism.* Ithaca: Cornell University Press.

Worobec, Christine D. 2020. "The Influences of A.V. Chayanov and Teodor Shanin on the English-Language Historiography of Peasants in the Russian Empire." *Russian Peasant Studies* 5 (4): 8–31. https://doi.org/10.22394/2500-1809-2020-5-4-8-31.

Yavlinsky, G, B. Fedorov, S. S. Shatalin, N. Petrakov, S. Aleksashenko, A. Vavilov, L. Grigoriev, et al. (1990) 1991. *500 Days: Transition to the Market.* New York: St. Martin's Press.

Yurchak, Alexei. 2006. *Everything Was Forever, until It Was No More.* Princeton: Princeton University Press.

Zagviazinskii, I. 1933. "Dogovor kupli-prodazhi v sovetskoi roznichnoi torgovle." In *Voprosy sovetskogo khoziaistvennogo prava,* edited by L. Ginzburg and I. Suvorov, 223–56. Moscow: Sovetskoe Zakonodatel'stvo.

Zakon Soiuza Sovetskikh Sotsialisticheskikh Respublik o trudovykh kollektivakh i povyshenii ikh roli v upravlenii predpriiatiiami, uchrezhdeniiami, organizatsiiami. 1983. Moscow: Izvestiia.

Zaslavskaya, T. I. 1980. "Ekonomicheskoe povedenie i ekonomicheskoe razvitie." *EKO: Ekonomika i organizatsiia promyshlennogo proizvodstva* 3 (69): 15–33.

Zaslavskaya, T. I. (1988) 1989. "Korennoi vopros perestroiki." In *Obratnogo khoda net,* edited by Gavriil Kharitonovich Popov, 46–49. Moscow: Izdatel'tvo politicheskoi literatury.

Zatulovskii, D. 1939. *Kak samomu izgotovit' turisticheskoe snariazhenie.* Moscow: Profizdat.

Zhevakina, Marinanna. 2020. "Sovetskie tsekhoviki: Etika 'levykh' otnoshenii." *Neprikosnovennyi Zapas* 5 (133): 207–17.

Žižek, Slavoj. 2009. *First as Tragedy, Then as Farce.* London: Verso.

Zubok, Vladislav. 2019. "Intelligentsia as a Liberal Concept in Soviet History, 1945–1991." In *Dimensions and Challenges of Russian Liberalism,* edited by Riccardo Mario Cucciolla, vol. 8, 45–62. Cham: Springer International.

INDEX

17th Party Congress (1934), 76
20th Party Congress (1956), 89, 93–97,
    111–112, 156–7n20
    See also cult of personality
22nd Party Congress (1961), 97–104,
    121, 156–57n20
23rd Party Congress (1966), 156n20
27th Party Congress (1986), 26, 118,
    122
500 Day Plan, 136
1932 decree "About the Protection
    of Socialist Property" 20, 69–71,
    79–80, 121, 150n17
    See also enclosure; anti-theft laws
1953 amnesty, 89–90, 96, 153n5
1983 Labor Collective Law, 121
1987 Law on State Enterprise, 118, 120,
    123–31
1988 Law on Cooperatives, 118
2022 war against Ukraine, 8, 139–41,
    145n6

Abalkin, Leonid, 25–26, 118–24
acquisition manager. *See snabzhentsy*
administrative-command system, 25,
    110–114, 132–135, 159n11
    See also totalitarianism
Aganbegyan, Abel, 122–25
Amfiteatrov, G. N., 99–100
Andropov, Yuri, 121
Anthem of the Soviet Union, 94, 111
anti-theft laws, 19–20, 69–70, 79–80, 121,
    151n20
Arendt, Hannah, 113
Aristotle, 124–25

barter, 24, 30, 43, 127, 130–131, 152n24,
    159n9
Beria, Lavrentiy, 90, 92, 94, 96, 153n5
    See also 1953 amnesty
Berliner, Joseph, 21, 76–77, 146n9

black market, 49, 85, 145n6
blat. See *economy of favors*
Brezhnev era, 92, 110–11, 147n5,
    156–57n20
Bukharin, Nikolai, 16–18
Burlatsky, Fyodor, 110

capitalism, 19, 76, 69, 142, 145n4
censorship, 90, 94, 105, 107–09, 111,
    135
    See also classified materials
central planning, 26–27, 76, 113, 120–24,
    147n4, 157n1
Chayanov, Alexander, 145–46n7
Chubais, Anatoly, 25
Chumak, Allan, 135
CIA, 92, 111–112
civil law. *See* property law: civil
Circus (1936 film), 73
clairvoyant. *See* extrasense
classified institutes, 40, 54, 107–09, 129,
    135, 155n18
    See also censorship
Cold War, 10–11, 95–96, 113, 157n22
collective farm. *See* kolkhoz
collectives, 22–26, 40–44, 62–64, 86,
    101–103, 119–22, 126, 137
collectivism, 13, 20, 23, 25, 72, 101–103,
    139–140
collectivization, 70–71, 95, 151n20
commodity deficit. *See* shortage
commons, 14, 20, 79–86, 125, 137–138,
    150n16, 159n13
communism, 19, 69, 98–100–103, 145n4,
    154n7
Communist Party, 19, 26, 62, 149n9,
    156–57n20, 158n6
communist youth. *See* Komsomol
comrades' courts, 101–102
    See also Third Party Platform;
    Foundations of Civil Jurisprudence

Constitution, 18, 20, 66–72, 99, 136, 139–40
Convicts (1936 film), 73–75, 78
cooperative: property, ventures, 67–69, 79–80, 123–124
corruption, 5, 9–11, 15, 32, 110
Counterplan (1932 film), 81, 152n22
crime, 100–02, 145n5, 149–50n15, 151n20, 154n11
cult of personality, 89, 93–96, 110–114
customary courts, 101–106, 154n11
customary rights, 14, 20–25, 79–87, 125–28, 149n11, 150n16, 151n20
cybernetics, 100, 135, 154n9, 157n1

de-Stalinisation, 89–90, 92, 94–97, 132, 137
Declaration of the Rights of Man and Citizen, 20, 143
democracy, 10, 13–14, 20, 94, 109–13, 159–60n14
destalinizatsiia. See de-Stalinisation
Digest of Laws of the Russian Empire, 68
dignity, 98, 101, 143
disenfranchisement, 69–70, 94
dispossession, 14, 19, 25, 64, 70–71, 93, 136, 143
See also enclosure
DIY. *See* self-made things
Djuna, 135

economy of favors, 7, 38, 43–44
enclosure, 19–20, 79–80, 143, 150n16, 150–51nn19–21
See also anti-theft laws
energo-informational radiation. *See* extrasense
Engels, Friedrich, 98, 100
enterprise-based distribution, 34, 62–63, 127–28, 130–31
esoterica. *See* extrasense
ethics as property. *See* dignity; *Foundations of Civil Jurisprudence*
excesses. *See* stockpiles
extrasense, 104, 108, 134–135

famine, 70–71
fifth column, 15, 25, 81, 89–91, 153n2
Firsov, Fred, 107–08, 155n16
forced labor, 71, 73–74, 89
See also Counterplan
formalism. *See* verbosity

Foundations of Civil Jurisprudence (1961), 98, 100–102
See also comrades' courts; Third Party Platform
Fuse shorts, 104

Gaidar, Egor, 25, 117
Garage (1979 film), 155n15
Ginzburg, Leonid, 69–70, 149n7
glasnost, 15, 94, 96, 109, 135
gleaning
as 1932 law, 70, 79
Biblical, 70, 80, 84
in socialist household, 19, 79–87, 125, 131
in perestroika, 124–132
Golden Billion: theory of, 141–142
Gorbachev, Mikhail, 24–27, 91–96, 109–123, 132–37, 159n10
grazhdanskoe pravo. See property law: civil law, dual-sectored law
Grossman, Gregory, 18, 38, 43, 147n4
See also second economy
group egoism, 126, 158n6
GULAG, 11, 61, 74, 90–91, 96, 105, 113
See also forced labor

Harvard Project on the Soviet Social System, 77, 149n13
Hayek, Friedrich, 13, 22, 120
Herzen, Alexander, 142–43, 145–46n7
history textbooks. *See* Stalin: omission from history
hoarding, 41, 77, 123, 158n5
See also stockpiles
honor and dignity. *See* dignity
household, 16–22, 75–78, 81–86, 117–25, 145–46n7, 151n21, 152n24
Huntington, Samuel, 9–10

immaterial
property relations, 101
values, 3
individual interests, 11–22, 99–106, 123, 137, 142–143, 154n7
Institute of Marxism-Leninism, 107, 155n16
Ioffe, Olympiad, 101–02, 149n12, 154n12
Ioffe Physics Institute, 45, 51, 54, 55, 108

Karpinskii, Len, 114, 134, 137
khozaistvennoe pravo. See property law: dual-sectored

khozaistvennyj mechanism, 158n4
khoziain, 19, 22, 73–78, 82–83, 118,
    125–26
    as sentiment (*chuvstvo khoziaina*), 109,
    118–19, 121–23, 127, 138
khozraschet, 23–24, 119
Khrushchev, Nikita, 89–103, 111–14,
    148n9, 153n4, 153n5, 156n20
Khrushchev's 1956 speech. *See* cult of
    personality
kolkhoz, 68–71, 121, 127
kollektiv. *See* collectives
Komsomol, 64, 103–05, 109
korruptsiia. *See* corruption

laboring family, trope, 67, 149n9
Leneva, Alena. *See* economy of favors
Lenin, Vladimir, 15, 92–95, 98, 111, 121
Leninist ideals, 94–95, 132
Liberation (1970–1971 film), 111
Liberman-Kosygin reforms (1965), 157n2
Lippmann, Walter, 22, 146n10

Magerovsky, Dmitrii, 69
Malenkov, Georgy, 81
marginalism, 16, 146n7
Marx, Karl, 12, 102, 143
Marxism-Leninism, 23, 107, 155n16
Mises, Ludwig von, 11–13, 17, 21, 120,
    137
Molotov, Vyacheslav, 24, 73, 152n1
money, 24, 40–62, 99, 104, 118, 123–24,
    130–31, 158–59nn7–9
Moral Codex of the Builder of Communism
    (1961), 102–04, 110
    See also Third Party Platform
moral economy, 14, 25, 35, 62
Morison, James, Rev., 70
mutual aid, 21–25, 102–103, 107, 132,
    152n24

Naishul, Vitali, 118, 127, 137
narodnik, 145–46n7
    See also peasant commune; Herzen,
    Alexander
nationalization, 70–71, 98
neoliberalism, 10–16, 22–25, 118, 137,
    143
neo-stalinism, 91, 111

obshchestvennoe, obshchestvo, obshchestvennost',
    69, 79, 101, 148n5
obshchina. *See* peasant commune

"one and the many," 11–12, 15–16, 19,
    109, 137
outdoor sport, communally organized,
    39–48

Pashukanis, Evgeny, 17–18, 98–99,
    145n5
Patrushev, Nikolai, 139
peasant commune, 142, 145–46n7,
    148n5
    in pre-Soviet law, 154n11
    See also narodnik
perestroika as trope, 14–15, 25, 34,
    62–66, 86–87, 91–93, 128–30
perestroika reform theory, 26, 109–15,
    118–27, 131–37
    alternative "bargaining model," 118,
    137
planned economy, 21–26, 41–42, 85–86,
    113, 126, 146n10, 147n4
Pogodin, Nikolai, 74
pol'zovanie, 68
    See also usufruct; *khoziain*; *vladelets*;
    sobstvennik
Polanyi, Karl, 4, 21, 120–26, 131, 145n2
Popov, Gavriil, 110, 133–34
pravila/poniatia (rules/norms), 48
price, 12–14, 24–26, 35, 42, 60–61,
    120–32, 137, 157n1, 159n9
primitive economy, 12
privatization, 10, 13, 25, 117, 137
procurement officer. *See snabzhentsy*
property
    communal, 19, 79–80
    immaterial, 101
    personal, 20–23, 71–72, 99–101, 145n7
    private, 12–24, 67–68, 79–80, 98–100,
    113, 145–46n7, 149n11, 150nn17–19
    socialist, 71, 80, 122, 134, 158n4
    See also enclosure; cooperative; usufruct
property law
    civil law, 20, 68, 98–101, 145n5
    early-Soviet, 67–69, 98–99, 148n2,
    152n23
    honor and dignity as personal
    property, 101
    khoziastvennoe pravo (dual-sectored law),
    69, 99–100, 149nn6–7
    late-Soviet (1961 reform), 98, 100–102
    perestroika, 122–24, 136–37
    pre-Soviet, 68, 148n2, 148n4, 149n11,
    150–51nn18–19
Putin, Vladimir, 11, 14, 93, 139

reciprocity, 4, 63–64, 103, 152n24
Reisner, Mikhail, 67
Rubinshtein, Boris, 18, 24, 69, 72, 76
rubles. *See* money
rules/norms. *See pravila/poniatia*
Russian ownership terms. *See khoziain;
    pol'zovanie; sobstevnnik; vladelets*
Russian populism. See *narodnik*
Ryzhkov, Nikolai, 131, 136

Sachs, Jeffrey, 26, 117
second economy, 38, 41–43
    See also black market; economy of
        favors; Grossman
secret plot. *See* fifth column
self-made things, 146–47n1, 147n2
    cemetery memorials, 36, 49, 125
    DIY guides, 46, 147–48n5
    ethics of, 48
    glass trinkets, 32–33, 57–59
    kitchen and household goods, 3–4,
        30–31, 50–53, 55–59
    materials gleaned from work,
        146n1
    sports gear, 39–48, 54, 125
self-regulating markets, 12–13, 119–121,
    137
Shatalin, Stanislav, 126, 136, 158n7
Shmelev, Nikolai, 120–23, 132–136
shortage, 14, 41, 76–78, 82, 120,
    125–130, 148n9
snabzhentsy, 82–84, 125, 146n9
sobstvennik, 75
    See also khoziain
social self-management, 26–27, 100–15,
    119–22, 131, 137, 142
    See also withering away of the state
socialism as anti-liberalism, 20, 71, 73,
    79
socialist accumulation, 19, 70–71, 112
socialist household, *sotsialisticheskoe
    khoziaistvo*, 16–27, 72–86, 124–32
socialist market, 120–26, 131, 137,
    158n7, 158n8, 159n11
Solzhenitsyn, Alexander, 105, 111
sotsialisticheskoe khoziaistvo. See socialist
    household
Soviet National Anthem. *See* Anthem of
    the Soviet Union
Soviet times as trope, 5, 33–37, 64–66,
    86–87, 138
stagnation, 95, 110, 132–135
Stalin
    as *khoziain*, 78, 80, 110

as trope in late-Soviet cult of WWII,
    111, 156–57n20
as trope in perestroika, 95–96, 110,
    114, 132–138
as trope in 2010s, 11, 89–93
his remarks on collectivism, 20, 72, 99
his remarks on enclosure, 19, 79,
    150n17
his remarks on socialist accumulation,
    71
omission from history, 92–95, 112,
    153n4, 156n20
See also Administer-command system;
    de-Stalinisation; neo-stalinism
Stalin museum in Gori, 88–89
Starikov, Nikolai, 91, 153n2
State and Revolution. See Lenin
stockpiles, 22–25, 41–59, 76, 81–86, 135,
    147–48n5
    in perestroika theory, 109, 123–132
    khoziain managing, 77–78, 82, 125, 127
striving: ethical, collectivist, personal, 17,
    22–23, 38–39, 43, 100–03, 114–15,
    152n24
Stuchka, Pyotr, 68, 78, 98
svoi, 18, 57, 145n6

textbooks. *See* Stalin, omission from
    history
Thaw era, 97–110, 153n6
    See also Third Party Platform
theft, 19, 61–62, 69–70, 79–80,
    149–50n15, 151n20
    See also anti-theft laws; crime
Third Party Platform, 97–106, 110, 119,
    153n6, 154n8
    See also 22nd Party Congress,
        Foundations of Civil Jurisprudence,
        Thaw era
Thompson, E. P., 14, 79, 84, 86
"Three Stalks of Grain" law. *See* 1932
    decree "About the Protection of
    Socialist Property"
    See also administrative-command
        system
tolkachi. See snabzhentsy
totalitarianism, 9–11, 112–14, 137,
    159n10
treason. *See* fifth column
tuneiadstvo (unemployment), 66–67,
    155n14

usufruct, 20–21, 68, 75–78
    See also civil law

verbosity, 109–112
vladelets, 68, 75, 122
    See also, usufruct; *khoziain*; *pol'zovanie*
Vyshinsky, Andrey, 20–24, 72, 154n7

Walter Lippmann Colloquium, 11, 22
White Sea Canal. *See Convicts*
withering away of the state, 15–19,
    98–103, 113, 136–138

WWII: in film and edutainment, 139–41
    See also Stalin as idiom of popular
    historiography

Yeltsin, Boris, 136, 159n14

Zagviazinskii, Ilya, 69
Zaslavskaya, Tatyana, 134, 147n4
Zhukov, Georgy, 91

www.ingramcontent.com/pod-product-compliance
Lightning Source LLC
Chambersburg PA
CBHW032350280326
41935CB00008B/517